IEEE Std 446-1995
(Revision of IEEE Std 446-1987)

IEEE Recommended Practice for Emergency and Standby Power Systems for Industrial and Commercial Applications

Sponsor

**Power Systems Engineering Committee
of the
Industrial and Commercial Power Systems Department
of the
IEEE Industry Applications Society**

Approved 12 December 1995

IEEE Standards Board

Abstract: This Recommended Practice addresses the uses, power sources, design, and maintenance of emergency and standby power systems. Chapter 3 is a general discussion of needs for and the configuration of emergency and standby systems. Chapter 9 lists the power needs for specific industries. Chapters 4 and 5 deal with selection of power sources. Chapter 6 provides recommendations for protecting both power sources and switching equipment during fault conditions. Chapter 7 provides recommendations for design of system grounding, and Chapter 10 provides recommendations for designing to reliability objectives. Chapter 8 provides recommended maintenance practices.
Keywords: batteries, emergency generators, emergency power, emergency system, emergency system design, engine generators, standby power, standby system, stored energy systems, transfer switch, uninterruptible power supplies, UPS, UPS batteries

Grateful acknowledgment is made to the following organizations for having granted permission to reprint illustrations in this document as listed below:

The Electrical Generating Systems Marketing Association (EGSA), 10251 W. Sample Rd., Ste. B, Coral Springs, FL 33065-3939, for **Table 3-1** from EGSA 109C-1994, Table 1, copyright 1994 by EGSA.

The National Fire Protection Association (NFPA), Quincy, MA 02269, for **Figure 3-5** from NFPA 70-1996, National Electrical Code®, Figure 517-30(b), copyright 1995 by NFPA.

The Automatic Switch Company (ASCO), Florham Park, NJ 07932, for **Figure 4-10**.

First Printing
July 1996
SH94381

The Institute of Electrical and Electronics Engineers, Inc.
345 East 47th Street, New York, NY 10017-2394, USA

ISBN 1-55937-598-1

Introduction

(This introduction is not a part of IEEE Std 446-1995, IEEE Recommended Practice for Emergency and Standby Power Systems for Industrial and Commercial Applications.)

In 1968 the Industrial and Commercial Power Systems Committee within the Industry and General Applications Group of the Institute of Electrical and Electronics Engineers recognized that a need existed for a publication that would provide guidance to industrial users and suppliers of emergency and standby power systems.

The nature of electric power failures, interruptions, and their duration covers a range in time from microseconds to days. Voltage excursions occur within a range from 20 times normal (or more) to a complete absence of voltage. Frequency excursions can vary as widely in many forms, from harmonics to direct current. These variables occur due to a multitude of conditions both in the power system ahead of the user's service entrance and following the service entrance within the user's area of distribution.

Such elements as lightning, automobiles striking power poles, ice storms, tornadoes, switching to alternate lines, and equipment failure are but a few of the causes of interruptions in the electric power supply ahead of the service entrance.

Within the user's area of distribution are such elements as short and open circuits, undersized feeders, equipment failures, operator errors, temporary overloads, single-phasing unbalanced feeders, fire, switching, and many other causes of power interruption or failure.

In the past the demand for reliable electric power was less critical. If power was completely interrupted too often, another source was found. If voltage varied enough to cause a problem, a regulator or a larger conductor was installed. As processes, controls, and instrumentation became more sophisticated and interlocked, the demand developed to shorten the length of outages. Increased safety standards for people required emergency and exit lighting. Many factories added medical facilities that needed reliable electric power.

With the advent of solid-state electronics and computers, the need for continuous, reliable, high-quality electric power became critical. Many installations required uninterruptible power, virtually free of frequency excursions and voltage dips, surges, and transients.

In 1969 a working group was established under the Industrial Plants Power Systems Subcommittee of the Industrial and Commercial Power Systems Committee to collect data and produce a publication entitled "Emergency Power Systems for Industrial Plants." Later that year the scope of the work was enlarged to include standby power since, in meeting various needs, the two systems were often found to be intertwined, or one system served multiple purposes.

As the work progressed, it became apparent that industrial and commercial needs contained more similarities than differences. Systems available to supply the required power to industry were found applicable to both fields. Once again the scope of the work was expanded to include commercial requirements. The existing working group was changed to the status of a subcommittee under the Industrial and Commercial Power Systems Committee to have direct responsibility, not only for the Orange Book Working Group, but for other matters concerning emergency and standby power. The proposed publication was redirected toward establishing recommended practices. As a result of subsequent organizational changes, this Emergency and Standby Power Systems Subcommittee is now under the Power Systems Engineering Committee of the Industrial and Commercial Power Systems Department.

This third revision of the IEEE Orange Book contains updating and expansion of existing material. In addition, a new chapter has been added that addresses design criteria for achieving reliability objectives.

This IEEE Recommended Practice continues to serve as a companion publication to the following other Recommended Practices prepared by the IEEE Industrial and Commercial Power Systems Department:

— IEEE Std 141-1993, IEEE Recommended Practice for Electric Power Distribution for Industrial Plants (IEEE Red Book).

— IEEE Std 142-1991, IEEE Recommended Practice for Grounding of Industrial and Commercial Power Systems (IEEE Green Book).

— IEEE Std 241-1990, IEEE Recommended Practice for Electric Power Systems in Commercial Buildings (IEEE Gray Book).

— IEEE Std 242-1986, IEEE Recommended Practice for Protection and Coordination of Industrial and Commercial Power Systems (IEEE Buff Book).

— IEEE Std 399-1990, IEEE Recommended Practice for Industrial and Commercial Power Systems Analysis (IEEE Brown Book).

— IEEE Std 493-1990, IEEE Recommended Practice for the Design of Reliable Industrial and Commercial Power Systems (IEEE Gold Book).

— IEEE Std 602-1996, IEEE Recommended Practice for Electric Systems in Health Care Facilities (IEEE White Book).

— IEEE Std 739-1995, IEEE Recommended Practice for Energy Management in Industrial and Commercial Facilities (IEEE Bronze Book).

— IEEE Std 1100-1992, IEEE Recommended Practice for Powering and Grounding Sensitive Electronic Equipment (IEEE Emerald Book).

The Orange Book Working Group for the 1995 edition had the following membership:

Neil Nichols, *Chair*

Chapter 1: Scope—**Neil Nichols**, *Chair*

Chapter 2: Definitions—**Neil Nichols**, *Chair;* Marco W. Migliaro; Joseph S. Dudor

Chapter 3: General need guidelines—**Gordon S. Johnson**, *Chair*

Chapter 4: Generator and electric utility systems—**Farrokh Shokooh,** *Chair;* Charles D. Hughes

Chapter 5: Stored energy systems—**Marco W. Migliaro**, *Chair;* J. H. Bellack; G. J. Davis; P. J. Demar; Joseph S. Dudor; Murray Leonard; Robert Soileau; Swagata Som

Chapter 6: Protection—**Pat O'Donnell**, *Chair;* René Castenschiold; Marco W. Migliaro; Neil Nichols; Charles D. Potts; Farrokh Shokooh; George Stromme

Chapter 7: Grounding—**René Castenschiold**, *Chair;* Norman Fowler; Daniel L. Goldberg; Gordon S. Johnson; Neil Nichols; Donald W. Zipse

Chapter 8: Maintenance—**Charles D. Potts**, *Chair;* René Castenschiold; Joseph S. Dudor; Norman Fowler; R. Gerald Irvine; Marco W. Migliaro; Gary Tupper

Chapter 9: Specific industry applications—**Eli Yagor**, *Chair*

Chapter 10: Design and operation considerations for improving the reliability of emergency power systems—**Gary Tupper**, *Chair;* Norman Fowler; Neil Nichols; Charles D. Potts; Max Don Trumble

The following persons were on the balloting committee:

When the IEEE Standards Board approved this recommended practice on 12 December 1995, it had the following membership:

National Electrical Code and NEC are both registered trademarks of the National Fire Protection Association, Inc.

Contents

IEEE Recommended Practice for Emergency and Standby Power Systems for Industrial and Commercial Applications

Chapter 1
Scope

This standard presents recommended engineering principles, practices, and guidelines for the selection, design, installation, application, operation, and maintenance of emergency and standby power systems. This information is primarily presented from a user's viewpoint; however, managing the effects of power system disturbances requires close cooperation between users, electric utilities, and equipment manufacturers.

This standard addresses the following questions:

— Is an emergency or standby power system (or both) needed, and what will it accomplish?
— What types of systems are available, and which can best meet the users' needs?
— How should the most suitable system be designed and applied to the existing power system?
— What are the maintenance and operating requirements for maintaining system reliability?
— Where can additional information be obtained?
— What are the design considerations for maintaining system reliability?

Definitions to specialized technical terms used throughout this standard are provided in Chapter 2. Emergency and standby power requirements of both industrial and commercial users are outlined and discussed, including a distinction made between mandatory laws, regulations, codes, and standards applicable to each. Knowledge of these requirements enables electric utility companies to meet specific power supply needs and equipment manufacturers to design efficient, practical, and reliable equipment and systems. Recommendations are made for various types of installations, based on technical and economic information on available hardware and systems provided by equipment manufacturers.

Technical guidelines for protecting and grounding emergency and standby power systems are presented in Chapter 6 and Chapter 7, respectively. Guidelines for the maintenance of specific types of equipment are presented in Chapter 8. Chapter 9 provides information on applications of emergency and standby power for specific industries. Chapter 10 presents design and operation guidelines that will improve emergency and standby power system reliability.

The following industries and fields are considered specialized and beyond the scope of inclusion and direct address by this standard: transport, government, military, and utility.

1

Chapter 2
Definitions

2.1 Introduction

This chapter is intended to provide terms and definitions applicable to this standard for the purpose of aiding in its overall understanding.

NOTE—The definitions of **emergency power system** and **standby power system** contained herein are based on the general functions of the two systems. They may not agree entirely with definitions developed by other bodies, which establish specific operating criteria or are used to establish regulatory codes.

2.2 Terms

2.2.1 absorbed electrolyte cell: A valve-regulated lead-acid (VRLA) cell whose electrolyte has been immobilized in absorbent separator (normally, glass or polymeric fiber). *Syn:* **starved electrolyte cell; absorbed glass mat (AGM) cell.**

2.2.2 absorbed glass mat (AGM) cell: *See:* **absorbed electrolyte cell.**

2.2.3 automatic transfer switch: Self-acting equipment for transferring one or more load conductor connections from one power source to another.

2.2.4 availability: The fraction of time within which a system is actually capable of performing its mission.

2.2.5 battery: Two or more cells electrically connected for producing electric energy.

NOTE—Also commonly used to apply to a single cell used independently.

2.2.6 battery rack: A structure used to support a group of cells.

2.2.7 bypass/isolation switch: A manually operated device used in conjunction with an automatic transfer switch to provide a means of directly connecting load conductors to a power source and of disconnecting the automatic transfer switch.

2.2.8 commercial power: Power furnished by an electric power utility company; when available, it is usually the prime power source. However, when economically feasible, it sometimes serves as an alternative or standby source.

2.2.9 current withstand rating: The maximum allowable current, either instantaneous or for a specified period of time, that a device can withstand without damage, or without exceeding the criteria of an applicable safety or performance standard.

2.2.10 dropout voltage (or current): The voltage (or current) at which a magnetically operated device will release to its de-energized position. It is a level of voltage (or current) that is insufficient to maintain the device in an energized state.

2.2.11 emergency power system: An independent reserve source of electric energy that, upon failure or outage of the normal source, automatically provides reliable electric power within a specified time to critical devices and equipment whose failure to operate satisfactorily would jeopardize the health and safety of personnel or result in damage to property.

2.2.12 flooded cell: *See*: **vented cell**.

2.2.13 forced outage: A power outage that results from the failure of a system component, requiring that it be taken out of service immediately, either automatically or by manual switching operations, or an outage caused by improper operation of equipment or human error. This type of power outage is not directly controllable and is usually unexpected.

2.2.14 frequency droop: The absolute change in frequency between steady-state no load and steady-state full load.

2.2.15 frequency regulation: The percentage change in emergency or standby power frequency from steady-state no load to steady-state full load:

$$\% R = \frac{F_{n1} - F_{f1}}{F_{n1}} \cdot 100$$

2.2.16 gel cell: *See:* **gelled electrolyte cell**.

2.2.17 gelled electrolyte cell: A valve-regulated lead-acid (VRLA) cell whose electrolyte has been immobilized by the addition of a gelling agent. *Syn:* **gel cell**.

2.2.18 harmonic content: A measure of the presence of harmonics in a voltage or current wave form expressed as a percentage of the amplitude of the fundamental frequency at each harmonic frequency. The total harmonic content is expressed as the square root of the sum of the squares of each of the harmonic amplitudes (expressed as a percentage of the fundamental).

2.2.19 immobilized electrolyte: Electrolyte in a cell that is retained by either using gelled or absorbed electrolyte technology.

2.2.20 load shedding: The process of deliberately removing preselected loads from a power system in response to an abnormal condition in order to maintain the integrity of the system.

2.2.21 oxygen index: The minimum concentration of oxygen, expressed as volume percent, in a mixture of oxygen and nitrogen that will just support flaming combustion of a material initially at room temperature, referred to in battery manufacturers' flammability designations for battery cases. *Syn:* **limiting oxygen index (LOI)**.

2.2.22 limiting oxygen index (LOI): *See:* **oxygen index**.

2.2.23 power failure: Any variation in electric power supply that causes unacceptable performance of the user's equipment.

2.2.24 power outage: Complete absence of power at the point of use.

2.2.25 prime mover: The machine used to develop mechanical horsepower to drive an emergency or standby generator to produce electrical power.

2.2.26 prime power: The source of supply of electrical energy that is normally available and used continuously day and night, usually supplied by an electric utility company, but sometimes supplied by base-loaded user-owned generation.

2.2.27 rated capacity (battery): The manufacturer's statement of the number of ampere-hours or watt-hours that can be delivered by a fully charged battery at a specific discharge rate and electrolyte temperature, to a given end-of-discharge voltage.

2.2.28 redundancy: Duplication of elements in a system or installation for the purpose of enhancing the reliability or continuity of operation of the system or installation.

2.2.29 scheduled outage: A power outage that results when a component is deliberately taken out of service at a selected time, usually for purposes of construction, preventive maintenance, or repair. This type of outage is directly controllable and usually predictable.

2.2.30 separate excitation: A source of generator field excitation power derived from a source independent of the generator output power.

2.2.31 shunt excitation: A source of generator field excitation power taken from the generator output, normally through power potential transformers connected directly or indirectly to the generator output terminals.

2.2.32 standby power system: An independent reserve source of electric energy that, upon failure or outage of the normal source, provides electric power of acceptable quality so that the user's facilities may continue in satisfactory operation.

2.2.33 starved electrolyte cell: *See:* **absorbed electrolyte cell**.

2.2.34 transient: That part of the change in a variable, such as voltage, current, or speed, which may be initiated by a change in steady-state conditions or an outside influence, that decays and/or disappears following its appearance.

2.2.35 uninterruptible power supply (UPS): A system designed to provide power automatically, without delay or transients, during any period when the normal power supply is incapable of performing acceptably.

2.2.36 valve-regulated lead-acid (VRLA) cell: A lead-acid cell that is sealed with the exception of a valve that opens to the atmosphere when the internal gas pressure in the cell exceeds atmospheric pressure by a pre-selected amount.

2.2.37 vented cell: A cell design that is characterized by an excess of free electrolyte, and in which the products of electrolysis and evaporation can freely exit the cell through a vent. *Syn:* **flooded cell; wet cell**.

2.2.38 wet cell: *See:* **vented cell**.

2.3 Bibliography

Additional information may be found in the following sources:

[B1] IEEE Std 100-1992, The New IEEE Standard Dictionary of Electrical and Electronics Terms (ANSI).[1]

[B2] Migliaro, M.W., and Alber, G., editors, "Glossary of Stationary Battery Terminology," Alber Technologies, Inc., Boca Raton, FL, 1992.

---

[1]IEEE publications are available from the Institute of Electrical and Electronics Engineers, 445 Hoes Lane, P.O. Box 1331, Piscataway, NJ 08855-1331, USA.

Chapter 3
General need guidelines

3.1 Introduction

While all who use electric power desire perfect frequency, voltage stability, and reliability at all times, this cannot be realized in practice because of the many causes of power supply disturbances that are beyond the control of the utility. For example, power failures can be caused by automobiles hitting poles; animals climbing across insulators; lightning striking overhead lines; and high winds blowing tree branches and other debris into lines.

The lightning, wind, and rain produced by thunderstorms and tornadoes can also cause power interruptions and transients. Figures 3-1 and 3-2 are both useful in determining the probability of such power failures (from thunderstorms and from tornadoes, respectively) depending upon the user's geographic location. More widely located storms, such as hurricanes, snowstorms, ice storms, and floods, also take their toll on power supply systems.

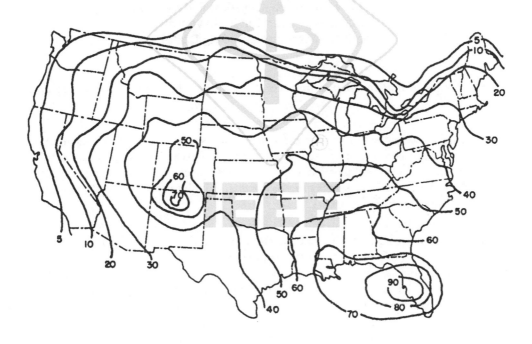

Figure 3-1—Average number of thunderstorm days per year

Although there is less chance for a power interruption caused by severe weather or other natural phenomena occurring on an underground system, and although an underground system has fewer dips, the duration of any interruption that occurs may be much longer because of

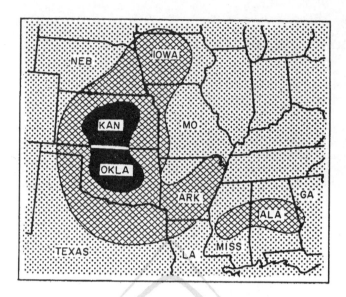

**Figure 3-2—Approximate density of tornadoes;
cross-hatched areas—100–200 in 40 years;
black area—over 200 in 40 years
(see 3.15, Standard Building Code)**

the greater length of time required to discover the source of the cable failure and to make repairs.

Even the operation of protective devices can cause power supply disturbances. As an example, overcurrent and short-circuit protective devices require excessive current to operate and are accompanied by a voltage dip on any line supplying the excessive current until the device opens to clear the fault. Devices opening to clear a lightning flashover with subsequent reclosing cause a momentary interruption.

Since utility companies have little practical control over disturbances on their systems, they are unwilling to accept responsibility for them or to make power quality or continuity guarantees. The following disclaimer is taken from a typical utility sales contract: "The power delivered hereunder shall be three-phase alternating current at a frequency of approximately 60 Hz and at a nominal voltage of 208/120 V wye. Except for temporary periods of abnormal operating conditions, variations from normal voltage shall not exceed 5% up or down. The utility will use reasonable diligence to provide a regular and uninterrupted supply of power, but in case such supply should be interrupted for any cause, the utility shall not be liable for damages resulting therefrom."

In several instances, utility companies have recognized the limitations of their power quality and have offered auxiliary equipment with special purchase agreements to satisfy the needs of those who use sensitive utilization equipment.

Utility companies are by no means the only source of power system disturbances. Disturbances and outages also occur in the plant system through the loss of power due to short circuits in wiring and failures of local generation including emergency and standby equipment. *Noise* is generated in otherwise acceptable electric power by motors, welders, switches, semiconductor-controlled rectifier (SCR) gating, dielectric heating, arcing short circuits, and a myriad of other sources.

Ordinary power meters and instrumentation cannot be used to measure power transients or disturbances. Recording devices with extremely fast response must be used to detect, measure, and record disturbance magnitudes and durations. Most disturbances will not only vary within a given 24 h period, but depending on the geographical area, could be subject to seasonal variations.

Any meaningful data with regard to power quality, or lack of it, will become obvious only after conducting a thorough and detailed measurement recording and analysis program. Such a program would include the monitoring of an incoming power line over a representative period of time. Since much of the instrumentation is costly (typically, $3000–$16 000) in relation to its limited duration usage, rental arrangements are often a popular choice.

Without a good power disturbance monitor to measure and record disturbances continuously, there is a tendency to make judgments regarding disturbances in the power source in terms of their effects upon various electrical loads. When the lights go out and the electrical equipment all stops working, this is usually a fairly reliable indication of a power interruption. However, if the lights merely flicker or the electronic equipment malfunctions, it is difficult to judge whether or not there has been a severe change in voltage for a very short time or a very small voltage change for a much longer time. One cannot determine, without a disturbance monitor, whether or not the disturbance was unusually severe or the electronic equipment was unusually susceptible to the disturbance. Without the necessary features in a disturbance monitor, one cannot tell if the source of the disturbance was external to the load equipment or was the load equipment itself.

The following list describes methods that can be used to reduce to acceptable limits, or even eliminate, the effects of power supply disturbances:

— Modification of the design of utilization equipment so as to be impervious to power disturbances and discontinuities;
— Modification of the prime power distribution system to be compatible with utilization equipment;
— Modification of both systems and equipment to meet a criterion that is realistic for both;
— Interposing a continuous electric supply system between the prime source and the utilization equipment; this will function as a *buffer* to external sources of transients, but depending on the design, could increase the magnitude of load-induced disturbances.

Almost any significant deviation from normal power parameters may be capable of causing problems with some electronic equipment. Steady or slow deviations that exceed the product design range of line voltage or frequency can affect the shaft speed of motors, the force and speed of actuators, and the conversion of ac voltage into regulated dc voltage for electronic circuit operation. As line voltage approaches product design limits, this often reduces the ability of the product to sustain, without incident, a line voltage transient as described in the following paragraph. Of course, some electronic circuits are more susceptible than others. This depends upon specific application and design.

Most frequent among excursions from normal line conditions are those classed as *voltage transients*. These often contain an initially fast voltage rise or fall (sometimes oscillatory) followed by a slower voltage rise or fall. Thus one transient event may contain both fast impulses and noise and a slower change in voltage.

Fast voltage impulses and noise generally have little direct effect upon the smooth, even flow of power to such devices as motors and ac to dc power conversion equipment. The flywheel effect of motors and the energy storage in filters for reducing radio frequency interference and ripple in rectified dc output current of ac to dc converters keep the fast voltage changes from affecting their outputs directly. Excessively large impulses or noise bursts and inadequate filtering may result in component voltage overstress or in the premature triggering of control circuit elements such as SCRs and TRIACs. Otherwise, very short-duration impulses and high-frequency noise have little effect upon electronic circuits via power supply paths. More often these disturbances reach sensitive electronic circuits by more subtle paths through circuit grounds where power and signal ground circuit paths intersect. This dictates that care be taken in the location of connections and routing of ground conductors in addition to the more obvious precautions taken to reduce the number and amplitude of transients.

For practical reasons and convenience, power disturbances should be defined in terms that are related to practical methods of measurement. When power disturbance limits are given in the specifications for electrical and electronic equipment, use of the same terminology and measurements will make problem-solving easier and in some cases will help identify the source of the disturbances.

For purposes of later discussions, disturbances in ac power are classified as deviations in one or more of the following areas:

- a) Voltage
  1) Steady-state values (slow average), including unbalance
  2) Outages and interruptions
  3) Surges and sags
  4) Impulses and noise

  NOTE—The term *transients* applies loosely to items 3) and 4).
- b) Wave shape
- c) Frequency
- d) Phase relationships

The steady-state value is measured with a true rms-actuated, rms-reading voltmeter or the equivalent. The instrument should be damped; otherwise the readings should be averaged over a 5–10 s averaging time so that a succession of readings will indicate the gradual, long-term changes in averaged rms voltage level. This is also known as slow-average rms voltage.

Most deviations in steady-state voltage are caused by voltage drops in power lines, transformers, and feeders as load is increased. When step voltage corrections are made by such means as transformer tap changing or by adding or removing capacitors, transients will be generated at the time of the step change. In addition, the change that corrected an undervoltage condition as the load increased will have to be reversed later when the load decreases. Otherwise, excessive overvoltage may result. Voltage is usually changed gradually in many small incremental steps. Occasional large step changes can occur.

The worst steady-state voltage deviations are likely to occur in areas where the total load approaches and even exceeds the capacity to generate or distribute power. In spite of short-time overload ratings, it becomes necessary to reduce load during periods of peak loading, such as during heat waves when air conditioning is added to all the other normal loads. Under such conditions, not only may there be an unusually large voltage drop between power source and load, but there may also be a planned voltage reduction to relieve utility system loading. This voltage reduction is known as a *brownout*. With reductions of 3%, 5%, or even 8% at points where voltage is regular, the voltage reduction at load points may be an additional 5–10%.

The most common protection against brownouts is some form of voltage regulation, preferably one that has sufficiently low internal impedance and fast response time to avoid disturbances created by load changes and by phase controlled load regulation (where used).

When a planned brownout fails to relieve the utility power system overload enough to supply energy at reduced voltage to all users, one remaining alternative is to shed loads in a rotating sequence known as a *rolling blackout*. Under some emergency plans, certain noncritical loads would be shed for the duration of the overload. A few known critical loads would not be disturbed. The remainder would be subjected to power interruptions lasting 10–20 min each on a rotating basis among groups of subscribers, sufficient to relieve the overload by means of the rolling blackout. Rolling blackouts in central Florida during the disastrous freeze of December 1989 extended beyond the maximum 20 min and resulted in severe damage to crops and tropical fish hatcheries.

Unequal loading on polyphase lines or single-phase three-wire lines is often the cause of voltage unbalance. Voltage control devices generally operate to regulate the average of the phase voltages, or sometimes just one of the phase voltages, on the assumption that the other phases will be equal to it. The most common corrective measure is to balance the loading among the phases. However, power sources with high internal impedance are more critical in a requirement to distribute loads evenly in order to avoid excessive voltage unbalance. Selection of a delta-connected primary with wye-connected secondary rather than a four-wire wye input and output will help distribute unequal phase loading.

Large computer installations with an uninterruptible power supply (UPS) capable of supplying the computer's power needs for 5–15 min would need supplementary standby power to operate auxiliary building services, such as air conditioning, and to replenish the storage battery energy in order that the computer system could continue to remain functional through an extended power outage. Diesel- or gas-turbine-driven generators fill this need.

11

Nonpermanent departures from the normal line voltages and frequency can be classified as disturbances. Disturbances include impulses, noise, transients, and even some changes in frequency or sudden phase shifts during synchronizing operations. Although the frequency and phase shift events may rarely be encountered when large loads are switched in power networks, these may frequently be encountered in small independent power sources during synchronizing and switching of loads from one source to another.

3.1.1 Short-duration disturbances

Most disturbances on a power system are of short duration. Studies show that 90% are less than one second. Voltage disturbances of more than once cycle duration are usually expressed in rms value. Those of less than once cycle are expressed in terms of the fundamental peak value. Subclauses 3.1.1.1–3.1.1.3 group disturbances according to their duration, usual description, and possible causes.

3.1.1.1 Less than 1 cycle—transient

Transients result from disturbances of all kinds. The most severe subcycle disturbances are natural lightning, electrostatic discharge, load switch, and short-duration faults.

3.1.1.2 Half cycle to a few seconds—swell or sag

Swells (increased voltage) or sags (decreased voltage) usually result from faults on the system with subsequent fuse or high-speed circuit breaker action and reclosing. On the loaded phases this results in a sag. On the unloaded phases the result may be a swell.

3.1.1.3 More than a few seconds—overvoltage or undervoltage

Overvoltage and undervoltage, usually attributed to severe faults accompanied by 50–100% voltage loss on one or more phases, often result in an outage in some circuit. Faults often involve all three phases and may be the result of a downed pole, a tree, or a crane on the line, a breaker lockout, or an in-line fuse blowing. If the critical load is on the cleared side of the fuse, the disturbance becomes an outage. If it is on the power source side of the fault clearing device, the normal voltage may be restored.

3.1.2 Frequency disturbances

In large power systems frequency changes are rare. However, with small engine generators, used for emergency supply, some frequency change is unavoidable when blocks of load are switched. With a modern synchronous governor, these disturbances should be under 5% frequency change and less than 5 s duration, even for full load switching.

IEEE Std 1100-1992[1] contains additional information on short-duration disturbances.

---

[1]Information on references can be found in 3.15.

3.1.3 Grounding

Grounding is an essential part of power systems and their connections to loads. Grounding ensures safety for personnel, provides a low-impedance return path, and serves as a constant potential signal reference. Chapter 7 contains the specific features of grounding emergency systems.

3.1.4 Single-phasing

System designers need to be aware that some systems can fail to properly respond to failure of one phase on a three-phase system. Two conditions that may cause improper sensing are three-phase motors that continue to run single-phase and ferroresonance.

Three-phase motors may continue to run when one phase of a three-phase system fails. Under that condition, the motor will induce a voltage on the failed phase so that the transfer switch sensing circuit may not detect the phase loss. However, this may cause the motor to overheat. To avoid this problem, one approach is to use negative sequence sensors on the motor and disconnect it. Another approach is to use close-differential voltage relays (approximately 95% voltage pickup and 90% dropout) on all three phases in the transfer switch control.

Ferroresonance is a condition that can induce a flash voltage on a disconnected leg of a transformer. This condition can cause improper recycling of emergency or standby system transfer switches. In a known case, the opening of a single utility supply fuse caused the transfer switch to recycle continuously. Since the transfer switch switched all the load to the emergency supply, the normal supply transformer was left with zero load. Ferroresonance produced an rms voltage approximately equal to the normal voltage on the open leg of the unloaded transformer. Therefore, the transfer switch sensed that normal voltage had returned, and it switched back to normal.

The cause of ferroresonance is the magnetizing reactance of the transformer combined with open line capacitance. The transformer was 225 kVA three-phase with grounded-wye primary/grounded-wye secondary. The connection between the transformer and the fuses was 25 kV #1 AWG cable of approximately 130 ft in length. Known practice indicates that these parameters do not produce ferroresonance in the heavily saturated region with associated damaging overvoltages. However, analysts have predicted distorted but nondamaging voltages on the open leg with 1.0–1.3 PU peak values (Smith, Swanson, and Borst 1975 [B18]).[2] The distortion from a sine wave is due to nonlinear (saturated) magnetic circuits.

In the above case, permanent resistive load on the transformer of slightly more than 1% of the rating, reduced voltages to well below the pickup point of the normal voltage-sensing relays on the transfer switch. Moving the transformer near the fuses (very short cable) also corrected the problem.

---

[2]The numbers in brackets preceded by the letter B correspond to those of the bibliography in 3.16.

Recommended practice for systems where single-phase switching, including fuse operation, can occur, is to maintain a small amount of untransfered load on the transformer secondary. Refer to IEEE Std 141-1993 for more information on industrial system connections.

3.1.5 Emergency power

Justification of the expenditure necessary to fulfill user needs for emergency and standby power systems falls into three broad classifications:

a)   Mandatory installations to meet federal, state, county, and municipal regulations;

b)   Maintenance of the safety of people during a power failure;

c)   Decreased economic losses due to fewer and shorter power failures.

Mandatory regulations for alternate power sources to ensure the safety of personnel and to prevent pollution of the environment continually increase. The National Electrical Code® (NEC®) (NFPA 70-1996) contains regulations for the safe installation of emergency and standby power systems. NFPA 99-1996, ANSI/NFPA 110-1993, and ANSI/NFPA 111-1993 contain testing, performance, and maintenance requirements. ANSI/NFPA 101-1994 lists occupancies that require emergency power. Those requirements usually concern the safety of occupants. Government authorities may adopt building codes and other regulations that make such systems mandatory.

Table 3-1 is a guide to codes and enforcement agencies for states and major cities in the USA. The enforcement agencies for each project should be consulted before and during the design to make sure that current applicable regulations are complied with.

Table 3-2 lists the needs in thirteen general categories with some breakdown under each to indicate major requirements. Ranges under the columns "Maximum tolerance duration of power failure" and "Recommended minimum auxiliary supply time" are assigned based upon experience. Written standards have been referenced where applicable.

In some cases, under the column "Type of auxiliary power system," both emergency and standby have been indicated as required. An emergency supply of limited time capacity may be used at a low cost for immediate or uninterruptible power until a standby supply can be brought on-line. An example would be the case in which battery lighting units come on until a standby generator can be started and transferred to the critical loads.

Following table 3-2, items from the "General need" column are presented in greater detail with recommendations as to the type of equipment or system that should be used (see 3.2–3.14).

Users of this standard may wish to skip the detailed presentation of each "General need" and go directly to Chapter 4. If so, care should be taken that all individual needs have been recognized and listed so that suitable power systems can be selected to meet all requirements.

Table 3-1—Codes of states and major cities

	Building	Electrical	Life safety	Enforcement	Phone
Alabama	SBC	NEC	NFPA 101	State Fire Marshal's Office.,PO Box 303352, Montgomery, AL 36130-3352	(205) 269 3575
Birmingham	SBC amend	NEC amend	NFPA 101	Chief Electrical Inspector, City Hall, Rm 207, 710 N. 20th St., Birmingham, AL 35203	(205) 254-2219
Alaska	UBC amend	NEC	None	State Fire Marshal, 5700 E. Tudor St., Anchorage, AK 99507-1225	(907) 269-5604
Anchorage	UBC amend	NEC amend	Ariz Fire Code	Building Official, PO Box 196650, Anchorage, AK 99519-6650	(907) 786-8307
Arizona	None	NEC	Ref in Bldg & Fire	Asst Fire Marshall,Dept of Bldg & Fire Safety, 1540 W VanBuren, Phoenix, AZ 85007	(602) 255-4072
Phoenix	UBC amend	NEC amend	NFPA 101	Assistant Director, Development Services Dept,200 W Washington, Phoenix, AZ 85003	(602) 262-6901
Arkansas	SBC amend	NEC	None	Elec. Administrator, 10421 W Markham, Rm. 301, Little Rock, AR 72205	(501) 682-4500
Little Rock	SBC	NEC	None	Dept of Neighborhood Planning, 723 W Markham St, Little Rock, AR 72201	(501) 371-4826
California	UBC amend	NEC amend	NFPA 101	State Fire Marshal, 7171 Bowling Dr, Suite 600, Sacramento, CA 95823	(916) 262-1875
Los Angeles	UBC amend	NEC amend	None	Chief, Mechanical, Div, Rm 485 City Hall, 200 N Spring St, Los Angelos, CA 90012	(213) 485-2301
San Diego	UBC amend	NEC amend	None	Dir Devel.Services Dept, 202 C St., MS9B,San Diego, CA 92101	(619) 236-6056
San Francisco	UBC amend	NEC amend	NFPA 101	Ch Elec Insp, Dept of Building Insp, 1660 Mission St., San Francisco, CA 94103	(415) 558-6030
San Jose	UBC amend	NEC suplmt	None	Chief Inspector Dept of Planning, 801 N 1st St, Rm 200, San Jose, CA 95110	(408) 277-4541
Colorado	UBC	NEC	NFPA 101	Lester Fields, Div of Housing, 1313 Sherman St, RM 323, Denver, CO 80203	(303) 866-2033
Denver	UBC amend	NEC suplmt	NFPA 101 amend	Director, Building Inspection Div, 200 W 14th Ave, Denver, CO 80204-2700	(303) 640-5843
Connecticut	NBC amend	NEC	NFPA 101 amend	Public Safety Building Offical, PO Box 2794,Middletown, CT 06457-9294"	(203) 238-6011
Delaware	None	NEC	NFPA 101 amend	State Fire Marshal's Office, R.D. 2, Box 166A, Dover, DE 19901"	(302) 739-4394
Wilmington	NBC amend	NEC amend	None	Dept Licences & Inspection, 800 French St, 5th Floor, Wilmington DE 19801	(302) 571-4423
Dist of Columbia	NBC amend	NEC	NFPA 1C1 amend	Admr, Bldg & Land Regulation Adm, 614 H St NW, Room 312, Washington, DC 20001	(202) 727-7340
Florida	SBC&SFBC	NEC	NFPA 1C1	Program Mgr, Dept of Community Affairs,The Rhyne Bldg, Tallahassee, FL 32399	(904) 487-1824
Jacksonville	SBC	NEC amend	NFPA 101	Sup Elect Section, Room 100 City Hall, 220 E Bay St., Jacksonville, FL 32202	(904) 630-1100
Miami	SFBC Dade	NEC w/excl	NFPA 101	Building Code Compliance Office, 140 W Flagler St, Suite 1603 Miami, FL 33130	(305) 375-2901
Orlando	SBC amend	NEC amend	NFPA 101	Bldg Official, Bur of Code Enforcement, 400 S Orange Av, Orlando, FL 32801	(407) 246-2271
Georgia	SBC	NEC amend	NFPA 101 amend	Commis'nr, Dept Comm Affrs, 1200 Equitable Bldg, 100 Peachtree St., Atlanta, GA 30303	(404) 656-5526
Atlanta	SBC	NEC amned	NFPA 101 amend	RL Dover, Electrical Division, 55 Trinity Av,SW, Suite 3900 Atlanta, GA 30335	(404) 330-6180
Hawaii	None	None	None	Local	
Honolulu	UBC amend	NEC amend	NFPA 101 limtd	Glenn Yokomichi, Elect Engr , City/County Bldg Dept, 650 S King St, Honolulu, HI 96813	(808) 527-6011
Idaho	UBC	NEC w/supl	NFPA 101	Elect Div Admr, Dept of Labor and Industrial Services, 277 N 6th, Boise, ID 83720	(208) 334-2183
Illinois	None	NEC local	NFPA 101	State Fire Marshal, 1035 Stevenson Dr, Springfield, IL 62706	(217) 785-4714
Chicago	CBC	CBC	None	Chief Electrical Inspector, Dept of Buildings, 121 N LaSalle St, Chicago, IL 60602	(312) 744-3457
Indiana	UBC amend	NEC amend	None	St Fire Marshall, Dept of Bldg Services, 402 W Washington St, Indianapolis, IN 46204	(317) 232-2226
Indianapolis	UBC amend	NEC amend	None	Dir.Tech. Services and Research Div, 402 W Washington St. Indianapolis, IN 46204	(317) 232-1402
Iowa	UBC amend	NEC amend	Iowa Fire M Rules	State Building Code Bureau, Wallace State office Building, Des Moines, IA 50319	(515) 281-3992
Des Moines	UBC amend	NEC amend	None	Ed McAtee, Senior Elect Inspector, Building Dept, 602 E 1st St, Des Moines, IA 50309	(515) 283-4925
Kansas	UBC	NEC	NFPA 101 amend	Ed Redmon, KS Fire Marshall, 700 SW Jackson St, Ste 600, Topeka, KS 66603-3714	(913) 296-3401
Wichita	UBC amend	NEC amend	NFPA 101	Supt Central Inspection, 455 N Main St, Wichita, KS 67202	(316) 268-4460
Kentucky	NBC (KYBC)	NEC amend	NFPA 101 (KYBC)	State Fire Marshal, The 127 Building, 1047 US 127 S, Frankfort, KY 40601	(502) 564-3626
Louisaina	SBC	NEC amend	NFPA 101	Chief Architect, State Fire Marshal's Office, 5150 Florida Blvd, Baton Rouge, LA 70806	(504) 925-4920
New Orleans	SBC amend	NEC amend	NFPA 101	Dir, Dept of Saf and Permits, Rm 7E05 City Hall, 1300 Perdido St, New Orleans, LA 70112	(504) 565-6111
Maine	None	NEC	NFPA 101	Admr Electrician Exam Bd Licenc & Enforce, State House Station # 35, Augusta ME 04333	(207) 582-8723
Maryland	NBC	NEC	NFPA 101amend	Ch Fire Prot Eng, Off St Fire Marshall, 101 Old Court Rd, Ste 300, Pikesville, MD 21032	(410) 764-4324
Baltimore	NBC amend	NEC amend	NFPA 101	Dennis Chojnowski, Permit Enforc, 417 E Fayette St, Rm 101, Baltimore, MD 21202	(410) 396-3462
Massachusetts	NBC amend	NEC amend	NFPA 101 limtd	Bd of Bldg Regulations, One Ashburton Place, Rm 1301, Boston, MA 02108	(617) 727-3200
Boston	NBC amend	NEC amend	NFPA 101 limtd	Buildings and Inspectional Serv, 1010 Massachusetts Av, Boston, MA 02215	(617) 635-5300
Michigan	NBC amend	NEC amend	Ref NFPA 101	St Bd of Construction Codes, 7150 Harris Dr, PO Box 30254, Lansing MI 48909	(517) 322-1739
Detroit	NBC amend	NEC amend	None	Head Engr, Mech. Elect. Div, 434 City/County Bldg, 2 Woodward Av, Detroit, MI 49226	(313) 224-3181
Minnesota	UBC amend	NEC amend	NFPA 101 limtd	St Bd of Electricity, Griggs Midway Bldg #S-128, 1821 University Av, St Paul, MN 55104	(612) 642-0800
Minneapolis	UBC amend	NEC amend	None	Supvr, Inspections Div, 300 Public Health Center, 250 S 4th St, Minneapolis, MN 55415	(612) 673-5845
Mississippi	SBC	NEC	None	St Bldgs only- Dir Office of Bldgs & Grnds, 1501 Walter Sillers Bldg, Jackson, MS 39201	(601) 359-3621
Jackson	SBC	NEC	None	Charles Dezrow, Deputy Dir, Bldg Permit Div, PO Box 17, Jackson, MS 39205	(601) 960-1159

Table 3-1—Codes of states and major cities (Continued)

	Building	Electrical	Life safety	Enforcement	Phone
Missouri	NBC St Facil	NEC St Facil	NFPA 101 St Fac	Office of Adm, Dept of Design & Construcion, PO Box 809, Jefferson City, MO 65102	(314) 751-4191
Kansas City	UBC amend	NEC amend	None	Director Codes Administration, 18th Floor City Hall, 414 E 12th St, Kansas City, MO 64106	(816) 274-1464
St. Loius	NBC amend	NEC	None	Supt. Electrical Section, Building Dept, Rm 425, 1200 Market St, St. Louis, MO 63103	(314) 622-3326
Montana	UBC amend	NEC amend	None	Bureau Chief Bldg Codes Bureau, Dept of Commerce, PO Box 200517 Helena, MT 59620	(406) 444-3933
Nebraska	UBC amend	NEC	NFPA 101 amend	Terry Carlson, Exec Dir, State Electrical Bd, 800 S 13th St., RM 109, Omaha, NB 68102	(402) 471-3550
Omaha	UBC amend	NEC	NFPA 101 amend	John Jesse, Superintendent, Permits and Inspection, 1819 Farnam St, Omaha, NB 68183	(402) 444-5350
Nevada	UBC amend	NEC	NFPA 101 refr	Bruce Nipp, St Public Works Bd, Capitol Complex 505 E King St, Carson City, NV 89710	(702) 687-3981
Las Vegas	UBC amend	NEC amend	NFPA 101 amend	John Tucker, Director Building and Safety, 400 E Stewart Av, Las Vegas, NV 89101	(702) 229-6251
New Hampshire	NBC	NEC	None	State Fire Marshal, Dept of Safety, 10 Hazen Dr,Concord, NH 03305	(603) 271-3294
New Jersey	NBC	NEC	none	Dept Comm Affrs, Div of Housing and Devel, 101 S Broad St, CN 802, Trenton, NJ 08625	(609) 292-7899
New Mexico	UBC amend	NEC amend	None	R. Pacheco,act. Bureau Chief, Electrical Bureau, 725 St. Michael's Dr, Santa Fe, NM 87504	(505) 827-7036
Albuquerque	UBC amend	NEC amend	None	D Steele, Ch Bldg Offical, Codes Administration, 600 2nd St NW, Albuquerque, NM 87102	(505) 764-1626
New York	U Fire & Bldg	NEC	U Fire & Bldg	Carl Sager, Director, Codes Division, Dept of State, 162 Washington AV, Albany, NY 12231	(518) 474-4073
Buffalo	NY Fire & Bldg	NEC	NY Fire & Bldg	David Pierowicz, Ch Elect Inspector, City Hall, Rm 601, 65 Niagara Sq, Buffalo, NY 14202	(716) 851-5902
New York City	NY City Bldg	NY City Elect	None	M Kahme,PE, Dir, Bur of Elec Contr, Rm 2324 Mun Bldg, 1 Center St, New York, NY 10007	(212) 669-8338
North Carolina	SBC amend	NEC amend	None	Alan Barringer, Ch Elect Engr, Dept of Insurance, 410 N Boylan Av, Raliegh, NC 27611	(919) 733-3901
North Dakota	UBC	NEC suppl	NFPA 101	Richard Haman, Exec Dir Electrical Board, 721 Memorial Highway, Bismark, ND 58504	(701) 328-2822
Ohio	NBC amend	NEC amend	None	Elmer Waltz, Div of Factory Bldg Insp, 2323 W 5th Av, PO Box 825, Columbus, OH 43216	(614) 644-2622
Cincinnati	NBC amend	NEC suppl	NFPA 101	Bob Lack, Ch Elec Insp, Dept Bldg & Insp, City Hall, Rm 316, Cincinnati, OH 45202	(513) 381-6080
Cleveland	NBC amend	NEC suppl	None	Ron Jennings, Ch Insp, Div of Bldg and Housing, 601 Lakeside Av, Cleveland, OH 44144	(216) 664-2618
Columbus	NBC amend	NEC amend	NFPA 101 amend	Dan Benninger, Ch Elec IInsp, Regulation Div,1250 Fairwood Av, Columbus, OH 43206	(614) 645-6076
Oklahoma	NBC	NEC	NFPA 101 amend	Office State Fire Marshal, 4545 N Lincoln Blvd, Suite 280, Oklahoma City, OK 73105	(405) 524-9610
Oklahoma City	NBC amend	NEC amend	None	RL Hood, Supt Insp Serv, Public Works Dept 420 W Main 8thFl. Oklahoma City, OK 73109	(405) 297-2948
Oregon	UBC amend	NEC amend	None	Junior Owings, Ch Elect Insp, Bldg Codes Div, 1535 Edgewater St NW, Salem, OR 97310	(503) 373-7509
Pennsylvania	None	None	State	Director, Bur Occup. & Industrial Safety, Rm 1529 7th & Forester St, Harrisburg, PA 17120	(717) 787-3323
Philadelphia	NBC amend	NEC amend	None	Ch Const Services, Dept of Lic & Inspec, 11th Fl . 1401 JFK Blvd, Philadelphia, PA 19103	(215) 686-5160
Pittsburgh	NBC amend	NEC	None	Chief Bur Bldg Inspection, Dept of Public Safety, 200 Ross St, Pittsburgh, PA 15220	(412) 255-2176
Rhode Island	NBC amend	NEC amend	None	J Cirillo, Commissioner, State Bldg Comm, 1 Capitol Hill, 2nd Floor, Providence,RI 02908	(401) 277-3529
South Carolina	SBC	NEC	None	AsstDepDir, BuildCodes&Related Servicesl, 3600 ForestDr, Suite100, Columbia, SC 29201	(803) 734-4182
Charleston	SBC	NEC	None	Building & FireOfficial, 75Calhoun St, Divison 320, Charleston, SC 29401	(803) 724-7431
South Dakota	SBC	NEC amend	None	Exec Dir, State Electrical Commission,302 S Paunee Ave, Pierre, SD 57501	(605) 773-3573
Tennessee	SBC	NEC suppl	NFPA 101	Elect Sec, Dept of Comm&Ins, Vol Pl, 3rd Fl, 500 J Robertson Pky, Nashville, TN 37243	(615) 741-7170
Memphis	SBC amend	NEC amend	NFPA 101	Bldg Off, Memphis/Shelby Cnty Code Enfor, 160 N Main St, Rm 750,Memphis, TN 38103	(901) 576-5341
Nashville	SBC amend	NEC amend	NFPA 101 amend	Dir, Dept of Codes Adm, Metro Howard Bldg, 700 2nd Av S, Nashville, TN 37210	(615) 862-6600
Texas	None	None	NFPA 101 limtd	Dept of Lic & Reg,Policy & Stds Div Box 12157, Capitol St, Austin, TX 78711	(512) 463-7356
Dallas	UBC amend	NEC amend	None	EconomicDevDept, Bldg Inspection Div, 320 E Jefferson Blvd, Room 105, Dallas, TX 75203	(214) 948-4480
El Paso	SBC amend	NEC amend	None	Ch Electrical Inspector, Public Inspection Dept, 2 Civic Center Plaza, El Paso, TX 79901	(915) 541-4900
Ft. Worth	UBC amend	NEC amend	None	Asst Dir/Bldg Official, City Dept of Devel, 1000 Throckmorton St, Ft. Worth, TX 76102	(817) 871-8025
Houston	UBC amend	NEC suppl	NFPA 101	Dept Public Works,Codes & Standards Group, PO Box 1562, Houston, TX 77251	(713) 754-0004
San Antonio	UBC amend	NEC amend	NFPA 101 limtd	Dir, Bldg Insp Dept, 114 W Commerce St, PO Box 83996, San Antonio, TX 78283	(210) 287-8232
Utah	UBC amend	NEC	NFPA 101 limtd	Dept of Commerce, Div of Occup & Prof Licens, PO Box 45805, Salt Lake City, UT 84145	(801) 530-6731
Salt Lake City	UBC amend	NEC	None	Sr Elect Inspector, Building & Housing Services, 451 S State St, Salt Lake City, UT 84111	(801) 535-7752
Vermont	NBC amend	NEC+state	NFPA 101 amend	Ch Electl Insp, Dept of Labor and Industry, National Life Bldg,Dwr 20 Montpelier, VT 05620	(802) 828-2106
Virgina	NBC amend	NEC amend	None	Asoc Dir, Code Enforc Office, Div of Bldg Regulation, 501 N 2nd St, Richmond, VA 23219	(804) 371-7160
Washington	UBC amend	NEC+state	None	Ch Elect Inspector,Div of Bldg & ConstrSafety Services, POBox44460, Olympia, WA 98504	(360) 902-5269
Seattle	UBC amend	NEC amend	None	Prin Engr, Dept of Construction & Land Use, 710 2nd Av, Suite 700, Seattle, Wa 98104	(206) 233-3892
West Virginia	NBC amend	NEC amend	NFPA 101 amend	Deputy State Fire Marshal, State Capitol, 2100 Washington St, Charleston, WV 25305	(304) 558-2191
Wisconsin	State BC	NEC amend	None	Div of Safety&Bldgs, PO Box 7969, 201 E Washington Av, Madison, WI 53707	(608) 266-3080
Milwaukee	Milwaukee BC	NEC suppl	None	Commissioner, Dept of Bldg Insp, 841 N Broadway Av, MB 1001, Milwaukee, WI 53202	(414) 278-2542
Wyoming	UBC	NEC	None	Dept Fire Prevention & Electrical Safety,1 W 25th St, Cheyenne, WY 82002	(307) 777-7119

Source: EGSA: 109C-1994 [B4]

Table 3-2—Condensed general criteria for preliminary consideration

Section	General need	Specific need	Maximum tolerance duration of power failure	Recommended minimum auxiliary supply time	Type of auxiliary power system		System justification
					Emergency	Standby	
3.2	Lighting	Evacuation of personnel	Up to 10 s, preferably not more than 3 s	2 h	x		Prevention of panic, injury, loss of life Compliance with building codes and local, state, and federal laws Lower insurance rates Prevention of property damage Lessening of losses due to legal suits
		Perimeter and security	10 s	10–12 h during all dark hours	x	x	Lower losses from theft and property damage Lower insurance rates Prevention of injury
		Warning	From 10 s up to 2 or 3 min	To return to prime power	x		Prevention or reduction of property loss Compliance with building codes and local, state, and federal laws Prevention of injury and loss of life
		Restoration of normal power system	1 s to indefinite depending on available light	Until repairs completed and power restored	x	x	Risk of extended power and light outage due to a longer repair time
		General lighting	Indefinite; depends on analysis and evaluation	Indefinite; depends on analysis and evaluation		x	Prevention of loss of sales Reduction of production losses Lower risk of theft Lower insurance rates

Table 3-2—Condensed general criteria for preliminary consideration (*Continued*)

Section	General need	Specific need	Maximum tolerance duration of power failure	Recommended minimum auxiliary supply time	Type of auxiliary power system		System justification
					Emergency	Standby	
3.2 (*Cont.*)	Lighting (*Cont.*)	Hospitals and medical areas	Uninterruptible to 10 s (NFPA 99-1996, ANSI/NFPA 101-1994); allow 10 s for alternate power source to start and transfer	To return to prime power	x	x	Facilitate continuous patient care by surgeons, medical doctors, nurses, and aids Compliance with all codes, standards, and laws Prevention of injury or loss of life Lessening of losses due to legal suits
		Orderly shut-down time	0.1 s to 1 h	10 min to several hours	x		Prevention of injury or loss of life Prevention of property loss by a more orderly and rapid shutdown of critical systems Lower risk of theft Lower insurance rates
3.3	Startup power	Boilers	3 s	To return to prime power	x	x	Return to production Prevention of property damage due to freezing Provision of required electric power
		Air compressors	1 min	To return to prime power		x	Return to production Provision for instrument control

Table 3-2—Condensed general criteria for preliminary consideration (*Continued*)

Section	General need	Specific need	Maximum tolerance duration of power failure	Recommended minimum auxiliary supply time	Type of auxiliary power system		System justification
					Emergency	Standby	
3.4	Transportation	Elevators	15 s to 1 min	1 h To return to prime power		x	Personnel safety Building evacuation Continuation of normal activity
		Material handling	15 s to 1 min	1 h To return to prime power		x	Completion of production run Orderly shutdown Continuation of normal activity
		Escalators	15 s to no requirement for power	Zero To return to prime power		x	Orderly evacuation Continuation of normal activity
3.5	Mechanical utility systems	Water (cooling and general use)	15 s	1/2 h To return to prime power		x	Continuation of production Prevention of damage to equipment Supply of fire protection
		Water (drinking and sanitary)	1 min to no requirement	Indefinite until evaluated		x	Providing of customer service Maintaining personnel performance
		Boiler power	0.1 s	1 h To return to prime power	x	x	Prevention of loss of electric generation and steam Maintaining production Prevention of damage to equipment

Table 3-2—Condensed general criteria for preliminary consideration (*Continued*)

Section	General need	Specific need	Maximum tolerance duration of power failure	Recommended minimum auxiliary supply time	Type of auxiliary power system		System justification
					Emergency	Standby	
3.5 (*Cont.*)	Mechanical utility systems (*Cont.*)	Pumps for water, sanitation, and production fluids	10 s to no requirement	Indefinite until evaluated		x	Prevention of flooding Maintaining cooling facilities Providing sanitary needs Continuation of production Maintaining boiler operation
		Fans and blowers for ventilation and heating	0.1 s to return of normal power	Indefinite until evaluated	x	x	Maintaining boiler operation Providing for gas-fired unit venting and purging Maintaining cooling and heating functions for buildings and production
3.6	Heating	Food preparation	5 min	To return to prime power		x	Prevention of loss of sales and profit Prevention of spoilage of in-process preparation
		Process	5 min	Indefinite until evaluated; normally for time for orderly shutdown, or To return to prime power		x	Prevention of in-process production damage Prevention of property damage Continued production Prevention of payment to workers during no production Lower insurance rates

Table 3-2—Condensed general criteria for preliminary consideration (*Continued*)

Section	General need	Specific need	Maximum tolerance duration of power failure	Recommended minimum auxiliary supply time	Type of auxiliary power system		System justification
					Emergency	Standby	
3.7	Refrigeration	Special equipment or devices which have critical warm-up (cryogenics)	5 min	To return to prime power		x	Prevention of equipment or product damage
		Depositories of critical nature (blood bank, etc.)	5 min (10 s per NFPA 99-1996)	To return to prime power		x	Prevention of loss of material stored
		Depositories of noncritical nature (meat, produce, etc.)	2 h	Indefinite until evaluated		x	Prevention of loss of material stored Lower insurance rates
3.8	Production	Critical process power (sugar factory, steel mills, chemical processes, glass products, etc.)	1 min	To return to prime power or until orderly shutdown		x	Prevention of product and equipment damage Continued normal production Reduction of payment to workers on guaranteed wages during nonproductive period Lower insurance rates Prevention of prolonged shutdown due to nonorderly shutdown

Table 3-2—Condensed general criteria for preliminary consideration (*Continued*)

Section	General need	Specific need	Maximum tolerance duration of power failure	Recommended minimum auxiliary supply time	Type of auxiliary power system		System justification
					Emergency	Standby	
3.8 (*Cont.*)	Production (*Cont.*)	Process control power	Uninterrupt- ible to 1 min	To return to prime power	x	x	Prevention of loss of machine and process computer control program Maintaining production Prevention of safety hazards from developing Prevention of out-of-tolerance products
3.9	Space conditioning	Temperature (critical application)	10 s	1 min To return to prime power	x	x	Prevention of personnel hazards Prevention of product or property damage Lower insurance rates Continuation of normal activities Prevention of loss of computer function
		Pressure (critical) pos/neg atmosphere	1 min	1 min To return to prime power	x	x	Prevention of personnel hazards Continuation of normal activities Prevention of product or property damage Lower insurance rates Compliance with local, state, and federal codes, standards, and laws

Table 3-2—Condensed general criteria for preliminary consideration (*Continued*)

Section	General need	Specific need	Maximum tolerance duration of power failure	Recommended minimum auxiliary supply time	Type of auxiliary power system		System justification
					Emergency	Standby	
3.9 (*Cont.*)	Space conditioning (*Cont.*)	Humidity (critical)	1 min	To return to prime power		x	Prevention of loss of computer functions Maintenance of normal operations and tests Prevention of explosions or other hazards
		Static charge	10 s or less	To return to prime power	x	x	Prevention of static electric charge and associated hazards Continuation of normal production (printing press operation, painting spray operations)
		Building heating and cooling	30 min	To return to prime power		x	Prevention of loss due to freezing Maintenance of personnel efficiency Continuation of normal activities
		Ventilation (toxic fumes)	15 s	To return to prime power or orderly shut-down	x	x	Reduction of health hazards Compliance with local, state, and federal codes, standards, and laws Reduction of pollution

23

Table 3-2—Condensed general criteria for preliminary consideration (*Continued*)

Section	General need	Specific need	Maximum tolerance duration of power failure	Recommended minimum auxiliary supply time	Type of auxiliary power system		System justification
					Emergency	Standby	
3.9 (*Cont.*)	Space conditioning (*Cont.*)	Ventilation (explosive atmosphere)	10 s	To return to prime power or orderly shutdown	x	x	Reduction of explosion hazard Prevention of property damage Lower insurance rates Compliance with local, state, and federal codes, standards, and laws Lower hazard of fire Reduce hazards to personnel
		Ventilation (building general)	1 min	To return to prime power		x	Maintaining of personnel efficiency Providing make-up air in building
		Ventilation (special equipment)	15 s	To return to prime power or orderly shutdown	x	x	Purging operation to provide safe shutdown or startup Lowering of hazards to personnel and property Meeting requirements of insurance company Compliance with local, state, and federal codes, standards, and laws Compliance with local, state, and federal codes, standards, and laws Continuation of normal operation
		Ventilation (all categories noncritical)	1 min	Optional		x	Maintaining comfort Preventing loss of tests
		Air pollution control	1 min	Indefinite until evaluated; compliance or shutdowns are options	x	x	Continuation of normal operation Compliance with local, state, and federal codes, standards, and laws

Table 3-2—Condensed general criteria for preliminary consideration (*Continued*)

Section	General need	Specific need	Maximum tolerance duration of power failure	Recommended minimum auxiliary supply time	Type of auxiliary power system		System justification
					Emergency	Standby	
3.10	Fire protection	Annunciator alarms	1 s	To return to prime power	x		Compliance with local, state, and federal codes, standards, and laws Lower insurance rates Minimizing life and property damage
		Fire pumps	10 s	To return to prime power		x	Compliance with local, state, and federal codes, standards, and laws Lower insurance rates Minimizing life and property damage
		Auxiliary lighting	10 s	5 min To return to prime power	x	x	Servicing of fire pump engine should it fail to start Providing visual guidance for fire-fighting personnel
3.11	Data processing	CPU memory tape/disk storage, peripherals	1/2 cycle	To return to prime power or orderly shutdown	x	x	Prevention of program loss Maintaining normal operations for payroll, process control, machine control, warehousing, reservations, etc.
		Humidity and temperature control	5–15 min (1 min for water-cooled equipment)	To return to prime power or orderly shutdown		x	Maintenance of conditions to prevent malfunctions in data processing system Prevention of damage to equipment Continuation of normal activity

Table 3-2—Condensed general criteria for preliminary consideration (*Continued*)

Section	General need	Specific need	Maximum tolerance duration of power failure	Recommended minimum auxiliary supply time	Type of auxiliary power system		System justification
					Emergency	Standby	
3.12	Life support and life safety systems (medical field, hospitals, clinics, etc.)	X-ray	Milliseconds to several hours	From no requirement To return to prime power, as evaluated	x	x	Maintenance of exposure quality Availability for emergencies
		Light	Milliseconds to several hours	To return to prime power	x	x	Compliance with local, state, and federal codes, standards, and laws Preventing interruption to operation and operating needs
		Critical-to-life machines and services	1/2 cycle to 10 s	To return to prime power	x	x	Maintenance of life Prevention of interruption of treatment or surgery Continuation of normal activity Compliance with local, state, and federal codes, standards, and laws
		Refrigeration	5 min	To return to prime power		x	Maintaining blood, plasma, and related stored material at recommended temperature and in prime condition

Table 3-2—Condensed general criteria for preliminary consideration *(Continued)*

Section	General need	Specific need	Maximum tolerance duration of power failure	Recommended minimum auxiliary supply time	Type of auxiliary power system		System justification
					Emergency	Standby	
3.13	Communication systems	Teletypewriter	5 min	To return to prime power		x	Maintenance of customer services Maintenance of production control and warehousing Continuation of normal communication to prevent economic loss
		Inner building	10 s	To return to prime power	x		Continuation of normal activity and control
		Television (closed circuit and commercial)	10 s	To return to prime power		x	Continuation of sales Meeting of contracts Maintenance of security Continuation of production
		Radio systems	10 s	To return to prime power	x	x	Maintenance of security and fire alarms Providing evacuation instructions Continuation of service to customers Prevention of economic loss Directing vehicles normally
		Intercommunications systems	10 s	To return to prime power	x	x	Providing evacuation instructions Directing activities during emergency Providing for continuation of normal activities Maintaining security
		Paging systems	10 s	1/2 h	x	x	Locating of responsible persons concerned with power outage Providing evacuation instructions Prevention of panic

Table 3-2—Condensed general criteria for preliminary consideration (*Continued*)

Section	General need	Specific need	Maximum tolerance duration of power failure	Recommended minimum auxiliary supply time	Type of auxiliary power system		System justification
					Emergency	Standby	
3.14	Signal circuits	Alarms and annunciation	1–10 s	To return to prime power	x	x	Prevention of loss from theft, arson, or riot Maintaining security systems Compliance with codes, standards, and laws Lower insurance rates Alarm for critical out-of-tolerance temperature, pressure, water level, and other hazardous or dangerous conditions Prevention of economic loss
		Land-based aircraft, railroad, and ship warning systems	1 s to 1 min	To return to prime power	x	x	Compliance with local, state, and federal codes, standards, and laws Prevention of personnel injury Prevention of property and economic loss

Readers using this recommended practice may find that various combinations of general needs will require an in-depth system and cost analysis that will modify the recommended equipment and systems to best meet the specific requirements.

Small commercial establishments and manufacturing plants will usually find their requirements under two or three of the general need guidelines given in this chapter. Large manufacturers and commercial facilities will find that portions or all of the need guidelines given in here apply to their operations and justify or require emergency and backup standby electric power.

3.2 Lighting

3.2.1 Introduction

Evaluation of the quality, quantity, type, and duration of emergency or standby power for lighting is necessary for each particular application. The different types of systems have various degrees of reliability that should be considered in the selection of the proper system.

3.2.2 Lighting for evacuation purposes

Interruption of power to a normal lighting system may cause injury or loss of life. Emergency lighting for evacuation purposes must energize automatically upon loss of normal lighting. Where legally required (ANSI/NFPA 101-1994) emergency systems are installed, lighting must be maintained for at least 1.5 h if battery-powered unit equipment is used. Emergency lighting must provide enough illumination to allow easy and safe egress from the area involved. All exit lights, signs, and stairwell lights should be included in both the emergency lighting system and the normal lighting system. Design of the emergency lighting system should include consideration of the need for lighting to silhouette protruding machines or objects in aisles.

3.2.3 Perimeter and security lighting

Emergency or standby power for perimeter and security lighting may be deemed necessary to reduce risk of injury, theft, or property damage. The power for perimeter lighting may not be required until several minutes after failure of normal power. In order to maintain perimeter lighting throughout the dark hours, a system should be capable of supplying power for 10–12 h for every 24 h the normal power source is off. For this reason, the unit battery equipment is not recommended for auxiliary perimeter lighting.

3.2.4 Warning lights

Emergency power should be available for all warning lights such as aircraft warning lights on high structures, ship warning lights on edges of waterways, and other warning lights that act to prevent injury or property damage. The power source selected should be capable of supplying emergency power throughout the duration of the longest anticipated power failure; therefore, the unit battery type is normally not suited for this application.

3.2.5 Health care facilities

Emergency lighting is of paramount importance in hospitals and similar institutions. The requirements for these areas are included in 3.12.

3.2.6 Standby lighting for equipment repair

Standby power for lighting should be installed in areas where the most probable internal power system failures may occur and in the main switchgear rooms. This requirement is justified by the necessity of having enough light to repair the equipment that failed and caused the loss of normal lighting.

3.2.7 Lighting for production

Interruption of power to a normal lighting system may cause serious curtailment or complete loss of production. Where there are no safety hazards or property damage associated with this need, the decision should be based on the economic evaluation of each particular application. Systems that provide power for emergency lighting may also provide high-level lighting to allow production to continue.

3.2.8 Lighting to reduce hazards to machine operators

A machine operator may be subjected to a high injury risk for the first few seconds after lighting has failed. Many machines present a safety hazard if suddenly plunged into darkness. Instantaneous emergency lighting is required for protection against this type of injury.

3.2.9 Supplemental lighting for high-voltage discharge systems

If mercury or other types of high-voltage discharge lighting are used for the regular system, consideration should be given to adding auxiliary lamps, such as incandescent or fluorescent. Some high-voltage discharge lamps require a cooling period before they restrike the arc and a warm-up period before they attain full brilliance. The total time required for full illumination after a momentary power interruption can range from 1 min for high-pressure sodium to 20 min for metal halide and mercury vapor.

3.2.10 Codes, rules, and regulations

Many states and municipalities have adopted their own specific codes regarding emergency lighting, in addition to those set down by the following organizations:

— The Occupational Safety and Health Act of 1970 (OSH Act) is charged with enforcing compliance and makes reference to the NEC and NFPA codes.
— NFPA 70-1996, the National Electric Code (NEC), Article 700, sets forth the standard of practice for emergency lighting equipment with regard to installation, operation, and maintenance.

— ANSI/NFPA 101-1994, the Life Safety Code, concerns itself with the specification of locations where emergency lighting is considered essential to life safety and specifics on exit marking.
— Underwriter's Laboratories, Inc., tests and approves equipment to uniform performance standards as established by ANSI/UL 924-1990.

3.2.11 Recommended systems

For short durations, primarily for personnel safety and evacuation purposes, battery units are satisfactory. For applications requiring longer service and heavier loads, an engine- or turbine-driven generator, which starts automatically upon failure of the prime power source, may be more suitable. ANSI/NFPA 101-1994 requires that emergency lighting facilities provide no less than an average of 10 lx ((1 fc) measured at any point along the path of egress at floor level. The standard allows illumination to decline to 6 lx (0.6 fc) average and 0.6 lx (.06 fc) minimum at the end of 1-1/2 h. The maximum top minimum illumination level may not exceed a a ration 40/1.

Table 3-3 summarizes the user's needs for emergency and standby electric power for lighting by application and areas.

3.3 Startup power

3.3.1 Introduction

Assume a cold boiler and a dead plant without electrical power or steam. From this premise, several very important issues must be considered:

— How will the plant be protected from freezing in cold weather? Even with gas heaters, will there be sufficient heat without fans and without interlocked make-up air units running?
— A steam turbine generator is on hand, but without forced draft, induced draft, boiler feed water, flame detectors, or control power. How can it be started?
— A gas turbine generator has been installed, but how can this be started without bringing it up in speed with a small steam turbine, an electric motor, or other prime mover? Gas compressors may be necessary and also require prime movers of some type.
— Steam-driven and electrically driven fire pumps are out of service. There may be no major fire protection until electric power or steam is restored.
— An uninterruptible power supply (UPS) of sufficient capacity is probably not on hand; otherwise, steam and electric power would not be down.

These statements illustrate the fact that adequate startup power is one of the most important considerations in the original design of any plant. Millions of dollars worth of equipment could be standing idle at a time of critical need if no allowance were made for starting the machines under expected conditions, such as a major power outage.

Table 3-3—Typical emergency and standby lighting recommendations

Standby[a]	Immediate, short-term[b]	Immediate, long-term[c]
Security lighting Outdoor perimeters Closed circuit TV Night lights Guard stations Entrance gates	Evacuation lighting Exit signs Exit lights Stairwells Open areas Tunnels Halls	Hazardous areas Laboratories Warning lights Storage areas Process areas
Production lighting Machine areas Raw materials storage Packaging Inspection Warehousing Offices	Miscellaneous Standby generator areas Hazardous machines	Warning lights Beacons Hazardous areas Traffic signals
Commercial lighting Displays Product shelves Sales counters Offices		Health care facilities Operating rooms Delivery rooms Intensive care areas Emergency treatment areas
Miscellaneous Switchgear rooms Landscape lighting Boiler rooms Computer rooms		Miscellaneous Switchgear rooms Elevator Boiler rooms Control rooms

[a] An example of a standby lighting system is an engine-driven generator.
[b] An example of an immediate short-term lighting system is the common unit battery equipment.
[c] An example of an immediate long-term lighting system is a central battery bank rated to handle the required lighting load only until a standby engine-driven generator is placed on-line.

3.3.2 Example of a system utilizing startup power

Starting major plant equipment without outside power is commonly referred to as a *black start* and is accomplished by using only the facilities available within the plant. One example of a system designed with black start capability, with a minimum electrical startup system, would be a large gas turbine driving a centrifugal compressor in the natural gas pipeline industry, where the high-pressure gas from the pipeline is used to drive expansion turbines and gas motors for cranking the turbine, operating pumps, and positioning valves. By utilizing the high-pressure gas for the large horsepower requirements, a small engine-driven generator, fueled by natural gas, is used to provide electric power for turbine accessories, battery charging, lighting, and powering other critical loads. When the turbine is running, a shaft-driven generator provides larger quantities of electric power for all station requirements; the small generator is placed on *standby*.

3.3.3 Lighting

In the design of the startup power system, first consideration should be given to installing battery-operated lights in the vicinity of the standby power source and switchgear.

3.3.4 Engine-driven generators

The battery-cranking power for the engine may also be used for some lights. Cranking may also be accomplished by compressed air supplied to a tank by the plant compressed-air system and prevented from leaving the tank into the plant system by a check valve.

The engines may be sized for short-term operation if some type of continuous power generation can be brought onto the line after startup. If no generation as a prime source of electric power has been installed, the diesel or engine generator should be sized for supporting all electrical needs for the generator auxiliaries, boilers, critical emergency lights, fire signals, exit lights, and other items listed in table 3-2.

3.3.5 Battery systems

Special consideration should be given to the design of the plant battery system or UPS, allowing for (1) adequate battery capacity to provide power for the necessary startup control systems, following a programmed safe stop; and (2), when possible, special disconnecting devices to automatically disconnect large power-consuming systems from the battery system to conserve battery capacity for restart.

With capacity for these minimum facilities in operation, consideration may then be given to installing sufficient capacity at the same time to support additional justified needs.

3.3.6 Other systems

Mobile equipment may suffice if it can reasonably be assumed to be available when needed. (Who has the highest priority when all have the need?) An alternate standby public utility line may also be available at a low cost from a separate source of supply. A neighboring plant with live generation may assist in an emergency.

3.3.7 System justification

A definite workable plan with the proper equipment should be evaluated, and action taken as justified, prior to the need.

3.4 Transportation

3.4.1 Introduction

This topic covers the moving of people and products by methods that depend upon electric power. The importance of maintaining power for these methods ranges from desirable to critical.

3.4.2 Elevators

Where two or more elevators are in use in buildings three or more stories high, the elevators or banks of elevators should be connected to separate sources of power. There are situations where standby power is required for all elevators within 15 s. Savings may be made by supplying power during outages of the normal supply to one-half the elevators installed, providing the traffic can be rerouted and the capacity of the elevators is adequate. Power must be transferred to the second bank of elevators within 1 min or so of the prime power loss to clear stalled elevators. Power may be left on this bank until normal power returns.

Where elevator service is critical for personnel and patients, it is desirable to have automatic power transfer with manual supervision. Operators and maintenance men may not be available in time, if the power failure occurs on a weekend or at night.

Where a single feeder supplies more than one elevator, selective coordination of the protective devices may enhance elevator availability. This is a requirement of the 1996 edition of the NEC, Section 620-26.

— *Typical elevator system.* Figure 3-3 shows an elevator emergency power transfer system whereby one preferred elevator is fed from a vital load bus through an emergency riser, while the rest of the elevators are fed from the normal service. By providing an automatic transfer switch for each elevator and a remote selector station, it is possible to select individual elevators, thus permitting complete evacuation in the event of power failure. The engine generator set and emergency riser need only be sized for one elevator, thus minimizing the installation cost. The controls for the remote selector, automatic transfer switches, and engine starting are independent of the elevator controls, thereby simplifying installation.

— *Regenerated power.* Regenerated power is a concern for motor generator-type elevator applications. In some elevator applications, the motor is used as a brake when the elevator is descending and generates electricity. Electric power is then pumped back into the power source. If the source is commercial utility power, it can easily be absorbed. If the power source is an engine-driven generator, the regenerated power can cause the generating set and the elevator to overspeed. To prevent overspeeding of the elevator, the maximum amount of power that can be pumped back into the generating set must be known. The permissible amount of absorption is approximately 20% of the generating set's rating in kilowatts. If the amount pumped back is greater than 20%, other loads must be connected to the generating set, such as emergency lights or "dummy" load resistances. Emergency lighting should be permanently connected to the generating set for maximum safety. A dummy load can also be automatically switched on the line whenever the elevator is operating from an engine-driven generator.

3.4.3 Conveyors and escalators

Escalators and personnel conveyors may require emergency power since physically handicapped persons ride up and would have great difficulty walking down, even though a normal person would be able to do so were the power off.

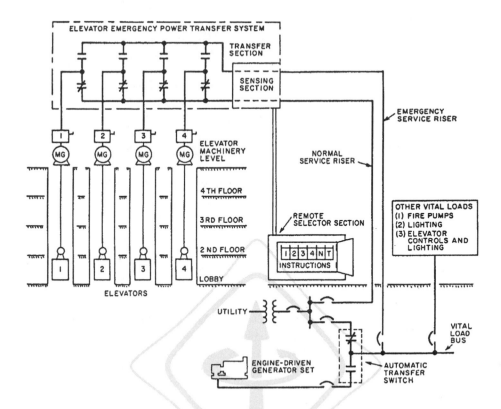

Figure 3-3—Elevator emergency power transfer system

Expanding systems require reevaluation of standby power needs each time equipment is added. Using conveyors to feed a few cattle or gather a few eggs may have once eased someone's labor, with labor filling in if needed. However, as these operations have become larger and larger, they have become more and more dependent upon electric power; therefore, the feasibility of electric power outage producing a disaster has increased, and the need for standby power more important.

3.4.4 Other transportation systems

Power for charging equipment for battery-powered vehicles is usually a noncritical requirement. Time available for the generation to come on-line varies from several minutes to several hours.

A few examples of transportation systems that may need standby power are the following:

— Conveyors for raw materials through to finished goods
— Warehouse high-stacking loading and unloading equipment, and conveyors delivering finished goods to shipping facilities
— Slurry pumps for long pipelines
— Livestock feeder conveyors

3.5 Mechanical utility systems

3.5.1 Introduction

Often the need for mechanical utilities is as great as that for electric power utilities. These are interdependent. We can speak of utility systems as a whole since, to most managers and corporate officials, these are all united in a group under the heading "utilities."

3.5.2 Typical utility systems for which reliable power may be necessary

Mechanical utility systems comprise the following services for which reliable electric power is usually required:

— Compressed air for pneumatic power
— Cooling water (including return pumps, pressure pumps, tower fans)
— Well water or other pumped sources for personnel use
— Hydraulic systems
— Sewer systems (sanitary, industrial, storm)
— Gas systems (natural, propane, oxygen), including compressors
— Fire pumps and associated water supplies
— Steam systems (low and high pressures)
— Ventilation (building and process)
— Vacuum systems
— Compressed air for instrumentation

Although this list is not exhaustive, it alerts a plant manager or engineer to the various needs and potential losses that may occur if electric power is not available.

Systems may be required for manufacturing and services to maintain other services. For example, electric power, water, and compressed air for boilers used to supply steam for the generation of electricity.

A 0.1–5 s power failure may cause plant operators to spend minutes or hours restarting equipment and making adjustments until all systems are again stable. Such disruptions to production should be prevented if economically justifiable.

3.5.3 Orderly shutdown of mechanical utility systems

An orderly shutdown of power to mechanical utility systems may be acceptable with a short-time smaller supply source of power provided for the following requirements:

— Maintaining temperature or pressure on vulcanizers until the product can be finished.
— Maintaining hydraulic pressure until a batch process is completed, or until the pressure can be released without loss.
— Operating pumps for a time until all process water has been shut off or has drained back into the sumps to prevent flooding. This becomes serious when the water is con-

taminated with oil and other waste when flooding occurs and special handling may be needed to comply with antipollution requirements.

— Maintaining ventilation to clear explosive atmospheres while a normal shutdown proceeds. Purging air is critical to some oven-drying processes.

— Preventing sanitary sewers from overflowing before personnel evacuation takes place.

— Running gas compressors for the finishing of a critical process.

This list is not exhaustive, but represents needs of various types, which should be sufficient to alert a plant engineer so that a plan may be prepared for an orderly shutdown. Management may then be justified to act on the plan and not be caught unprepared in an emergency situation.

3.5.4 Alternates to orderly shutdown

An orderly shutdown may not be acceptable. Then an alternate may be selected, such as the following:

— *Maintaining utilities without an interruption.* Full capacity standby power must be available as well as uninterruptible power for boiler controls, on-line computers, and essential relays and motor starters.

— *Accepting an outage but returning on standby power.* Full capacity power must be available. Startup of functions will be required since magnetic motor starters and relays will have dropped out. Although power is off for 0.1–5 s, it will take 15–30 min or more for return to normal operation.

3.6 Heating

3.6.1 Maintaining steam production

Continuous-process plants require uninterrupted steam production. Minimum requirements for continuous steam production are sufficient combustion air, air to instruments and actuators, water and fuel supplies, plus a continuous power supply to most flame supervision systems. The maximum interruption tolerable is that duration during which the inertia of the fans or pumping equipment will maintain flows and pressures above minimum limits. Table 3-4 illustrates how this can be achieved.

3.6.2 Process heating

Process heating is defined as heat required to maintain certain process materials at the required temperature. Noncritical heating processes, due to the inherent heat capacities of such systems, can withstand a power interruption of considerable duration, i.e., 5 min to a maximum of several hours.

Table 3-4—Systems for continued steam production

Components	Allowable outage duration	Systems
Flame supervision systems	Nil	Mechanical stored energy systems Motor-generator set ride-through UPS systems
Motor controls and instrumentation	Nil	Same as above
Boiler fans	1/2 to 2 s	Multiple utility services, either on-line and relayed, or off-line, switched, and transferred
Air compressor	To 30 min, depending on storage; nonessential air users should be automatically shut off	Multiple utility services Turbine- or engine-driven generator, off-line Turbine (combustion, steam, water), off-line
Water pump	To 5 min, depending on water drum capacity and upsets in steam production caused by power disturbance	Multiple utility services either on-line and relayed, or off-line, switched, and transferred Turbine (combustion, steam, water), off-line, automatic start
Oil pumps (for burners)	To 15 cycles, more with flywheel	Multiple utility services, on-line and relayed Turbine (combustion, steam, water), on-line
Electric oil supply pumps	Several minutes	Turbine- or engine-driven generator, off-line Multiple utility services, on- or off-line

Any of the following systems would be adequate for this application:

— Engine-driven generators, off-line
— Multiple utility services, on-line and relayed, or off-line, switches, and transfers
— Turbine (combustion, steam, water), off-line or on-line
— Mechanical stored-energy system, with auxiliary motor generator sets off-line

Other heating processes, such as cord and fabric treating and drying, are of such a critical nature that loss of heat will cause an out-of-specification product within 10 s, but the gas or oil burners and flame detectors are sensitive to drops in voltage of about 40% for a second or less. In this case, an uninterruptible supply for the controls and an engine generator for a 10 s main power supply or an alternate feed system may be required.

Infrared drying of enamel on automobiles and appliances is a form of heating by electric energy that must be maintained. A short interruption, perhaps 10 s, may be acceptable to bring on-line standby generation or perform automatic switching to an auxiliary power source.

Losses may be substantial if power is lost during the heat treating of metals and when either direct or indirect melting of metals is in process. Two evaluations must be made: one based on not losing the flame on the fuels used, and the other based on accepting an interruption for a short period with a restart necessary. Uninterruptible power is several times more expensive than switching or emergency power, but saves the product and prevents process interruption. Switching or emergency power is less expensive, but product or process losses may exceed the initial savings in the chosen electric supply system.

Induction and dielectric heating are other forms of electrical heating that may or may not allow short interruptions to be tolerated. Most processes, whether in production or in other fields, could tolerate an interruption of sufficient duration to come on-line with switched sources or an engine- or turbine-driven generator.

3.6.3 Building heating

Buildings, even in the coldest regions, can usually be without heating for a minimum of 30 min. The same systems listed for noncritical heating processes will be suitable for this application.

3.7 Refrigeration

3.7.1 Requirements of selected refrigeration applications

Requirements for refrigeration are usually noncritical for short power interruptions of several minutes to several hours. The need may become extremely critical as the length of time of the outage increases. Consider these refrigeration needs:

— Production of ice cream or the freezing of foods may stop in the middle of the process. Not only will all production be lost during a power failure, but damage may result to the product in process.
— Material in storage may be in jeopardy as temperatures rise. Cafeterias, frozen food lockers, meat cooling and storage facilities, dairies, and other food operations require refrigeration and will soon be in trouble as the length of the power outage increases.
— Scientific tests of long duration may require accurately maintained low temperatures. Short outages of electric power may destroy the tests and require repeating. An

expensive and time-consuming process should be provided with a standby power system.

— Medical facilities require refrigeration for blood banks, antibiotics, and for long-range laboratory experiments and cultures that could be spoiled.

— As the state of the art of superconductivity develops, improves, and spreads to applicable fields, power for cryogenic refrigeration equipment operation will probably become critical.

Where present refrigeration units are electrically driven, when new units of moderate size are to be installed in permanent locations, and when other needs exist (as is usually the case) for emergency or standby power, a common engine-driven generator or alternate utility source should be considered.

Because of the slow rise in temperature of cold-storage facilities, a savings may be made by the use of a smaller than normal standby electric generator. By switching power to various units in turn, an acceptable storage temperature may be maintained until normal electric power has been reestablished.

3.7.2 Refrigeration to reduce hazards

Certain chemical processes are exothermal and release heat during the chemical reaction. Loss of the cooling or refrigeration system may cause severe damage or even an explosion.

3.7.3 Typical system to maintain refrigeration

A manual starting of an engine-driven generator, turbine, or alternate utility supply will usually suffice, providing a suitable alarm is installed to notify responsible persons of a loss of refrigeration.

3.8 Production

3.8.1 Justification for maintaining production in an industrial facility during a power failure

Production continuation in an industrial facility during a power failure is justified by the total sum of many tangible and intangible savings. The following paragraphs discuss various considerations that can affect these savings.

Is there a guaranteed wage clause in the labor contract? If so, there will be a direct loss in wages paid for which no production is received. Where power requirements are low and the heavy-power-demanding machines are left shut down until normal power is returned, a small electric supply system can be justified to supply finishing areas, inspection areas, office areas, and other areas where most employees work.

Who is waiting for the product? There are periods when the products are being routed to warehouses and machines are not running at capacity previous to the outage. In this case, the cost of machine downtime is lower than it would be for a product that a customer will not receive, or will receive late, if production is at full capacity and an outage occurs.

What is the cost of the product spoiled in process? In the rubber industry, material may become sealed in vulcanizers, extruders, or mixers at high temperatures and will be difficult and expensive to remove. Steam or water pressure may drop to zero and prevent proper cures with losses due to poor or ruined products.

If all electric power is lost during certain processes in the making of sugar, glass, steel, pharmaceuticals, rubber, paper, chemicals, and some other materials, the product may have to be scrapped.

What is the cost of consequential damages? While the material ruined may be scrap, there may be as many problems and costs associated with its removal as with the loss itself. Some material must be dug out or removed by hand, piece by piece, until lines are cleared or chambers are empty and clean so that an orderly startup can follow.

What is lost in reestablishing work efficiency? A 1/2 h electric power interruption disorganizes the workers. Experience indicates that, following the interruption, it will take men and women at least two or more hours to settle down, go to work, and reach the production level at which they were operating just prior to the power failure. It may take days to reestablish normal procedures in scheduling of incoming and outgoing materials and in telegrams, letters, notices, and calls explaining delays and changing promises.

A less tangible item lost is that of goodwill. For example, in the film processing industry, the customer may not consider the replacement of the exposed film with unexposed as adequate compensation for "once in a lifetime" pictures that were spoiled due to a power failure.

Real and potential costs and losses must be calculated or estimated and added together to justify an emergency and standby power system for industrial and commercial facilities.

A reasonable estimate of the costs associated with each past power failure should be calculated and recorded in a journal with the date, duration, and conditions existing at the time. As time goes on, this could be valuable factual backup information for budget requests.

3.8.2 Equations for determining cost of power interruptions

A rough estimate of the direct cost of a power failure from a cash flow viewpoint may be calculated as follows:

total cost of a power failure $= E + H + I$

where

E = cost of labor for employees affected (in dollars)
H = scrap loss due to power failure (in dollars)
I = cost of startup (in dollars)

The value of E, H, and I may be calculated as follows:

$E = AD \, (1.5 \, B = C)$
$H = FG$
$I = JK \, (B = C) = LG$

where

A	=	number of productive employees affected
B	=	base hourly rate of employees affected (in dollars)
C	=	fringe and overhead hourly cost per employee affected (in dollars)
D	=	duration of power interruption (in hours)
F	=	units of scrap material due to power failure
G	=	cost per unit of scrap material due to power failure (in dollars)
J	=	startup time (in hours)
K	=	number of employees involved in startup
L	=	units of scrap material due to startup

After the cost of downtime has been calculated, the savings in utilities should be subtracted to arrive at a total cost of downtime.

3.8.3 Commercial buildings

For commercial establishments, a similar example may be assembled based on the length of the power interruption, labor cost, loss of profit on sales, loss due to theft, and startup costs.

3.8.4 Additional losses due to power interruptions

In addition to losses relating to cash flow are those more difficult to calculate but which should be included when available and applicable, such as

— Prorated depreciation of capital costs
— Depreciation in quality in process materials
— "Cost" of money invested in unused materials or machines

Other losses may occur under special or unusual conditions. In an industrial plant operating at 100% capacity, any loss in production results in the loss of the profit of the item or service. The prorated cost of fixed and variable overhead becomes a loss. Customers may switch to competitors. Expenditures for standby power have additional justification under this condition.

3.8.5 Determining the likelihood of power failures

Next, the likelihood of a power failure must be determined by studying the record of the plant or utility company electrical supply, or by transmitting the service requirements to the local utility and obtaining their recommendations. Examples of recorded power failures are shown in table 3-5.

Rather than complete power failures, as recorded in table 3-5, table 3-6 covers short-term dips.

Table 3-5—Example of recorded power failures

Date	Time	Duration	Transmission line
9 March	09:52	10 min	14
11 June	21:53	12 s	14
11 June	22:13	9 s	14
15 July	20:40	5.5 s	13 + 22
17 July	19:13 20:44	1–2 min	14 (9 times)

Table 3-6—Example of recorded short-term dips

Date	Time	Line	Duration (cycles)	Line-to-ground dip (per unit)			Voltage after
				E_z	E_b	E_c	
14 April	21:50	32	18	0.86	0.81	0.75	1.0
30 April	15:53	System	43	0.83	0.92	0.92	1.0
9 May	07:52	23, 24	32	0.90	0.85	0.83	1.0
9 May	07:54	20	24	0.31	0.31	0.58	1.0
9 May	07:55	22	46	1.00	1.00	0.69 0.40 0.50 0.06	
17 May	00:43	13, 22	21	0.50	0.69	0.31	1.0

A projection should be made, working with the utility company, as to whether or not the power reliability will improve or decline. Since the cost of a power failure, as defined in this standard, is paid by the user, it is important that he or she relate the reliability of power duration and quality to the need for justification.

3.8.6 Factors that increase the likelihood of power failures

As designed load is reached or exceeded, the probability of a power failure increases. A similar probability exists as systems become more complex and as system equipment ages.

3.8.7 Power reserves

Power reserves in the user's area should be investigated. Adequate reserve margins above peak load demands provide a guide to power reliability because the margin provides for some contingencies.

3.8.8 Examples of standby power applications for production

The following typical examples were taken at random from users who found, after evaluation, purchase, and installation, that a standby power system was justified:

— A drug company installed a special engine generator backup system based on the need for constant temperatures in manufacturing processes. The value of processes saved during blackouts soon exceeded the cost of the equipment installed by more than 10 times.

— A photographic film processing company specified a 45 kW engine generator when the film processing machines were ordered. Film must continue to progress to each step of the process within 30 s or loss of quality will result.

— A 400 kW, 480 V, three-phase engine generator was installed in a highly automated egg farm. Electric service continuity was mandatory for egg production and the welfare of the "machines" (chickens). During the first year, two electric service outages occurred and the automatic emergency generator reliability supplied power.

3.8.9 Types of systems to consider

An engine- or turbine-driven generator or an alternate independent utility source usually will fulfill the requirements for standby power. More than a standby system may be required for critical loads. Motor starters, contactors, and relays held closed by a solenoid or electromagnet have no ride-through and are especially sensitive to short-time power outages or voltage dips. Their dropout characteristics vary with respect to voltage level and the length of duration of the voltage dip. As a guide, a voltage dip to 60% or 70% of rated voltage for 0.5 s will de-energize many of the devices. The longer the duration of the voltage dip, the more devices will de-energize. Depending on the application of these devices, an emergency or UPS system may be justifiable, especially where boiler controls, critical chemical processes, safety devices, and other critical systems are required to be maintained (Funk and Beatty 1987 [B6]).

Devices much more likely to fail or malfunction due to voltage excursions are modern electronic switching devices, which tolerate almost no time delay, and pressure, temperature, and flow transmitters and receivers of the electronic type. Automatic controllers for process control, data reduction, and logging are in this same category (Gilbert 1960 [B7]).

A UPS system for critical on-line computer or boiler control loads may be required since a 0.5 cycle outage may mean restarting the plant. In combination, the UPS system may be of short duration since the standby equipment should be designed to be on-line in from 10–60 s.

Factory clocks used for production control, or for the basis of incentive wage payments, should be arranged to maintain accurate time by the use of batteries for power during the time of any power interruption.

Support of production facilities will justify most or all of the user's needs detailed in this chapter. The evaluation, justification, and decision to purchase and install a standby, emergency, or UPS system, or a combination of these systems, must include the consideration of all the electric power requirements for all listed needs in the case of a power failure.

3.9 Space conditioning

3.9.1 Definition

Space conditioning is a controlled environment, either to maintain standard ambient conditions or some artificial alteration of a standard environment in a building, room, or other enclosure.

3.9.2 Description

A controlled environment may include any of the following variables:

— Temperature
— Vapor content
— Ventilation
— Lighting
— Sound
— Odor
— Gas
— Dust
— Organisms

3.9.3 Codes and standards

Codes apply primarily where personnel safety is involved, but still very little reference is made specifically to power supply requirements. Most requirements of the OSH Act are dedicated to ventilation of areas where hazardous gas, contaminants, and other similar elements and conditions can exist that would endanger personnel safety. Sections 1910.1006 and 1910.96 of the OSH Act give such requirements. Where *adequate* ventilation is referenced, conditions exist that may warrant backup or uninterruptible power supplies to provide this ventilation.

3.9.4 Application considerations

Air-conditioning loads for personal comfort are not normally considered critical and are even shed under overload conditions in some cases. Where equipment is sensitive to temperature, however, such as where solid-state electronic components exist, air conditioning can be critical. Where continuous backup or standby power is not available, a self-contained emergency or standby generator would apply. An UPS specifically for this purpose is not normally necessary since loss of power would cause no instantaneous temperature change. Likewise, where moisture and humidity cause serious equipment and operating problems, heating might require some type of backup power supply.

Table 3-2 shows examples of tolerable outage time for various applications. Ideally, tests should be run by the designer or planner to determine the maximum transfer times tolerable. Amount of power needed, acceptable outage time, and economics will determine the applicable power supply. Often, economics dictate that power for space conditioning be incidental to total power supply requirements, and the user must evaluate the ultimate consequences of loss of power. An adequate alarm system might be a consideration in this case.

Alarm and signal circuits often require as much or more reliability than equipment providing critical space conditioning. A UPS would be necessary where even a temporary loss of power would endanger personnel or cause severe equipment damage.

3.9.5 Examples of space conditioning where auxiliary power may be justified

Typical situations and facilities in which a comprehensive study of the need for supplemental electric power is warranted are as follows:

— Commercial and laboratory botanical installations may require programmed cyclic control of temperature, humidity, and lights to develop the crop yield or desired experimental results. The loss of temperature or humidity control for 6–8 h can result in total loss of a crop. A greenhouse must have maintained temperature in order to produce.

— Tropical animal raising requires control of ventilation, temperature, humidity, and lighting. All are completely dependent on electric power. A loss of heat or cooling can result in death or illness to all animals being raised. Lighting and temperature changes from the established cycle can induce unwanted breeding periods in many exotic creatures. Egg production may be greatly curtailed by temperature changes or loss of light.

— Agricultural operations are often located in remote areas where long utility lines are susceptible to damage.

— Final operations and packaging of materials susceptible to contamination are conducted in *clean-room*-type environments. A power interruption will shut down the total operation, and contamination may result as people exit, unless the room is kept under positive pressure to prevent in-drafts from bringing in contaminants. Such contaminants will necessitate a complete recleaning of the room before it can be used again.

— In large processing plants, priorities may be established for essential loads. Nonessential loads may be dropped automatically by load-shedding systems in the event of a power failure, and other limited emergency sources must be relied upon. A reevaluation of these priorities should be undertaken. Critical temperature controls may have been placed in an air-conditioned space. These controls must function to achieve an orderly process shutdown, but can fail due to overheating caused by lack of ventilation or cooling.

— Windowless buildings or inside rooms may become unsafe for occupancy during an extended power interruption. Power supplies to keep these areas ventilated should be installed if evacuation of all personnel is not acceptable.

3.9.6 Typical auxiliary power systems

Needs may require any one or more types of emergency and standby power systems available. An engine driven generator or combustion turbine should be considered for these applications. Switching to a separate alternate electric utility line would involve a lower capital cost, should such a line be readily available. In addition, a short-time UPS system may be required for critical applications to supply power during engine startup or switching.

3.10 Fire protection

3.10.1 Codes, rules, and regulations

Various codes, standards, laws, rules, and regulations contain either advisory or mandatory statements related to emergency and standby power systems for fire protection. See California Administrative Code, Title 24, Part 3, Basic Electrical Regulations (Article E700, Emergency Systems); ANSI/NFPA 101-1994; pp. 19 and 20 of IEEE Committee Report 1974 [B9]; and Katz 1968 [B12]. There appears to be more written on the subjects of wiring system reliability and needs than on the source of electric power supply or the checking and maintenance of the complete installation. All three are vital.

Article 760 of the NEC lists some requirements for protecting circuitry in alarm and signal systems. Article 230-94 of the NEC pertains more to the power supply by allowing a fire alarm circuit to be connected to the supply side of a service overcurrent device if it has separate overcurrent protection.

The requirements of all local, state, and national standards and codes should be determined. The insurance company that will underwrite the insurance can provide valuable assistance in making sure that all requirements are met.

A common-sense approach to fire protection should be used even beyond the minimum standard of meeting the letter of the law and insurance requirements. The primary goal is to avoid a destructive fire, or, in the event that a fire has started, to limit it to a local area with minimum damage to property and no harm to personnel. In-depth knowledge of the industrial facility and of processes by plant engineers and other responsible plant personnel should be utilized to reduce the likelihood of a fire or the extent of a fire's damage, should one begin.

3.10.2 Arson

Arson may be a source of a fire; power for plant security, lighting, signaling, and communication covered in subsequent subclauses should be regarded as contributing to the reduction of possible loss by fire from this cause.

3.10.3 Typical needs

The user's possible specific needs in combination with the general need of emergency and standby power systems for fire protection include

— Power, usually batteries, to crank the engine on an engine-driven fire pump
— Sprinkler-flow alarm systems
— Communication power to notify the fire department and to assist in guiding their activities
— Lights for the firemen to work by in the buildings, around the outside area, and mobile on company trucks
— Power for the boilers that supply steam-driven fire pumps
— Motors driving fire pumps, well pumps, and booster pumps
— Air compressors associated with fire water tanks
— Smoke and heat alarms
— Deluge valves
— Electrically operated plant gates, drawbridges, etc.
— Communications, such as public address systems for directing evacuation of personnel
— Fire and hazardous gas detectors

3.10.4 Application considerations

A fire almost always warrants initiation of an emergency shutdown in a plant either by operator-initiated devices or by automatic operation. The circuit required for shutdown is obviously critical, as are all main circuits for the above-mentioned fire protection equipment. Uninterruptible power supplies should be first choice for these applications. Where automatic fire protection is employed, like sprinkler systems, CO_2 discharge, etc., nuisance initiations must be prevented, a condition that lends itself to application of uninterruptible power supplies.

It is common practice in large plants to back up an electrically driven fire water pump with a mechanically driven one such as a diesel drive. If all ac power is lost in an emergency shutdown operation, fire protection is maintained. In this case, the ac power supply to the motor-driven pump is not absolutely critical. If a mechanical drive pump is not available, the motor-driven pump would normally be supplied by an emergency generator.

Under emergency conditions, such as fire, communications are sometimes vital to personnel and equipment safety. Under emergency conditions, communications should not be subjected to an outage of any kind. Even momentary outages of a few cycles might cause erroneous communications, especially where remote supervisory control is employed.

3.10.5 Feeder routing to fire protection equipment

Electric power distribution systems supplying fire equipment should be routed so as not to be burned out by a fire in the area they are protecting.

Protection of control circuitry, as well as main fire protection circuitry, can be enhanced by underground conduits, separate conduit and wire from other circuits, and fire-resistant insulated cable such as type MI.

3.11 Data processing

3.11.1 Classification of systems

Most data processing installations can be grouped into two general classes of operation in accordance with their usage. These classifications are off-line and on-line. These categories will be helpful in identifying a data processing system's vulnerability to electrical power disturbances, since an off-line process will rarely require power buffering or backup sources or equipment. Conversely, it is common for an on-line system to warrant the additional expense of buffering or backup equipment.

3.11.1.1 Off-line data processing systems

These systems are generally set up to perform one or more programs at a time in a sequential or batch type. Usually such systems have a program operator for automatic processing of control cards for a given job run. Often, 24 h operation for a heavily loaded system may be necessary. In the off-line category, for the most part, are business, scientific, and computer center applications. Systems of this type are particularly vulnerable when the programs are lengthy (several hours in duration). Thus the insertion of several natural breaks or checkpoints in the program for segmentation of long programs is highly desirable. Programming can be designed to save intermediate results at a checkpoint and to have the option of restarting at the last checkpoint that preceded the power interruption. Such a practice in program interruption can be valuable in protecting against peripheral equipment failure. Many current programs are being designed without checkpoint techniques even though the practice has been found to be feasible. Data-dependent programs have running times that vary in duration of the magnitude of input data and, accordingly, it is difficult to limit the run to much less than a 20 min period.

3.11.1.2 On-line data systems

On-line data systems, or as they are often called, *real-time* systems, are systems that are time- and event-oriented. They must respond to events that occur randomly in time, often coincidentally. An awareness of the system of events that occur that are external to the computer and beyond its influence is a requirement. In this category are such applications as industrial process monitoring and control systems, airline passenger reservations systems, vehicular traffic control, certain specialized scheduling applications, international credit card and bank associated credit/transaction systems, and many others. With these systems, the computer outage problem due to power interruption is usually more critical than in off-line applications. Furthermore, there is generally no merit in segmenting programs. In most cases, any outage or power interruption will result in the loss of some data that were available only during the time period of the outage. The form of the input data is not conveniently available for a rerun, but may come from sensors such as thermocouples or pressure transducers that are scanned by a computer. When a computer controls a process, potential problems resulting from a power disturbance are generally serious enough in terms of product damage or equipment malfunctioning to warrant the use of a reserve or backup power source. Furthermore, any solution, to be adequate, must accomplish the necessary switching to the backup source without power interruption to the computer. It is obvious that the potential losses to several hundred users, or input stations, to a time-shared computer system would warrant the providing of a backup source that can practically guarantee uninterruptible power. In cases where equipment or process monitoring must be made, as through data logging, protection from destruction of only the core memory content during a power interruption may be adequate. Automatic restart upon return of power is possible to minimize time that the equipment is down and can often be utilized with the additional provision for a manual means of updating the system data or information not gathered or scanned during an interruption.

3.11.1.3 Single-phase versus three-phase

The foregoing discussion has categorized data processing equipment and resulting electrical loads by their respective functional usage, that is, whether they are off-line or on-line systems. In most cases, large systems are involved. A further differentiation that can be made is by the magnitude of load. As with most power utilization equipment, smaller power consuming devices can generally be supplied from a single-phase source. The differentiation between single-phase versus three-phase power consuming systems is often necessary since the methods of protecting against input power disturbances and outages can be quite different for each system. Some of the data processing systems that use single-phase power will employ microprocessors or minicomputers. Others may consist of multiple single-phase load units distributed in their connection to three-phase power so as to achieve a reasonable load balance when all units are operating. This may result in load unbalance when some of the units are turned off.

In general, computers and peripheral units that draw less than 1.5 kVA will often be single phase. Those that draw more than 10 kVA often require three-phase power. In most cases, single-phase loads can be connected to three-phase sources provided load unbalance at maximum load is not excessive, generally taken as 25% or less.

3.11.2 Needs of data processing equipment from a user's viewpoint

In general, data are gathered in analog or digital form and converted to one or the other system. (Refer to definitions in the preceding paragraphs.) These data in electrical form are then processed through one or several programs by an electronic computer, minicomputer, or microprocessor. The results are traced or printed out, or a signal is generated and fed back to form a closed-loop system that provides control to match preset conditions. Both types of outputs are commonly available and used.

3.11.2.1 Real-time data processing

Both industrial and commercial users apply real-time data processing systems with a computer on-line. Failure of the data processing system often causes loss of valuable data or interruption of a critical process, either of which may result in extensive financial losses and require hours, days, or even weeks to fully recover. Failure of computers providing control may also jeopardize the safety of personnel. These failures can occur as a result of an electric power failure. Thus a reliable high-quality primary power supply is frequently justified to minimize loss of money and to prevent injury or loss of life.

3.11.2.2 Process or operational controls

A short list of control operations that frequently include data processing equipment, mini-computers, or microprocessors will suffice to alert users to the types of hazards and losses that may occur as a result of a power failure. Applications are categorized for both industrial and commercial classifications.

— *Industrial applications.* Materials handling; regulating control and status monitoring of pipelines, compressor, and pumping stations at remote locations; mixing compounds; grinding, drilling, machining; twisting textile fibers; steel mill processing; refining (oil); automatic testing and gauging; fabric processing; power flow and load dispatching; safety and security monitoring; process control and data acquisition.

— *Commercial applications.* Controlling elevators; automated checkstand combined with inventory control; newspaper production machines; airline passenger reservations; computer-aided emergency vehicle dispatching; environmental, life safety, security monitoring and control for buildings; typesetting; accounting; traffic control—cars, rail, and airplane; stock exchanges and broker transactions; corporation computers for engineering, scientific, and business matters; hospital diagnostic equipment and individual intensive care systems; banking, financial, and credit transactions.

3.11.2.3 History of developing needs

With the advent of the electronic computer as a part of data processing and process control, an increased emphasis has been placed on the need for emergency and standby power systems to assure a continuous flow of energy. Coupled with this need is a superimposed problem, namely, the suppression of most short-time switching interruptions, voltage surges, dips, and frequency excursions. Often the suppression of transient disturbances and the need for emergency or standby power can be satisfied through a single installation of supplementary or auxiliary equipment. These transient disturbances have been a part of the electric power supply in the past, but caused few problems until electronic equipment came into extensive use. In some instances the solid-state power control equipment has caused problems, particularly on small, independent power systems.

3.11.3 Power requirements for data processing equipment

By the proper selection of an electric supply system, the power needs associated with data processing with a computer can be met, namely, a reliable source of noise-free electric power at all times and of a much higher quality than previously demanded by most devices.

The problem is how to reconcile commercial short-duration power interruptions with relatively short time domains in electronic circuits. In early stages of data processing equipment and computer equipment development, it was not unusual to experience problems with hardware and software when power disturbances of microseconds in duration were experienced. Most equipment built in that era was extremely vulnerable to such short-time disturbances. The goal of most manufacturers in today's technology is to build from 4 ms to 1 cycle of carryover, or ride-through time, into their equipment.

Table 3-7 shows computer input power quality parameters for several manufacturers. The user should consider table 3-7 only as a source of some examples since computer designs vary with size of computers, their processing power, and the technology available when the design was created. They are continually changing and the parameters of power needs are changing rapidly with the designs. Some of the paragraphs that follow expand on the individual parameters that are presented in the table. Although there is a degree of variance among computer manufacturers, the following represents the principle power parameters that are considered important by most major companies. While several of these parameters, such as frequency variation, can be relatively insignificant when power is derived from a commercial power source, they can become an important design consideration when supplemental or independent power sources are applied as a means of power quality improvement.

3.11.3.1 Steady-state voltage

208Y/120 V single- and three-phase voltage is the most common electronic equipment utilization voltage with some single-phase 120, 120/240, or 240 V. Some equipment is reconnectable for use at several voltages by use of an internal tapped transformer. Tolerance on the 60 Hz voltage varies among manufacturers; however, limits as listed in ANSI C84.1-1989 are +6% and −13%.

A growing trend is to provide regulated low-voltage direct current for logic circuits by rectifying the output from 400–40 000 Hz electronic inverters. These devices, though lacking ride-through ability when installed without the addition of sizable banks of energy storage capacitors, do offer a compact and convenient source of regulated low-voltage dc power. With proper design and redundance, their reliability is at least equal to that of a central motor-generator.

As discussed later, where 400 Hz or other special frequency power must be distributed to computer equipment from a location remote from the computer equipment, special considerations must be made for voltage drop (increases with higher frequency systems). Conductors are ordinarily installed in nonferrous raceways.

Table 3-7—Typical range of input power quality and load parameters of a major computer manufacturer

Parameters	Range
1) Voltage limit, steady-state (all phases)	+6%, −13%
2) Voltage disturbances (all phases)	Surge +15% for 0.5 s maximum Sag −18% for 0.5 s maximum Transient overvoltage 150–200% for 0.2 ms
3) Harmonic content	5% maximum with equipment operating
4) Electromagnetic compatibility	1 V/m maximum
5) Frequency limits	60 Hz ± 0.5
6) Frequency rate of change	1 Hz/s (slew rate)
7) Three-phase voltage unbalance	2.5% of arithmetic average
8) Three-phase load unbalance	5–20% maximum for any one phase
9) Power factor	0.8–0.9
10) Load demand	0.75–0.85 (of connected load)

NOTE—Parameters 1), 2), 5), and 6) depend upon the power source. Parameters 3), 4), and 7) are a function of the interaction of the source and the equipment load. Parameters 8), 9), and 10) are a function of the equipment. The harmonic content of the voltage is computed as the sum of all harmonic voltages added vectorially.

3.11.3.2 Voltage transients

Computer manufacturers usually specify maximum momentary voltage deviations within which their equipment can operate without sustaining errors or equipment damage. The transient conditions are defined in terms of amplitude and time duration. Historically, an example was a range from ±5% of undefined duration to −30% for 500 ms, and +130% for 5 ms. Another example is ±20% for 30 ms. A few manufacturers also specify a duration limit for total voltage loss of from 1 ms to 1 cycle. A figure of 8.3 ms (half-cycle) for older equipment was typical. These values should not be confused with impulse tolerances, which are of much shorter duration (microseconds) and higher level (500%) and are usually part of the noise susceptibility and electromagnetic compatibility (EMC) tests.

Figure 3-4 shows an envelope of voltage tolerances that is representative of the present design goal of a cross section of the electronic equipment manufacturing industry. Shorter duration overvoltages have higher voltage limits. Some computer manufacturers specify a maximum allowable limit for volt-seconds, typically 130% of nominal volt-seconds (area under the sine wave).

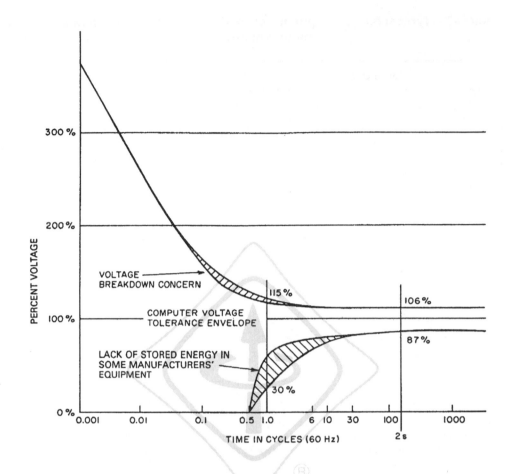

NOTE: Newer data is expected to be included in next revision of IEEE Std 1100-1992.

**Figure 3-4—Typical design goals of
power-conscious computer manufacturers**

3.11.3.3 Frequency

The manufacturer's tolerance on 60 Hz equipment ranges from ±0.5 Hz to ±1%, with the majority of the equipments limited to ±0.5 Hz. Time-related peripheral devices are most sensitive to frequency (clocks, card readers, magnetic tapes, disks). Ferroresonant (ac/dc) supplies, which are widely used by some manufacturers in peripherals, are also frequency-sensitive since they operate on a tuned circuit principle. They can generally tolerate variations of only ±1%. Some auxiliary motor-generators and other power supplies can tolerate variations as wide as ±3 Hz; however, for satisfactory operation of the entire system, the ±0.5 Hz tolerance should be maintained at all times for all parts of the system. Deviation from the tolerance may cause equipment malfunction or damage. Power of 400 Hz or 415 Hz is used primarily in computer mainframes or in other areas where high-density power is needed. The higher frequency allows design of a smaller and more compact power supply and components that result in reduced heating losses. The deriving of 400 Hz power does involve additional costs. Also, distribution of 400 Hz power presents some special problems. Thus, for many of the peripheral manufacturers, 60 Hz power is still preferred. Some equipment, such as large CPUs, use both 400 Hz and 60 Hz power, with 60 Hz mainly for cooling fans and blowers. The current trend is to use 400 Hz power in the larger data processing systems, with 60 Hz limited to the smaller systems and peripherals. Development and wider usage of 60–400 Hz or higher frequency static inverters to replace motor-generator sets and to be placed in individual equipments would reverse the trend back toward 60 Hz input in equipments. Several major computer hardware manufacturers predict the use of frequencies considerably above 400 Hz for future generation computer systems. Inverter frequencies of 20 kHz are commonly used now, and some state-of-the-art inverters operate at 100 kHz and higher.

The voltage quality and characteristics of 400 Hz power are extremely critical, with frequency generally not as critical a parameter. Most manufacturers who consider the 400 Hz source an integral part of the computer would prefer to furnish conversion equipment as part of the computer installation. Furthermore, because of the special problems associated with the distribution of 400 Hz power, conversion equipment is generally located relatively close to the utilization equipment.

In addition to being sensitive to the limits of ±0.5 Hz, some system peripherals are also sensitive to the rate of change within this band. Although extensive information is not available, a variation of 0.05 Hz/s has been cited by one manufacturer as a limit for some units of his system. A typical limit is 1.5 Hz/s, measured as rate of change in a 10 cycle running average. The limit is most significant when turbine or engine generators are applied where small load step applications may cause the rate to be exceeded.

3.11.3.4 Distortion

The maximum harmonic distortion permitted on input lines ranges from 3–5%, with the majority at +5%. The percentage is usually specified as total line-to-line distortion, with a maximum of 3% for any one harmonic.

Excessive harmonic content can cause heating in magnetic (iron) devices, such as transformers, motors, and chokes. The harmonic distortion will also appear as additional ripple in the output of some ac/dc power supplies and also cause threshold limits to vary in peak and average sensing circuits. Either can contribute to data errors.

It should be noted that elements of the load may introduce considerable distortion or noise into the power source. This reflected noise, although not in the source, may require suppression through filtering to avoid interference with other loads also connected to the system.

The voltage envelope should be sinusoidal, with a crest factor of 1.414 ± 0.1. Waveform deviation should be limited to ±10% line-to-neutral. The variation in the amplitude (in time) of the wave should not exceed ±0.5%.

Excessive modulation of the voltage can produce pulsing and speed variations in motors and can introduce additional ripple in the output of ac/dc power supplies.

Some computer units have half-wave rectifier units and SCRs (half-wave phase control). These are capable of creating a dc component of load current and greater current in the neutral than in the phase conductors. Power sources for such loads must be capable of handling them.

3.11.3.5 Phase angle displacement

Although some manufacturers build only single-phase equipment, the majority of equipment, particularly for larger systems, is three-phase. The maximum deviation from normal 120° spacing ranges from ±2.5° to ±6°. Unequal phase displacement, whether in the source or due to unequal loading, can further contribute to phase voltage unbalance.

3.11.3.6 Voltage balance

Unequal distribution of single phase, as is frequently encountered in computer systems, will increase the amount of voltage unbalance. Wherever possible, effort should be made to distribute load evenly between the phases.

Excessive phase voltage unbalance can cause excessive heating to three-phase devices such as motors. Similarly, relays and other electromechanical devices may be damaged due to continuous operation at high (or low) voltage. In addition, high *ripple* may be observed in some three-phase ac/dc power supplies if the voltage unbalance to the supply is high. Percent voltage unbalance is defined by ANSI/NEMA MG 1-1993, Part 14.35.2, as

$$\text{percent voltage unbalance } = 100 \times \frac{\text{maximum voltage deviation from average voltage}}{\text{average voltage}}$$

3.11.3.7 Environmental considerations

It is well known that electronic equipment is capable of reaching design performance levels only when proper cooling is introduced. The principal thrust of this discussion involves the electrical power needs of data processing equipment. However, it must be recognized that cooling of that equipment can be an overriding and sometimes limiting factor in the operation of data processing equipment, principally because most cooling and ventilating equipment is electrically powered. In addition to comfort air conditioning for the computer room, the computer's central processing unit (CPU) logic and chassis often have special cooling requirements and many have overtemperature alarms or cutoffs. With larger systems and increased capabilities, computers have, for technical reasons, also grown more compact, leading to increased power densities in terms of watts per cubic foot. The result has been a progression in chassis cooling from natural convection, to forced air, to chilled water, and in some cases, to a refrigerant-cooled chassis. However, intermediate-sized computer installations are frequently cooled by forced air through ducts or under floor areas. Small computers and peripherals may contain their own internal fans and draw cooling air from the room where they are installed.

The methods of cooling of a computer system can also heavily influence how long a computer system can operate without electrical power to cooling apparatus. Assume that computer power could be maintained through the use of batteries, standby generators, or other auxiliary equipment, which is described later. It then becomes important to consider the design/selection of computer system cooling systems and their need for auxiliary power supplies. Obviously, there is no need to provide battery ampere-hour capacity, which can extend computer operating time beyond the time that a computer system can operate before it must shut down due to overheating.

Most manufacturers are reluctant to cite these times for their computer hardware since many variables within a facility can exist. For forced-air cooling, many claim up to 15 min can elapse before overheating and equipment shutdown occurs due to operation of overtemperature sensors. For those systems that use chilled-water cooling, approximately 2–3 min has been given as the length of time that the chilled supply can be cut off. For refrigerant cooling, about 15 min is often considered the maximum.

Most larger systems shut down automatically when a high temperature is reached and many provide a warning alarm when approaching a high temperature.

3.11.3.8 Humidification

The need for, and extent of, introduction of humidification into a data processing equipment room will vary considerably with the geographic area. Humidity control is required to ensure orderly movement of papers, cards, and magnetic tapes in the operation of the computer and its peripherals. Low humidity allows the building up of static electrical charges, which in turn causes cards and tape to stick together, jam, etc. Extremely high humidity can result in condensation of moisture on chilled chassis plates, resulting in rust and corrosion. Most data processing equipment manufacturers recommend that a humidity range of 40–60% be maintained in equipment rooms. As with cooling apparatus, discussed in the preceding paragraph, humidity-generating equipment can be as important as cooling equipment. Any reserve or standby equipment must be sized for not only the supply of electrical power to data processing equipment, but also for the length of time the equipment can operate without supplemental humidification or dehumidification and attendant problems.

3.11.4 Factors influencing data processing systems on incoming or supplementary independent power sources

Much of the foregoing discussion has been dedicated to the various influences that the source of electrical power has on data processing equipment and systems. It should be recognized that the same equipment and systems can, in various ways, interact with and influence the source power system and other utilization equipment served by it. Some of these influences become important if supplementary independent power sources are used as an enhancement of power source quality, particularly where emergency and standby power is applied.

3.11.4.1 Load magnitude

The size of the electrical load of a data processing system depends on the makeup, complexity, and even on the function of the system. A typical small system may vary from 10–50 kVA, and larger systems, from 100–300 kVA. Some multiple systems may be as large as 2000 kVA. As systems become larger, some manufacturers elect to power the mainframes with 400 Hz power derived from the 60 Hz source, often through separate motor-generator sets.

A principal computer manufacturer states that approximately 30–35 W/ft^2 per computer floor space should be allowed in planning for ultimate computer electrical power consumption. This load density is exclusive of any attendant space conditioning, humidification, or dehumidification loads that would be required.

3.11.4.2 Load growth

For an established system, most load growth will result from the incremental and often unpredictable addition or expansion of peripheral devices (tapes, disks, cardpunch, etc.). However, not all system growth results in electrical load growth. For example, the replacement of several smaller disks by a larger (in a computing sense) disk device may actually require less power. Major load growth occurs when an entire system performance capability is upgraded, which usually results in a new mainframe and some peripherals.

3.11.4.3 Power factor

The characteristic power factor of a computer system is relatively high. The power factor of the 60 Hz portion of the load generally ranges from 80–85%, and the power factor of the 400 Hz (motor-generator set) load is generally around 90%. Depending on the amount of 60 Hz load, and on whether or not a motor-generator set is used, the overall combined power factor is usually in the range of 80–90%. During initial powering up or startup, the power factor may drop as low as 50% for short periods.

3.11.4.4 Load unbalance

Most equipment manufacturers attempt to balance their equipment load in the design of the equipment and in load connection in the planning phase. However, load unbalance may run from 5–30% (phase-to-phase) steady state and up to 100% dynamic, as in startup. The effect of load unbalance is to produce unbalanced phase voltages. See the discussion of voltage balance in the preceding paragraphs.

3.11.4.5 Startup

The powering up of a computer system may place severe demands on the power source. In that regard, independent power sources are more vulnerable than a commercial power source from the utility company. Efforts are made by manufacturers to reduce inrush by various methods. Energizing of large loads is often sequenced in steps, manually or automatically.

Special motor-starting techniques can be used to reduce inrush in the starting of large motors, disks, and motor-generator sets.

The user often can employ operational procedures designed to ease startup and step loading. As an example, large groups of peripherals may be started manually, in sequence, rather than simultaneously. Large 400 Hz loads, such as mainframes powered by motor-generator sets, may be brought on-line slowly by controlled buildup of the generator output to give the logic load a cushioned start as well as reduced inrush.

Even with reduction methods, high inrush currents are common with many pieces of computer equipment. One manufacturer's central processor whose steady-state load is 24 kVA presents a 1500% (of steady state) transient for approximately 100 ms, which decreases to 600% in 300 rms. Another manufacturer, requiring 60 kVA steady state, presents a 400% transient. Still another manufacturer, requiring about 8 kVA steady state, presents a 1000% transient for a half-cycle, dropping to normal not later than the next cycle. The startup of a 40 kVA motor-generator set can require up to 200% for 2–10 s, even with special starting methods. High inrush puts an added requirement on the design of the power source, especially on devices, such as ride-through motor-generator sets and static inverters. Current-limiting protection for inverters is typically 125–175%. Voltage output will drop during current-limiting output.

3.11.4.6 Step or pulsing loads

Even when a system is on-line and drawing steady-state power, it may present severe load transients due to the operational demands of the computer. Step changes in load as high as 200–300% may be possible when starting an additional unit. Frequently, step changes in load can be minimized within the equipment through judicious programming that avoids simultaneous energizing or operation of several processes or pieces of equipment.

Pulsing loads can cause problems and occur when a number of devices that have power peaks, which are coincident and repetitive, are connected to the same power source. As an example, the programming of multiple tape units to rewind simultaneously should be avoided. Line printers, whose steady-state load is small, may step 100–200% when striking a full line of print. The cumulative effect of a large number of printers in synchronism can place a severe strain on the power system. If the power source includes a rotating device with speed control, it is possible for the load to cause oscillations in the control and output. Although extremely rare, the problem should be considered if there could be a large number of synchronized pulsing loads.

3.11.4.7 Load-generated harmonics and noise

Certain elements in the load, such as saturated magnetic circuits (transformers, motors), may cause distortion of the voltage waveform. Problems often result from the reflection into the source of load-generated noise, such as switching spikes caused by turning devices on or off or by the firing of high-speed solid-state devices (SCRs, diodes) that are a part of the computer load. The spikes, of microsecond width, may run several hundred volts on the 120 V line. These disturbances may have to be eliminated by filtering to avoid interference with other parts of the load.

The load factor for an on-line system may approach 100% due to the continuous nature of its operation. Off-line systems will generally be lower, depending on their daily scheduling and use.

Demand factor is the ratio of the actual steady-state running load to which a power system will be subjected to the total connected load.

Demand factor is important since connected kVA loads are generally available from the equipment manufacturer as nameplate ratings of individual components and can be taken as the worst-case condition. Thus, an arithmetic total of the loads can be computed. However, some computer system manufacturers provide data on the actual running loads, as seen by the total system, when operating the individual components as a system.

Through experience and data obtained from several of the computer systems manufacturers, some of the larger computer systems having connected loads in the area of 300 kVA, experience demand factors of between 75% and 85%. In other words, the running loads can be predicted to run between 225 kVA and 255 kVA for such a system. Thus users should be aware that nameplate ratings indicate power for a fully featured machine and actual loadings may be significantly less for individual user's systems.

Larger systems, consisting of many components, will probably have lower demand factors when compared with smaller systems with fewer components because of inherent diversity among components.

3.11.4.8 Grounding

Most computer manufacturers have preferred methods of system and equipment grounding for their hardware. Some systems require special grounded signal reference grids with single-point grounding and strict control of the paths through which equipment ground and power system ground are interconnected. These grounds are always connected one to the other to be electrically safe and to conform with the codes. The paths may be separated up to some point. Also, since computers and office machines are accessible to people, particular attention must be given to the safety grounding of all equipment. If, for the sake of radio frequency noise reduction, the equipment grounding green wire is isolated from the building/raceways, it must be run with power conductors and carried back to the service equipment grounding conductor. Furthermore, special semiconductive flooring may be employed for computer rooms, which enables draining off of static charges and minimizes the shock hazard to personnel. Some equipment manufacturers recommend grounding of equipment to the floor grid. The manufacturers installation instructions are not always correct and may contribute to problems. See Chapter 7 for grounding of emergency and standby power systems.

3.11.5 Justification of supplemental power

Insurance companies provide loss of power and loss of production insurance that can give a cost guideline on how much can be spent to improve the power supply.

The various units of a computer system are not equally sensitive to power supply disturbances. Power requirements for equipment such as air conditioning, lights, and drive motors are much less restrictive than for the logic, memory, control disk, and tape units. For economic reasons, the power loads should be separated into those requiring buffer or filter action with a UPS and those that require no buffering and can accept a 0.5 s–1 min power interruption while switching to a standby source of electric power.

Assuming that such a separation of computer or data processing equipment, or both, is possible, the next step would involve the selection of a system or equipment that would best solve the user's problems.

In summary, the following steps are intended to serve as a checklist toward problem-solving where power problems are present. Care is required and computer manufacturer's advice should be heeded in arranging and coordinating the ground references where more than one power source supplies power to computer units in a common system.

a) Survey power quality requirements of all installed equipment to determine maximum degree of sensitivity of the individual components. These data are often not available from manufacturer's published literature.

b) Check to see if the local utility company has operating records. If no records are available, the user may choose to install a power disturbance monitor to detect and record transient power deficiencies at the point of usage and obtain a profile of power transients for a minimum two-week period. The results of such recordings should be used with the recognition that such seasonal conditions of lighting and other weather-related problems may not have been accounted for.

c) Review and analyze the monitor's records to identify the magnitude, number, time, date, and characteristics of the recorded transients, interruptions, and prolonged outages.

d) Classify the transients according to their origin: from the utility; from the operation of electrical equipment in the computer's vicinity; from the operation of computer units and their accessories.

e) As appropriate, prepare engineering design and cost estimates of a power-buffering system of required capacity (kVA). The chosen power-buffering system should accommodate both future expansion and possible replacement with more recently marketed computer models.

f) Evaluate actual and intangible losses due to interruptions or malfunctions of the electronic data processing equipment from all causes, including losses attributable to power supply deficiencies or failure.

g) Compare expected losses without power-buffering equipment to the cost of owning and operating various types of a power-buffering system as insurance against transient-caused interruptions or malfunctions of computer equipment.

h) If the previous step justifies an investment in a power-buffering system, proceed with
the project.

3.11.6 Power quality improvement techniques

Any attempts to categorize power improvement equipment should logically attempt also to
define the time duration effectiveness of the equipment. The simplest and least costly equipment is limited in effectiveness to extremely short-duration power disturbances. As the time
span for protection of disturbances increases to *outage*-type disruptions, the sophistication
and associated cost for related equipment, as a general rule, will also increase. The following
list broadly classifies equipment from the very short duration to an indefinite time period. A
broader classification of equipment could be the distinction between passive and dynamic
systems.

Equipment systems:

— Power conditioners
— Short time (up to 15 s, but typically 0.1 s) ride-through
— Extended time (up to 30 min) ride-through
— Indefinite time

The time interval for most of the equipment listed can usually be extended to an indefinite
time period through the use of a supplemental standby power source such as a second utility
company power feeder or on-site generation. To maintain power input to the load within tolerance, the supplementary equipment must be capable of *riding through* the inherent sensing
and transfer time switching associated with a second incoming feeder. With standby generation systems, ride-through time must at least equal prime mover starting time, including synchronizing and transfer switching times for those systems.

Short-time ride-through can be accomplished with *mechanical stored energy systems*, which
are described in 5.4.

Extended ride-through time can be achieved through operation of the equipment in conjunction with stored energy equipment, such as batteries.

In general, *power conditioning* equipment is limited to improvement of short-duration power
problems. In installations where electrical noise and voltage are principal problems, an isolation transformer can be an effective solution in noise attenuation and voltage control.

Isolation transformers can simultaneously isolate and change voltage, for example, from
480 V three-phase to 208Y/120 V, or can have a one-to-one transformation ratio. An ordinary
transformer with separate primary and secondary circuits will provide some isolation. However, effectiveness is greatly improved if they are equipped with special shielding between
the primary and secondary windings. This special shielding will reduce the noise amplitude
and inhibit the passage of noise through the transformer. Performance of three-phase transformers will be greatly enhanced in handling harmonic currents and unbalanced load if the
transformer is connected delta-primary/wye-secondary on a three-legged core. Such trans-

formers can be equipped with primary taps to adjust output voltage when input is constantly high or low. A typical tap range is +5% to –5% in 2.5% steps.

Beyond the isolation transformer is a wide range of voltage correction or stabilizing equipment, each having distinct and unique operating characteristics. Commercially available equipment that would fall into the power conditioner classification are listed in table 3-8. Typical reported response times are listed for each device. It is obvious, because of the relatively slow response times, that the use of several of the devices would be restricted to simple voltage regulation and would have questionable value against short-term disturbances. In addition, some of the devices have inherently high internal impedance. Any sensed voltage drop is ultimately corrected by its voltage-regulating capability. However, under stepped load change, the dynamic voltage change may be unacceptable for the time required for the regulator to respond. If multiple loads are to be supplied by one device and one of the loads is switched, one must be assured that the magnitude of voltage change before the regulator can react will be within acceptable limits.

Table 3-8—Performance of power conditioning equipment

Equipment type	Response time	Typical internal impedance (%)
Regulator, low impedance	11 ms	3–5
Transformer, constant voltage	25 ms	
Reactor, electronic saturable	30 ms	20–30
Regulator, electronic magnetic	160 ms	
Regulator, electromechanical	5+ s	3–5
Regulator, induction	5+ s	10
Tap changer, mechanical	60 s	3–5

Dynamic regulation and response time are the major considerations. It is stressed that because of relatively slow response times some of the equipment is effective only for voltage adjustment or correction. Also, steady-state regulation is normally published, but dynamic regulation to step changes in voltage input and load current is often omitted. Without a detailed analysis of equipment operating characteristics, often from actual test data, a user could mistakenly think that he is getting protection against short-duration line input voltage disturbances and the effects of changing load. In general, equipment is available to accept line voltage variations of a 15% overvoltage to a 20% undervoltage condition with output regulated to ±5% of rating. Such a regulated output is generally sufficient for electronic data processing equipment. In a situation in which an ac line regulator appears to be needed, the application should be reviewed with the manufacturer of the data processing equipment.

3.11.7 Selection factors for supplemental power

The true nature of the data processing operation must be examined in combination with its extent of usage. On-line systems generally require a higher degree of power protection than off-line systems. Certainly, a 24 h around-the-clock operation would be more vulnerable than a one-shift-a-day operation.

Whether on-line or off-line, the consequences of a power failure should be determined in terms of cost, value of lost data, necessity of reruns, inconvenience to and loss of revenue from customers, possible equipment damage, repair cost, and general annoyance. It is some-times found, particularly in off-line operations, that the consequences of an outage do not jus-tify the often considerable expenditure for a protective system. The decision must be based on how much a user should pay for insurance in light of the benefits to be derived.

To evaluate the effects of outages, an estimate of the number of outages and their duration predicted over a period of at least one year should be obtained from the utility, based on their past operating experiences.

A comparison of what is predicted with what is acceptable in terms of power limits should indicate if supplemental protection is needed.

3.11.7.1 Protection time

Assuming that the predicted available power is not acceptable in terms of duration or fre-quency of disturbances or disruption, it must then be determined how much protection is appropriate and what solutions are available to the user.

Table 3-9 has been prepared to indicate what effect three types of power-line disturbances will have on data processing and computer equipments. Also shown for each type of distur-bance are several of the available solutions that can be applied for enhancement of the power quality. Note that in this comparison the disturbance durations are for less than 1 cycle, from 1 cycle–10 s, and for more than 10 s. Table 3-10 presents similar data in a slightly different manner and shows, for each of the categories of disturbances, how effective each of the avail-able solutions will be as a power quality improvement measure.

3.11.7.2 Reliability

An indication of reliability can be expressed in hours of mean time between failure (MTBF). Data for calculating the MTBF can be obtained from IEEE Std 500-1984. Equipment and reliability can be enhanced by redundant systems and components and provision for isolation or bypass of defective parts or subassemblies.

Table 3-9—Summary of typical power-line disturbances

Type of voltage disturbance	Voltage level of disturbance	Duration of disturbance	Typical effects on computer equipment	Typical power enhancement projects
Outage	Below 85% V rms	More than 10 s	Built-in voltage sensors will power down computer equipment in an uncontrolled manner. Processing is interrupted usually resulting in excessive restart/rerun time, possible loss of data, or damage to hardware.	Uninterruptible power supply system, standby diesel generators, dual power feeders, general improvements to power distribution system.
Momentary under- and overvoltage (sags and surges)	Below 85% V rms and above 105% V rms	From 16.7 ms (1 cycle) to 10 s	Equipment may power down depending on duration and magnitude of disturbance. If so, processing is interrupted usually resulting in excessive restart/rerun time. In severe cases, loss of data and damage to hardware may occur.	Solid-state switching between dual feeders, motor generator sets, fast response line voltage regulators, balance computer load on three-phase power, improve computer equipment grounding, general improvement to power distribution system.
Transient overvoltages (impulses or spikes)	100% V rms or higher (measured as instantaneous voltage above or below the line V rms)	Less than 16.7 ms (1 cycle)	Data disruptions leading to errors, unready indications, etc., may cause individual equipment to stop processing. However, direct effects on the system are not normally detectable. Rarely, a severe transient will cause equipment to power down. Damage to electronic components may also occur if the equipment is not properly grounded or otherwise protected from transient overvoltages.	Isolation transformers, transient suppressors, power-line filters, primary and secondary lightning arrestors, balance computer load, improve computer equipment grounding.

Table 3-10—Relative effectiveness of power enhancement projects in eliminating or moderating power disturbances (U.S. Navy)

Disturbance type	Uninterruptible power supply (UPS) system and standby diesel generator	Uninterruptible power supply (UPS) system	Dual power feeders		Motor-generator	Solid-state line voltage regulator	Specialty shielded isolating transformer	Suppressors, filters, and lightning arresters	Balance computer load on three-phase supply, improve grounding
			Secondary spot network	Secondary selective[a]					
Transient and oscillatory overvoltage	All source-caused transients and no load-caused transients	All source transients and no load transients	None	None	All source transients and no load transients	Most source transients and no load transients	Most source transients and no load transients	Most	Some[b]
Momentary undervoltage or overvoltage	All	All	None	Most	Most	Some (depends on response time)	None	None	Some[b]
Outage	All	Only outages of a duration equal to the discharge time of the battery	Most	Most	Only *brown-out*	Only *brownout*	None	None	None

[a] Includes special application of a solid-state switch between two independent sources.
[b] These improvements do not eliminate or moderate power-line disturbances, but they do make the computer equipment significantly less susceptible to under- and overvoltages. Assistance of the computer manufacturer is generally required to identify grounding problems.

A typical reliability prediction assumes that if the UPS system fails, there is to be a high probability that the static switch will operate and that main power of suitable quality will be available to handle the load. The probability of simultaneous failures of the UPS and static switch or main power yields an exceptionally low failure rate corresponding to MTBFs of 10 years or longer. However, the probability of switch failure is greater when it is called upon to operate than when quiescent. Also, the duration of the failure in a static switch may be extended due to an inability to detect failure.

As with reliability, data on equipment life expectancy are difficult to obtain. Often, because of the rapid advancement of data processing technology, the protected equipment obsolescence will generally occur before the life of the protecting equipment is exceeded.

Dynamic or rotating apparatus is capable of withstanding short time and sustained overloads better than static equipment. Furthermore, most static assemblies are more vulnerable to shock or high-inrush loads than dynamic equipment. Dynamic or rotating equipment does not lend itself well to expansion through paralleling due to complex control problems. Conversely, most static systems are easily expanded through the addition of parallel modules or additional batteries.

Because some systems have inherent lower overall efficiencies, increased heat losses will be evident. The first cost of supplemental cooling and ventilating equipment, with ongoing operating and maintenance costs, must be considered. Furthermore, the need of additional auxiliary or standby power capability to drive the cooling and ventilating equipment, when normal power curtailment occurs, must also be examined.

3.11.7.3 Other factors

Most equipment will occupy building interior space, which not only costs money but will require environmental treatment or tempering. Such space is often treated as leasable space an, as such, its cost considered as an ongoing cost in any comparative analysis.

Delivery, setup, checkout, and debug time can often be an important and deciding factor when the dependence and prime emphasis is placed on having a data processing system or computer and its capabilities in service on an around-the-clock basis.

Some of the solutions for improvement of power quality will require the installation of an auxiliary power source with some form of prime mover. Other sections in this standard provide detailed guidance toward a prime mover selection. The most popular choice is the diesel engine, with gas turbine usage increasing.

Often it is to the advantage of the user to provide for a separation of the source for the data processing equipment or its power improvement equipment from the source for the facility's environmental equipment. Since the only objective of the auxiliary power source is to provide an almost immediate source of power, reliability in starting is the most important characteristic. Usually, the unit is called on to start after a sustained period of idleness. The time period for starting could be important since the equipment could be called on to operate in conjunction with a stored energy type of ride-through system. Often data processing equipment is installed in a relatively quiet atmosphere so that whichever choice of prime mover is made, some form of acoustic treatment will probably be required.

3.11.8 IEEE Std 1100 (the IEEE Emerald Book)

IEEE Std 1100-1992 contains a thorough treatment of the power requirements for sensitive electronic equipment. The book covers fundamentals, instrumentation, and recommended design and installation practices.

3.12 Life safety and life support systems

3.12.1 Introduction

Emergency power for life safety systems is required in many different types of commercial and industrial facilities. For example, an alternative power source is needed to illuminate exits and to operate alarm systems in most public buildings. These needs generally relate to fire safety as set forth in ANSI/NFPA 101-1994.

In contrast, emergency power requirements for life support systems, such as a heart-lung machine or medical diagnostic equipment, are generally limited to health care facilities. These requirements result from operational needs unique to the health care environment.

Emergency power for both life safety and life support equipment is addressed in this subclause primarily from the viewpoint of the user.

3.12.2 Health care facilities

Typical examples of both life safety and life support emergency power requirements are found in large health care facilities. An appreciation for both of these needs can therefore be obtained by reviewing a hospital's emergency power system.

Hospitals are increasingly dependent on electrical apparatus for patient life support and treatment as illustrated in the following paragraphs.

Electronic monitoring systems are being used to conduct therapy for critically ill patients. In the operating suite, during open-heart surgery, an electronic heart-lung machine maintains extracorporeal circulation. In the intensive care unit, patients depend on ventilators powered by electricity. Cardiac-assist devices augment a patient's own circulation in the coronary care unit. Continuous lighting is needed to observe patients in primary care areas, and power is needed to maintain refrigerated storage of vital supplies such as blood and tissue banks.

In addition to these examples of direct dependency on electric power in patient care, the sustained loss of electrical power can also result in an undesirable traumatic experience for some seriously ill patients.

Hospitals also must have a highly reliable supply of emergency power for life safety systems to ensure that the lives of sick or disabled persons are protected during emergencies.

Interruption of normal electrical services to hospitals may be caused by a variety of phenomena. These include storms, floods, fires, earthquakes, explosions, traffic accidents, electrical equipment failure, and human error. Several large area blackouts have been experienced in the recent past with prolonged local outages. As a consequence of the "energy crisis" the incidence of such failures is thought by many authorities to be on the rise. Alternative sources of power for supplying vital life safety and life support systems must be provided to protect patients relying on these systems.

3.12.2.1 Power continuity requirement

The acceptable duration for an interruption of normal power service to critical hospital loads is the subject of many state codes and regulations. National standards often referenced by the states and specifically addressing this issue are NFPA 99-1996 and the NEC, Article 517.

NFPA 99-1996 requires that all health care facilities maintain an alternate source of electrical power. With few exceptions, this source must be an on-site generator capable of servicing both essential major electrical equipment and emergency systems.

For hospitals, NFPA 99-1996 provides the following criteria with respect to the emergency system: "Those functions of patient care, depending on lighting or appliances that are permitted to be connected to the Emergency System are divided into two mandatory branches; the Life Safety and the Critical. The branches of the Emergency System shall be installed and connected to the alternate power source . . . so that all functions specified . . . shall be automatically restored to operation within 10 seconds after interruption of the normal power."

To meet the "10 second criteria" the emergency system must include independent distribution circuits with automatic transfer to the alternate power source. Two-way bypass and isolation transfer switches are recommended for the emergency branches. Figure 3-5 shows the emergency system wiring arrangement from a typical hospital. The hospital emergency system installation must follow Articles 518 and 700 of the NEC.

The *life safety branch* of the emergency system, as described in NFPA 99-1996, includes illumination for means of egress and exit signs (ANSI/NFPA 101-1994 requirement), fire alarms and systems, alarms for nonflammable medical gas systems, hospital communication systems, and task illumination selected receptacles at the emergency generator set location.

NFPA 99-1996 contains a complete listing of circuits to be connected to the critical branch feed areas and functions related to patient care. For most of these critical loads the "10 second criteria" is considered to be sufficient. However, an instantaneous restoration of minimal task lighting, using battery systems, is recommended in operating, delivery, and radiology rooms where the loss of lighting due to power failure might cause severe and immediate danger to a patient undergoing surgery or an invasive radiographic procedure.

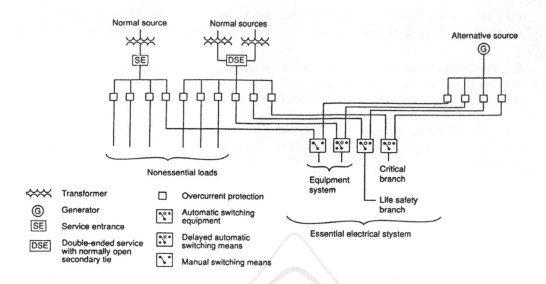

Figure 3-5—Typical hospital wiring arrangement

Examples of the types of life support and life safety equipment available with built-in battery backup power are as follows:

— *Life support.* Aortic balloon pumps, ECG and EEG monitors, portable defibrillators, portable respirators, task lighting
— *Life safety.* Fire monitoring and alarm systems, communication systems, safety lighting

Periodic tests and maintenance are essential to assure the reliability of the alternate source of power and other elements of the emergency system. Regular performance of maintenance is subject to the approval of the authority having jurisdiction. A record of procedures must be kept. Power outages in the past have shown the uselessness of having unmaintained emergency and standby systems that fail in time of need. Basic maintenance and test requirements for essential electrical systems in hospitals are also included in NFPA 99-1996.

Since emergency and standby power systems are mandatory in most areas, the hospital electrical system designer must review the state and city building laws and regulations. These laws often reference the NEC, NFPA 99-1996, and ANSI/NFPA 101-1994, as well as other national standards such as the Uniform Building Code. Insurance and building inspectors should also be consulted. In addition, installation, operation, and maintenance of the emergency power system is a factor in accreditation by the Joint Commission on Accreditation of Hospitals.

3.12.2.2 Power quality requirements

There is another power problem in hospitals that is not covered by any of the previously referenced codes and standards. It is the adverse effect of poor power quality on sensitive electronic loads. With the growing dependence on electronic equipment in medical facilities, users are finding that the "10 second criteria" no longer provides an acceptable functional capability. These loads are disturbed by transient overvoltages that are measured in microseconds and dips in steady-state voltage lasting only a few cycles of the 60 Hz wave. See 3.11 for a detailed description of typical power-line disturbances and their effect on sensitive electronic equipment.

Some examples of sensitive hospital loads and the probable results of poor power quality (evidenced by power-line disturbances) are shown in table 3-11.

Table 3-11—Sensitive hospital loads

Sensitive load	Probable result of severe power disturbances
ICU patient monitoring systems	Incorrect trend analysis or false alarm Lost time for restart and reprogramming Loss of data
Lab equipment blood gas analyzers	Depending on complexity, may result in extensive reprogramming and set-up lost time
Blood cell counter	Automatic power down for self-protection, which disrupts or delays test runs
Nuclear monitoring	Disruption of test and inability to retest due to patients' radiation exposure limit
X-ray/ultrasonic scanner	Varies from no effect to breakdown depending on equipment susceptibility
Hospital information systems (HIS) computers	Typical computer subject to disruption resulting in restart and reprogramming lost time and loss of memory (see 3.11)

This problem can be diminished if the manufacturer of sensitive or critical medical equipment thoughtfully designs the equipment to tolerate power-line disturbances. For example, built-in batteries can power equipment or at least maintain critical data during momentary interruptions in the normal supply. In addition, the susceptibility to transient overvoltage can be reduced if the equipment power supply design includes proper isolation and built-in transient overvoltage protection. These preventive measures by the medical equipment manufacturer are considered to be an efficient method of avoiding power quality-related problems.

Computer systems adapted to hospital applications typically do not have built-in protection from power-line disturbances. Nevertheless, just as in the business sector, computer systems will inevitably play a dominant role in hospitals. Organizations such as the Society for Computer Medicine provide a forum for identifying and putting into practice hospital computer applications. These applications have been summarized as "patient care computing" and include patient monitoring, laboratory, radiology, diagnostic support, patient data base acquisition, patient scheduling, and so on.

With the increased dependence on computer systems in hospitals, more priority will certainly be placed on supplying continuous and disturbance-free power in the future. For computers and other life safety and life support systems where it is impractical for the equipment manufacturer to provide built-in solutions to power-quality problems, the user may find the need for power interface systems in his facility. Power interface systems bridge the gap between equipment susceptibilities and power-line disturbances. For overvoltages or electrical noise problems, isolation transformers or transient suppressors may be an effective deterrent when installed in the building power source. Required stored energy to ride-through low-voltage and momentary interruptions may be obtained from a power buffering motor-generator set or, when the need for power continuity warrants, an UPS (battery system). These interface systems are addressed in Chapter 4 and stored energy systems in Chapter 5.

A large health-care facility involved in extensive life-support-related functions will probably require a combination of both emergency power and power interface systems. In this case, a central system approach to satisfy special power requirements may be more cost effective than one that addresses individual equipment separately.

It is strongly recommended that the user with an apparent power-quality problem consult and secure the services of qualified engineers familiar with the unique power-quality requirements of his facility.

3.12.3 Other critical life systems

Other critical life systems not necessarily unique to hospitals are subject to similar special laws and regulations regarding emergency power. Some examples follow:

— Controls for pressure vessels, such as boilers or ovens, where a failure may result in a life endangering explosion or fire
— Air supply systems for persons in a closed area
— Fire pumps, alarms, and systems
— Communications systems in hazardous areas
— Industrial processes in which the interruption of power would create a hazard to life

To meet these or other specialized emergency power requirements, the assistance of an engineer who is experienced in the particular problem area should be obtained.

3.13 Communication systems

3.13.1 Description

Communication systems are those facilities that require electric power for verbal, written, or facsimile transmission and reception. Common systems of this type are

— Telephone
— Facsimile
— Teletypewriter
— Paging
— Radio
— Television

Needs of one or all of the above communication systems during a power failure may well justify the cost of one or more emergency and standby power systems, possibly in conjunction with any other critical loads.

3.13.2 Commonly used auxiliary power systems

Battery or battery and converter equipment are practical sources of power using a float-charging system. Small engine generators are practical and economical. In the size ranges usually required from 1–5 kW, the installed cost ranges from about $1000/kW and up, depending upon the quality of the equipment, battery life, gasoline storage problems, and amount of automatic equipment deemed to be necessary or convenient.

3.13.3 Evaluating the need for an auxiliary power system

The need of an emergency or standby power system for communications should include satisfactory answers to the following questions:

a) Will the communication equipment be required
    1) To issue orders for an orderly shutdown of processes and equipment?
    2) To announce instructions to personnel? A typical announcement might be to wait by the machines or to check out for the duration of the shift.
    3) To call for help, issue warnings, and coordinate the work should there be a fire, civil disturbance, vandalism, or other threat to personnel safety or plant security?
b) How will vital messages be received or sent for remote plants concerning production, inventory, or sales changes?
c) How will key personnel be found, or instructed; and how will these persons report conditions to a central responsible source of control?

Many other questions may be asked, but the maintaining of communications under emergency conditions will save vital time and expedite the return to normal conditions with reduced confusion.

For industrial plants, the telephone system is usually powered both regularly and on a standby and emergency basis by the telephone company, normally by batteries or by standby generation. In some plants there is a separate in-plant telephone system that may be powered by batteries under a float charge that will maintain the communication system for several hours during a prolonged power interruption. The user should check to see that his system will function for the required time with loss of normal power.

Usually various bells, horns, and other call devices connected to the telephone system are powered by the lighting circuits and will stop functioning if there is a power interruption, even though the receiver and transmitter work. If required, these should be wired to the backup power system.

Teletype equipment functions much the same as the telephone system so that the signal may be present but the printout device will not operate without local power.

Paging systems in plants are frequently extensive, using many hundreds of watts of audio power and several kilowatts of 120 V power. The need to use the system during a power interruption should not be overlooked.

Radio systems are common in industrial plants. While the mobile units for personnel as well as in-plant and out-of-plant car and truck units are generally self-powered by batteries, the main base station usually is connected to the nearest commercial power source. While mobile units may or may not be able to speak to each other, the system as a whole usually stops functioning if the base station power fails. Consideration of emergency and standby power for this base station should not be overlooked.

In some plants and commercial buildings, paging or broadcasting is done by dialing through the telephone system. In this case, both the telephone and paging or radio systems should be supplied with emergency power.

3.14 Signal circuits

3.14.1 Description

A signal circuit supplies power to a device that gives a recognizable signal. Such devices include bells, buzzers, code-calling equipment, lights, horns, sirens, and many other devices.

3.14.2 Signal circuits in health care facilities

Signal circuits in medical buildings that should be provided with continuous emergency power within 10 s (ANSI/NFPA 101-1994) include the following:

a) Fire alarm systems:
   1) Manually initiated
   2) Automatic fire detection
   3) Water flow alarm devices used with sprinkler systems

b) Alarms required for systems used for piping of nonflammable medical gas
c) Paging system
d) Nurse's station signaling system from patient areas
e) Alarm systems attached to equipment required to operate for the safety of major apparatus
f) Signaling equipment for elevators in buildings of more than four stories

3.14.3 Signal circuits in industrial and commercial buildings

Signal circuits for commercial buildings and industrial plants that may require continuous emergency power within 1 min include the following:

a) Fire alarm system
b) Watchman's tour system
c) Elevator signal system
d) Door signals (into restricted areas such as boiler rooms and laboratories with electric door locks)
e) Liquid level, pressure, and temperature indications

3.14.4 Types of auxiliary power systems

The emergency supply for the signal circuits can be engine-driven generators, multiple utility services, or floating battery systems with auxiliary power. Most signal circuits operate down to 70% rated voltage and therefore require no special voltage-sensing relays on the transfer device.

It is recommended that an emergency source of electric power be supplied for every part of a fire alarm and security system. A local battery supply on float charge, close to the power need, in continuous service is very reliable. A usually acceptable substitute is an automatic transfer to a battery system when prime power fails.

Signal circuits are usually a small electrical burden and integral part of a total load that also requires an emergency source. Therefore, the selection of emergency system and hardware generally depends upon the requirement of other related loads.

3.15 References

This chapter shall be used in conjunction with the following publications:

ANSI C84.1-1989, American National Standard Voltage Ratings for Electric Power Systems and Equipment (60 Hz).[3]

ANSI/NEMA MG 1-1993, Motors and Generators.[4]

---

[3]ANSI publications are available from the Sales Department, American National Standards Institute, 11 West 42nd Street, 13th Floor, New York, NY 10036, USA.
[4]NEMA publications are available from the Sales Department, American National Standards Institute, 11 West 42nd Street, 13th Floor, New York, NY 10036, USA.

ANSI/NFPA 30-1993, Flammable and Combustible Liquids Code.[5]

ANSI/NFPA 101-1994, Code for Safety to Life from Fire in Buildings and Structures.

ANSI/NFPA 110-1993, Emergency and Standby Power Systems.

ANSI/NFPA 111-1993, Stored Electrical Energy Emergency and Standby Power Systems.

ANSI/UL 924-1990, Safety Standard for Emergency Lighting and Power Equipment.[6]

California Administrative Code, Title 24, Part 3, Basic Electrical Regulations, Article E700, Emergency Systems, Document Section, Sacramento, CA.[7]

EGSA 101G-1995, Electrical and Mechanical Terminology and Definitions.[8]

IEEE Std 100-1992, The New IEEE Standard Dictionary of Electrical and Electronics Terms (ANSI).[9]

IEEE Std 141-1993, IEEE Recommended Practice for Electric Power Distribution for Industrial Plants (IEEE Red Book) (ANSI).

IEEE Std 241-1990, IEEE Recommended Practice for Electric Power Systems in Commercial Buildings (IEEE Gray Book) (ANSI).

IEEE Std 493-1990, IEEE Recommended Practice for the Design of Reliable Industrial and Commercial Power Systems (IEEE Gold Book) (ANSI).

IEEE Std 500-1984 (Reaff 1991), IEEE Guide to the Collection and Presentation of Electrical, Electronic, Sensing Component, and Mechanical Equipment Reliability Data for Nuclear Power Generating Stations (ANSI).

IEEE Std 1100-1992, IEEE Recommended Practice for Powering and Grounding Sensitive Electronic Equipment (The Emerald Book) (ANSI).

NFPA 70-1996, National Electrical Code®.

NFPA 99-1996, Health Care Facilities Code.

---

[5]NFPA publications are available from the Sales Department, American National Standards Institute, 11 West 42nd Street, 13th Floor, New York, NY 10036, USA.

[6]UL publications are available from Underwriters Laboratories, Inc., 333 Pfingsten Road, Northbrook, IL 60062-2096, USA.

[7]This document can be obtained from the Department of General Services, P.O. Box 1015, North Highlands, CA 95660, USA.

[8]EGSA publications are available from the Electrical Generating Systems Association, 10251 W. Sample Rd., Suite B, Coral Springs, FL 33065, USA.

[9]IEEE publications are available from the Institute of Electrical and Electronics Engineers, 445 Hoes Lane, P.O. Box 1331, Piscataway, NJ 08855-1331, USA.

Occupational Safety and Health Act (OSH Act) of 1970 (29 USC 651 et seq.), Public Law No. 91-596, Chapter XVII of Title 29 (Labor) of The Code of Federal Regulations, Parts 1900-1999, established on April 13, 1970 (36 FR 7006) as amended by Public Law No. 101-552, Nov. 5, 1990. Amendments to Occupational Safety and Health Act of 1970, as published in the Federal Register, Washington, DC, Office of the Federal Register, National Archives and Records Service, General Services Administration.[10]

Standard Building Code, Southern Building Code Congress International.[11]

Uniform Building Code, International Congress of Building Officials.[12]

3.16 Bibliography

Additional information may be found in the following sources:

[B1] Beeman, D. L., Ed., *Industrial Power Systems Handbook.* New York: McGraw-Hill, 1955.

[B2] Burch, B. F., Jr., "Protection of Computers against Transients, Interruptions, and Outages," Presented at the 1967 IEEE Industry and General Applications Group Annual Meeting, Pittsburgh, PA, Oct. 4, 1967.

[B3] Castenschiold, R., "Criteria for Rating and Application of Automatic Transfer Switches," *IEEE Conference Record of 1970 Industrial and Commercial Power Systems and Electric Space Heating and Air-Conditioning Joint Technical Conference*, IEEE 70C8-1GA, pp. 11–16.

[B4] EGSA 109C-1994, Safety Codes Required by States and Major Cities.

[B5] Ferency, N., "Is a UPS Really Necessary?" *Electronic Products Magazine,* pp. 126–127, Apr. 17, 1972.

[B6] Fischer, E. I., "Emergency Power Facilities for a Research Laboratory," *Conference Record of the 1966 IEEE Industry and General Applications Group Annual Meeting*, IEEE 34-C36, pp. 305–324.

[B7] Funk, D. G., and Beatty, J. M., *Standard Handbook for Electrical Engineers*, 12th ed., New York: McGraw-Hill, 1987, Section 21.

---

[10]This publication is available from the Publications Dept., Occupational Safety and Health Administration (OSHA), 200 Constitution Ave., NW, Washington, DC 20210.

[11]This publication is available from the Southern Building Code Congress International, 900 Montclair Rd., Birmingham, AL 35213.

[12]This publication is available from the International Conference of Building Officials, South Workman Mill Rd., Whittier, CA 90601.

[B8] Gilbert, M. M., "What the Chemical Industry Can Do to Minimize Effects from Electrical Disturbances," Presented at the AIEE and ASME National Power Conference, Paper CP 60-1161, Philadelphia, PA, Sept. 21–23, 1960.

[B9] Heising, C. R., and Dunki-Jacobs, J. R., "Application of Reliability Concepts to Industrial Power Systems," *Conference Record of the 1972 IEEE Industrial Applications Society Annual Meeting*, IEEE 72CH0685-81A, pp. 289–295.

[B10] IEEE Committee Report, "Protection Fundamentals for Low-Voltage Electrical Distribution Systems in Commercial Buildings," IEEE JH 2112-1, 1974.

[B11] Jenkin, M. A., "Functions of Patient Care Computing," *Medical Instrumentation*, vol. 12, July–Aug. 1978.

[B12] Kaufman, J. E., Ed., *IES Lighting Handbook*. New York: Illuminating Engineering Society, 1972, Section 14, pp. 14-10 to 14-12.

[B13] Katz, E. G., "Evaluation of Hospital Essential Electrical Systems," *Fire Journal*, vol. 62, Nov. 1968.

[B14] Key, T. S., "Diagnosing Power Quality Related Computer Problems," *IEEE I-CPS Conference Record*, 78CH1302-91A, pp. 48–56, June 1978.

[B15] Knight, R. L., and Yuen, M. H., "The Uninterruptible Power Evolution—Are Our Problems Solved?" *Conference Record of the 1973 IEEE Industry Applications Society Annual Meeting*, IEEE 73CH0763-31A, pp. 481–485.

[B16] Miller, N. A., "Noninterruptible Power Supplies for Essential Control Systems in Power Plants," Presented at the IEEE IAS–IEC Group Meeting on Heating, Chicago Chapter, June 7, 1972.

[B17] Oliver, R. L., "Plant Engineering at RCA," *Plant Engineering*, Apr. 1969.

[B18] *Readers Digest Almanac*. Pleasantville, NY: The Readers Digest Association, 1972, p. 790.

[B19] Smith, D. R., Swanson, S. R., and Borst, J. D., "Overvoltages with Remotely Switched Cable-Fed Grounded Wye-Wye Transformers," *IEEE Conference Record*, 1975 Winter Power Meeting, New York, NY.

[B20] Tucker, R. Line Voltage Regulators, "Less Costly Alternative to UPS," *Electrical Consultant,* Aug. 1974.

Chapter 4
Generator and electric utility systems

4.1 Introduction

4.1.1 Overview

When an equipment problem is experienced, due to failure of the electric power supply, the options are to either tolerate the problem and do nothing, modify the equipment or system to perform satisfactorily during a power failure, or alter or supplement the power supply to prevent potential occurrences of failure. In many cases, the best decision is to modify the equipment or system, but this chapter does not examine these cases.

If the electric power user's study has shown that the most beneficial approach is to alter or supplement the power supply source, another study should be undertaken to determine the proper systems, configuration, and hardware that will meet the determined power requirements for the lowest cost.

This chapter describes combinations of systems and hardware that have been proven reliable in preventing the following types of electric power failure:

— Long-time interruption (hours)
— Medium-time interruption (minutes)
— Short-time interruption (seconds)
— Over- or undervoltage
— Over- or underfrequency

4.1.2 Guidelines for use

Emergency power systems are of the following two basic types:

— An electric power source separate from the prime source of power, operating in parallel, that maintains power to the critical loads should the prime source fail
— An available reliable power source to which critical loads are rapidly switched automatically when the prime source of power fails

Standby power systems are made up of the following main components:

— An alternative reliable source of electric energy separate from the prime power source
— Starting and regulating control if on-site standby generation is selected as the source
— Controls that transfer loads from the prime or emergency power source to the standby source

For reasons of economy, the user would be prudent to establish, from the previous chapters of this recommended practice, specific needs for emergency and standby power before specifying and purchasing equipment, since equipment costs are proportional to the following requirements and specifications:

— Longer equipment life
— Increased capacity
— Closer frequency regulation
— Closer voltage regulation
— Freedom from voltage or frequency transients
— Increased availability
— Increased reliability
— Increased temporary overload capability
— Quiet operation
— Safety from fuel hazards
— Pollution-free operation
— Freedom from harmonics
— Close voltage and frequency regulation with wider-range rapid load changes

Consideration should be given to load growth. Future power requirements frequently need to be connected to the emergency and standby system. It may be desirable to add additional existing power loads to the more reliable power bus as soon as the advantages are realized in practice. If additional capacity cannot be justified initially, the equipment and system should be selected and designed for future economic expansion compatible with the initial installation.

Operating costs of the systems and hardware are usually secondary to the initial costs of purchasing equipments, but should be included as a factor in the selection. These include cost of fuel, inspection frequency, ease of maintenance, frequency of testing, cost of parts, and taxes.

Installation quality should be high to prevent losing the reliability of electric power designed into the system and purchased in the hardware (IEEE Committee Report 1974 [B6]).[1] One should guard against introducing voltage transients into the emergency and standby power distribution system. Satisfactory voltage levels should be maintained under all loading conditions.

For industrial plants, electric systems should conform to IEEE Std 141-1993.[2] For commercial buildings, electric systems should conform to IEEE Std 241-1990. Grounding practices should follow the recommendations in IEEE Std 142-1991 and Chapter 7 of this book. Additional shielding, bonding, grounding, and even filtering may be required to maintain the quality of the emergency and standby power supply.

When energized sources of power are available for emergency use, a light should be included in the system to show that the source is energized and an alarm, to signal loss of available

---

[1]The numbers in brackets preceded by the letter B correspond to those of the bibliography in 4.7.
[2]Information on references can be found in 4.6.

power. These should be located where responsible persons can take action, should an alarm sound. An alternate utility source (see 4.3) or battery system is typical of line sources normally requiring these signals.

Users should take these additional steps to assure performance reliability:

— Establish regular inspections using a check sheet and recording exceptions;
— Perform regular preventive maintenance and repair items of exceptions found during the inspections;
— Set up a trial at regular intervals simulating a power failure but timed so as not to encounter hazards or losses should the system not operate as anticipated.

There are mathematical methods for quantitatively determining the reliability of an emergency or standby power system. Once the need is established, it may be advisable to calculate the system reliability, especially for emergency systems involving possible injury or loss of life. One such method is detailed in both Heising and Johnston 1972 [B5] and in Sawyer 1972 [B10].

4.2 Engine-driven generators

4.2.1 Introduction

These units are "work horses" that fulfill the need for emergency and standby power. They are available from small 1 kVA units to those of several thousand kVA. When properly maintained and kept warm, they dependably come on line within 8–15 s. In addition to providing emergency power, engine-driven generators are also used for handling peak loads and are sometimes used as the preferred source of power.

They fill the need of back-up power for uninterruptible power systems. Where well-regulated systems, free from voltage, frequency, or harmonic disturbances, are required, such as for computer operations, a *buffer* may be needed between the critical load and the engine-driven generators.

4.2.2 Diesel-engine generators

A typical diesel engine-driven generator rated 500 kW is shown in figure 4-1. Typical ratings of engine-driven generator sets are given in table 4-1. Individual models by various companies may be different. Lower speed units are heavier and more costly, but are more suitable for continuous duty.

Diesel engines are somewhat more costly and heavier in smaller sizes, but are rugged and dependable. The fire and explosion hazard is considerably lower than for gasoline engines. Sizes vary from about 2.5 kW to several MW.

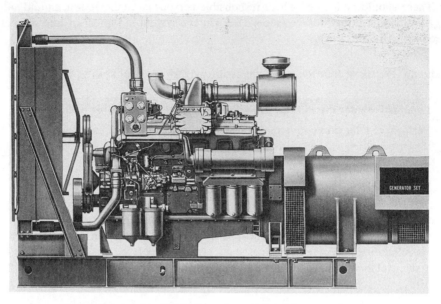

Figure 4-1—Typical diesel engine-driven generator

Table 4-1—Typical ratings of engine-driven generator sets

Nominal rating (kW)	Prime power rating (kW)	Standby rating (kW)	Power factor	Prime mover			Speed (r/min)
				Gasoline	Diesel	Natural gas/ LP gas	
5				×	×	×	3600
10	10	10	1.0	×	×	×	1800
25	25	30	0.8	×	×	×	1800
100	90	100	0.8	×	×	×	1800
250	225	250	0.8	×	×	×	1800
750	665	750	0.8	×	×	×	1800
1000	875	1000	0.8	×	×	×	1800

4.2.3 Gasoline-engine generators

Gasoline engines may be furnished for installations up to about 100 kW output. They start rapidly and are low in initial cost as compared to diesel engines. Disadvantages include a higher operating cost, a greater hazard due to the storing and handling of gasoline, short storage life of the fuel, and generally a lower mean-time between overhaul. The short fuel storage life restricts gasoline engines' use for emergency standby.

4.2.4 Gas-engine generators

Natural gas and liquid petroleum (LP) gas engines rank with gasoline engines in cost and are available up to about 600 kW and higher. They provide quick starting after long shutdown periods because of the fresh fuel supply. Engine life is longer with reduced maintenance because of the clean burning of natural gas. However, consideration should be given to the possibility of both the electric utility and the natural gas supply being concurrently unavailable. Unless engine compression ratios are increased, engines lose approximately 15% in power when operated on natural gas, compared to gasoline. Considerations in selecting natural or LP gas-fueled engines are the availability and dependability of the fuel supply, especially in an emergency situation. Reference should be made to the National Electrical Code (NEC) (NFPA 70-1996), Sections 700-12 and 700-11, to determine whether an on-site fuel supply is required.

4.2.5 Derating requirements

As noted in figure 4-30 in 4.4.3, altitude will cause a serious derating of the prime mover to deliver the torque required for the full generator output. Oversizing of the engine is a must for higher altitudes. The generators are less critical in output capacity if adequate cooling air is supplied to carry away the heat generated by the losses.

A general rule for derating engine power loss with altitude increase is to derate about 4% for each 1000 ft increase in altitude. Turbo-charged engines usually do not need to be derated below a specified minimum altitude, typically 2500–5000 ft above sea level. Also, an average derating factor for high ambient temperature is 1% for each 10 °F above 60 °F. Temperature derating is not considered as important as altitude derating.

4.2.6 Multiple engine-generator set systems

Automatic starting of multiple units and automatic synchronizing controls are available and practical for multiple unit installations. Advantages of several smaller units over one large unit should be considered since emergency and standby power can be available while one unit is being maintained or overhauled. Starting is usually reliable; especially if the units are warm and maintained by regular exercising, the likelihood of all of the units not starting is extremely low as compared to a single unit.

Smaller units also allow the "building block" concept. As capital is made available and the need of increased capacity grows, additional units of identical size and type may be added, thus simplifying the parts, maintenance, and training problems. The trend toward larger emergency power supplies also justifies the use of multiple sets to provide the additional power. Figures 4-2, 4-3, 4-4, and 4-5 illustrate typical multiple-set systems.

One very important consideration in the selection of smaller versus larger units is the service to which they will be subjected. Smaller units are nearly all higher speed (1800 r/min) engine-driven sets, and if these units are to be run continuously for long periods of time, the engine should be evaluated very thoroughly. Refer to table 4-1 for the comparison between prime power and standby ratings. Units may be operated at the standby rating for the duration of a power outage but should not be used at that rating for continuous operation. Generators for standby use are frequently operated at higher output and temperature rise than are those for continuous use.

4.2.7 Construction and controls

The basic electrical components are the engine-generator set and associated meters, controls, and switchgear. Most installations include a single generator set designed to serve either all the normal electrical needs of a building or a limited emergency circuit. Sometimes the system includes two or more generators of different types and sizes serving different types of loads. Also, two or more generators may be operating in parallel to serve the same load.

4.2.8 Typical engine-generator systems

This information is designed to help in selecting the electrical components of a generator installation. No attempt has been made to cover every situation that might arise.

The figures in this chapter show a circuit breaker at each generator set. The NEC, Article 445, permits a number of forms of generator protection, including inherent protection. Therefore, a circuit breaker or other form of overcurrent protection may or may not be used. For an in-depth discussion of generator protection, see Chapter 6.

In figures 4-2, 4-3, 4-4, 4-5, and 4-6, the following abbreviations are used:

— ATD = automatic transfer device (automatic transfer switch or electrically operated circuit breaker)
— CB = circuit breaker
— EG = engine-driven generator set
— LDC = load-dumping contactor, electrically operated, mechanically field
— PC = paralleling contactor

Figure 4-2 shows a standby power system in which, if power fails from the normal source, both engines automatically start. The first generator to reach operating voltage and frequency will actuate load dumping circuits and cause the remaining load to transfer to this generator. When the second generator is in synchronism, it will be paralleled automatically with the first. After the generators are paralleled, all or part of the dumped load is reconnected if the standby capacity is adequate.

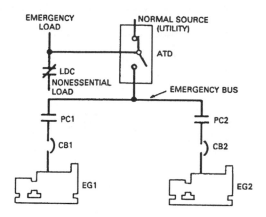

Figure 4-2—Two engine-generator sets operating in parallel

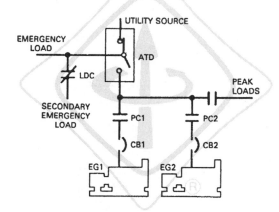

Figure 4-3—Peaking power control system

If one generator fails, it is immediately disconnected. A proportionate share of the load is dumped to reduce the load to where the remaining generator can handle it. When the failed generator is reinstated, the dumped load is reconnected. When the normal source is restored, the load is retransferred and the generators are automatically disconnected and shut down.

With the system shown in figure 4-3, idle standby generator sets can perform a secondary function by helping to supply power for peak loads. Depending on the load requirements, this system starts one unit or more to supply peak loads while the utility service supplies the emergency circuits. When the second generator is in synchronism, it will be paralleled automatically with the first. If the utility service fails, the peak loads are automatically disconnected and the generators pick up the emergency loads through the transfer device. Use of the standby generator(s) for peak shaving may increase wear and consequently shorten the overall time between overhauls. With proper maintenance, however, the reliability of the system is not hindered. Peak shaving use may require a different air quality permit.

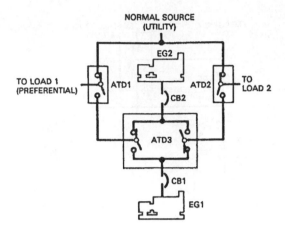

Figure 4-4—Three-source priority load selection system

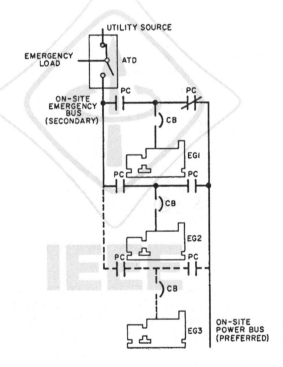

Figure 4-5—Combination on-site power and emergency transfer system

Figure 4-4 shows a standby power system where there is a split emergency load with one load being more critical than the other.

When the prime source fails, both generators start. If Load 1 is the preferential load, the generator that reaches operating speed first is put on the line by ATD3 to feed Load 1 through ATD1. When the other generator reaches operating speed, it then feeds Load 2. If the genera-

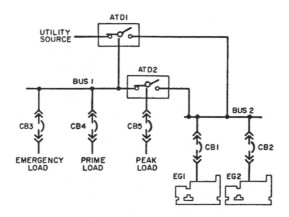

Figure 4-6—Dual engine-generator standby system

tor feeding Load 1 fails at any time, the other generator will be transferred from Load 2 and take over Load 1. When the prime source is restored, both loads are retransferred to the normal source and the generators shut down.

The system shown in figure 4-5 provides switching and control of utility and on-site power. Two on-site buses are provided: (1) an on-site power bus (preferred) supplies continuous power for computer or other essential loads, and (2) an emergency bus (secondary) supplies on-site generator power to emergency loads through an automatic transfer device if the utility service fails.

In normal operation, one of the generators is selected to supply continuous power to the preferred bus (in figure 4-5, EG1). Simplified semiautomatic synchronizing and paralleling controls permit any of the idle generators to be started and paralleled with the running generator to change generators without load interruption. Anticipatory failure circuits for low oil pressure and high coolant temperature permit load transfer to a new generator without load interruption. However, if the generator enters a critical failure mode, transfer to a new generator is made automatically with load interruption.

Many loads, such as lighting, fire alarms, heating, and air-conditioning, are fed by the utility service through the transfer device. If the utility fails, idle generators are automatically started and assume these loads through the automatic transfer device.

Figure 4-6 is similar to figure 4-3 wherein idle standby generator sets can perform a secondary function by helping to supply power for peak loads. Depending on the load requirements, this system starts one or both generators to feed the peak load by switching ATD2 while the utility service continues to supply the emergency and prime loads. The second generator is paralleled automatically with the first.

If the utility service fails, the emergency and prime loads are automatically transferred to the emergency generators. Depending on generator capacity, the peaking load may be left on, or CB5 may be dropped for the emergency.

4.2.9 Special considerations

Unusual conditions of altitude, ambient temperature, or ventilation may require either a larger generator to hold down winding temperatures or special insulation to withstand higher temperatures. Generators operating in the tropics are apt to encounter excessive moisture, high temperature, fungus, vermin, etc., and may require special tropical insulation and space heaters to keep the windings dry and the insulation from deteriorating.

4.2.10 Engine-generator set rating

For some buildings the maximum continuous generator load will be the total load when all equipment in the building is operating. For others, it may be more practical and economical to set up an emergency circuit or circuits so that only certain essential lights and equipment, and perhaps just one elevator, can be operated when the load is on the standby generator. Reference should be made to NEC, Sections 700-5 and 701-6, to determine whether an on-site fuel supply is required.

4.2.11 Motor-starting considerations

The successful start of a motor on an engine-driven generator requires that the motor develops enough torque for its driver's load and the system voltages be maintained above critical limits. Most motors behave as a constant impedance load during starting, which means that starting torque is proportional to the square of the terminal voltage. If the terminal voltage of a motor during startup is 80% of its rated value, the starting torque is 64% of its rated locked-rotor torque. Therefore, the purpose of a motor-starting study is to find a maximum voltage dip that the system and the motor can withstand.

Since the starting power factor of motors is low (typically from 20% to 50%) and locked-rotor currents are high (typically from 500% to 700%), the starting power demand of motors is mostly reactive and can be as high as ten times the full load reactive power demand of the motor. For example, a 100 hp motor with 600% LRC, 80% full-load PF and 20% starting PF will require the following complex power (kW and kvar) from the system at full-load (FL) and starting (LR) conditions (assuming full-load $kVA = hp$, and the system impedance is negligible):

$$S_{FL}(kVA) = 100(0.8 + j0.6) = 80 + j60$$

$$S_{LR}(kVA) = 600(0.2 + j0.98) = 120 + j588$$

$$\frac{kvar_{LR}}{kvar_{FL}} = \frac{588}{60} = 9.8$$

$$\frac{kW_{LR}}{kW_{FL}} = \frac{120}{80} = 1.5$$

Depending on the size of the motor with respect to the engine generator, motor starting can represent a small or a large disturbance to the generator. In extreme cases, starting a very large motor can be almost as severe as a short-circuit condition for the generator. Under a short-circuit condition, the generator reactance jumps down from its steady-state value (Xd) to subtransient value (Xd'') and then changes to transient value (Xd') and gradually back to its steady-state value (Xd). Therefore, to correctly model a motor acceleration on an engine generator, the generator model should include its field and damper windings, so that both the subtransient and transient behaviors are modeled. In additon to this, the rotor model used for the motor should include the effect of speed on the rotor reactance and resistance. This means that a transient stability program, which can include the effect of generator exciter and governor systems, should be used for motor acceleration studies.

For a snapshot study where the objective is to calculate the maximum voltage dip during starting, simple models for the generator and motor can be used. For this purpose, the generator can be modeled as a constant voltage source behind its transient reactance and the starting motor is modeled as a constant locked-rotor impedance.

Engines driving generators should be sized to handle the continuous kW load, plus motor starting requirements and the generator losses. It is important to note in the example calculation above that the initial starting kW exceeds the kW_{FL} by 50%. During acceleration the kW requirement may become twice the initial requirement when the motor reaches breakdown speed, as determined by the breakdown torque rating. The generator engine must be capable of driving the starting kW requirements. In sizing the engine generators for motor starting, the locked-rotor kVA rating of the motors should be compared with the maximum motor-starting kVA capability of the generator. Manufacturers' data can usually be obtained, giving the maximum rating in kVA of the engine generator as well as its continuous rating. The maximum starting kvar rating would be the maximum amount of the short-duration kVA available for motor-starting duty without exceeding a specified voltage dip.

Generator set manufacturers are usually willing to furnish a guide for calculating motor-starting effects. A rule of thumb of 0.5 hp/kW is frequently used; however, the final decision should be based upon the manufacturer's data. When motor-starting kVA or continued kW exceed the rated values of the generator set, the effects of the resulting voltage and frequency deviation on equipment other than the motor being started should be evaluated (that is, motor starters, relays, computers, communication equipment, etc.).

Generators are usually sized for the maximum continuous kVA demand. Should there be unually high inertia loads to start without benefit of reduced-voltage starting, or if voltage and frequency regulation other than specified cannot be tolerated during the startup period, a higher rated generator may be required.

4.2.12 Load transient considerations

A voltage regulator with sufficient response is required to minimize voltage sags or surges after load transients. The engine-generator set should be of sufficient capacity and design capability to minimize the effect of load transients. Many industrial applications can tolerate large voltage sags (usually down to 80%, but as low as 65% in special cases) as long as they are not so low as to cause motor contactors to drop out or automatic brakes to set. Solid-state controls and computers may be affected. The effect of non-linear loads on the generator set controls should be evaluated.

4.2.13 Manual systems

Manually controlled standby service is the simplest and lowest cost arrangement and may be satisfactory where an attendant is on duty at all times and where automatic starting and transfer of the load is not a critical requirement.

4.2.14 Automatic systems

In order for engine-driven generators to provide automatic emergency power, the system should also include automatic engine starting controls, automatic battery charger, and an automatic transfer device. In most applications, the utility source is the normal source and the engine-generator set provides emergency power when utility power is interrupted or its characteristics are unsatisfactory. The utility power supply is monitored and engine starting is automatically initiated once there is a failure or severe voltage or frequency reduction in the normal supply. The load is automatically transferred as soon as the standby generator stabilizes at rated voltage and speed. Upon restoration of normal supply, the transfer device automatically retransfers the load and initiates engine shutdown. See 4.3.8 for special consideration in retransferring motor loads.

4.2.15 Automatic transfer devices

Transfer equipment for use with engine generator sets is similar to that used with multiple-utility systems, except for the addition of auxiliary contacts that close when the normal source is interrupted. These auxiliary contacts initiate the starting and stopping of the engine-driven generator. The automatic transfer device may also include accessories for automatic exercising of the engine-generator set and a 5 min unloaded running time before shutdown. For additional information on automatic transfer devices, refer to 4.3.

4.2.16 Engine-generator set reliability

To keep the engine in good condition, whenever it starts it should run for a sufficiently long time so that all parts reach their normal operating temperatures. In case emergency power is called for only briefly, it is desirable that the engine continue to run for about 15 min after normal power has been restored. A programmed control should be added that starts the engine once a week and operates it for a set period of time under load.

Reliability and satisfaction of the standby power supply partially depends on the engine generator installations. The following key points should be considered:

a) Systems dependent upon a municipal water supply are not dependable because the supply can be interrupted in an emergency. A radiator cooling system or a heat exchanger cooled system with an independent cooling water supply should be specified.

b) Antifreeze protection may be required. A room heater, electric immersion heater, or steam jacket improves starting reliability and solves the antifreeze problem at the same time. A loss-of-heat alarm may be required.

c) A silencer on the intake and exhaust may be required by law and will reduce noise levels.

d) Fuel supply systems must meet local laws, regulations, and insurance requirements. The capacity stored depends on available guaranteed quick delivery replacement, including Sundays and holidays and under all weather conditions.

e) Fuel supplies stored underground are desirable. Above ground, antifreeze protection may be required.

f) Gasoline and diesel fuels deteriorate if they stand unused for a period of several months. Normal testing and running on line may be used to keep fuel fresh. Inhibitors may be added to the fuel. Fuel used for several purposes will tend to be fresh. A fuel test program should be established to ensure fuels are fresh and reliable.

g) Engine vibration transferred to the building should be dampened by rubber pads or springs, and flexible couplings should be used on fuel, exhaust, water, and conduit lines.

h) Equipment mounting should conform to local seismic requirements.

i) Starting aids are of three types, of which item 3) is frequently preferred:

1) Air heated before it reaches the cylinders

2) Volatile starting fluid injected into the engine air

3) Engine block maintained warm

4.2.17 Air supply and exhaust

Exhaust piping inside the building should be covered with gas-tight insulation to protect personnel and to reduce room temperature. The exhaust piping must be of sufficient diameter to avoid exhaust back pressure. Consideration should be given to dissipating the exhaust away from air intakes and minimizing air pollution.

Some means of providing free flow of fresh air into the generator room is necessary to keep the atmosphere comfortable for personnel and to make clean, cool air available to the engine. The most effective and lowest-cost method is usually to use a *pusher*-type fan on the radiator and connect the radiator to the outside through a duct. The intake opening should be approximately 25–50% larger than the duct.

4.2.18 Noise reduction

Vibration must frequently be isolated from structures to reduce noise. Noise-reducing mufflers are rated according to their degree of silencing by such terms as *industrial*, *residential*, or *critical*, and are usually required to meet noise standards. An intake muffler is not usually installed since an engine normally is supplied with at least one intake air cleaner that also serves as an intake silencer.

4.2.19 Fuel systems

To simplify the fuel supply system, the fuel tank should be as close to the engine as possible. When gasoline or LP fuel is used, it normally cannot be stored in the same room with the engine because there is a danger of fire or fumes. However, when diesel fuel is used, it can sometimes be stored in the same room as the engine. If a remote tank is used, a transfer tank located near the engine is recommended. The building code or fire insurance regulations should be checked to determine whether the fuel storage tank may be located beside the generator set, in an adjacent room, outside, or underground.

An engine equipped to operate on gasoline, LP gas, or diesel fuel stored on-site is a self-contained system that does not depend on outside municipal or utility services. It is dependable and affords independent standby protection.

4.2.20 Governors and regulation

Governors work in droop or isochronous modes of operation. In a droop mode, the engine's speed decreases as the load increases, while in an isochronous mode the governor maintains the same stead speed at any load, up the the full load:

$$\text{speed droop} = \frac{\text{no-load r/min} - \text{full-load r/min}}{\text{full-load r/min}} \cdot 100\%$$

Typical speed droop setting for a droop-operated generator is 3–5%. Thus if speed and frequency at full load are 1800 r/min and 60 Hz, respectively, at no load they will be 1872 r/min and 62.4 Hz, with 4% droop.

When a generator is parallel with the system for maintenance periods, the governor is set on droop mode, i.e., it is base-loaded. Under an isolated condition, it is desirable to operate the governor under an isochronous mode so that the system frequency is kept constant.

Under steady load, frequency tends to vary slightly above and below the normal frequency setting of the governor. The extent of this variation is a measure of the stability of the governor. An isochronous governor should maintain frequency regulation within ± 1/4%.

When load is added or removed, speed and frequency dip or rise momentarily, usually 1–3 s, before the governor causes the engine to settle at a steady speed at the new load. For generators operating in parallel with a primary source of power, the governor may be arranged to automatically switch from droop to isochronous mode upon loss of the primary source.

4.2.21 Starting methods

Most engine-generator sets utilize a battery-powered electric motor for starting the engine. A pneumatic or hydraulic system normally is used on large units where battery starting is impracticable.

4.2.22 Battery charging

In addition to the battery-charging generator on the set, a separate automatic battery charger is recommended for maintaining battery charge when the generator is not running. Failure to keep the battery properly maintained and charged is the greatest cause of emergency system failure.

4.2.23 Advantages and disadvantages of diesel-driven generators

In evaluating the merits of diesel engine versus gas turbine prime movers, the following advantages and disadvantages of each should be considered:

— *Fuel supply.* Gas turbines and diesel engines can generally burn the same fuels (kerosene through #2 diesel).

— *Starting.* Where the application requires acceptance of 100% load in 10 s, diesel generator sets can be provided that can meet this requirement. Most gas turbine generators sets require more than 30 s.

— *Noise.* The gas turbine operates quieter and has less vibration than the diesel engine.

— *Ratings.* The gas turbine is not readily available in sizes less than 500 kW, while diesel engine units range from 15 kW or lower.

— *Cooling.* Diesel engines in the larger sizes normally require water cooling, while gas turbines are normally air-cooled.

— *Installation.* Gas turbines are considerably lighter and smaller in size. Turbines also require less total cooling and combustion air and produce minimal vibration. Installation costs are normally less and rooftop applications are more feasible.

— *Cost.* First cost for diesel engines is lower than gas turbines, but overall installed cost sometimes becomes comparable due to the lower installation costs of the gas turbines.

— *Exercising.* The cyclic operating requirements under load are more rigid for diesel units than for gas turbines.

— *Maintenance.* The gas turbine is a more simple machine than a diesel engine. However, repair service for a diesel engine is generally more readily available than for a gas turbine.

— *Efficiency.* The diesel engine operates more efficiently than a gas turbine under full load. However, the reduced exercising requirements for the gas turbine normally make the turbine the lower fuel consumer in standby applications.

— *Frequency response.* The gas turbine generator is superior in full-load transient frequency response.

4.2.24 Additional information

Engine generator specifications are treated in greater detail in EGSA 101P-1995.

4.3 Multiple utility services

4.3.1 Introduction

Multiple utility services may be used as an emergency or standby source of power. In this case, an additional utility service from a separate source is required along with the required switching equipment. Figure 4-7 shows automatic transfer between two low-voltage utility supplies. Utility Source 1 is the normal power line and Utility Source 2 is a separate utility supply providing emergency power. Both circuit breakers are normally closed. The load must be able to tolerate the few cycles of interruption while the automatic transfer device operates.

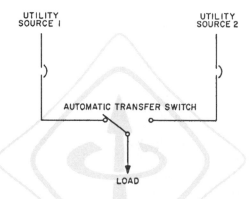

Figure 4-7—Two-utility-source system using one automatic transfer switch

4.3.2 Closed-transition transfer

If the utility will permit the two sources of supply to be connected together momentarily, the transfer device may be provided with controls for both open (normal supply opened before the emergency supply is closed) and closed (emergency supply closed before the normal supply is opened) transition. With closed transition, the utility can notify the customer to transfer to the emergency source in order to take the normal supply out of service for maintenance and repair without the momentary interruption that occurs with open transition. Closed transition requires the sources to be synchronized with proper phase angle and phase sequence. Short-circuit duty will be increased during closed transition.

4.3.3 Utility services separation

Use of multiple utility service is economically feasible when the local utility can provide two or more service connections over separate lines and from separate supply points that are not apt to be jointly affected by system disturbances, storms, or other hazards. It has the advantage of relatively fast transfer in that there is no 5-15 s delay as there is when starting a standby engine-generator set. A separate utility supply for an emergency should not be relied upon unless total loss of power can be tolerated on rare occasions. Otherwise, use of engine-generator sets is recommended. Also, in some installations, such as hospitals, codes require on-site generators.

A no-potential alarm should be installed on the emergency supply so that the utility can be notified and emergency precautions taken if the emergency supply is lost. Additional reliability has been obtained in rare instances where the services are available from different utility companies.

4.3.4 Simple automatic transfer schemes

Automatic switching equipment may consist of three circuit breakers with suitable control and interlocks, as shown in figure 4-8. Circuit breakers are generally used for primary switching where the voltage exceeds 600 V. They are more expensive but safer to operate, and the use of fuses for overcurrent protection is avoided. Relaying is provided to transfer the load automatically to either source if the other one fails, provided that circuit is energized. The supplying utility will normally designate which source is for normal use and which is for emergency. If either supply is not able to carry the entire load, provisions must be made to drop noncritical loads before transfer takes place. If the load can be taken from both services, the two R circuit breakers are closed and the tie circuit breaker is open. The three circuit breakers are interlocked to permit any two to be closed but prevent all three from being closed. The advantage of this arrangement is that the momentary transfer outage will occur only on the load supplied from the circuit that is lost. However, the supplying utility may not allow the load to be taken from both sources, especially since a more expensive totalizing meter may be required. A manual override of the interlock system should be provided so that a closed transition transfer can be made if the supplying utility wants to take either line out of service for maintenance or repair and a momentary tie is permitted.

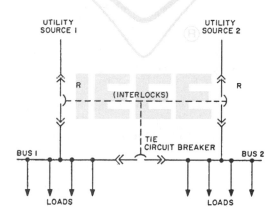

**Figure 4-8—Two-utility-source system where
any two circuit breakers can be closed**

If the supplying utility will not permit power to be taken from both sources, the control system must be arranged so that the circuit breaker on the normal source is closed, the tie circuit breaker is closed, and the emergency source circuit breaker is open. If the utility will not permit dual or totalized metering, the two sources must be connected together to provide a com-

95

mon metering point and then connected to the distribution switchboard. In this case, the tie circuit breaker can be eliminated and the two circuit breakers act as a transfer device. Under these conditions, the cost of extra circuit breakers can rarely be justified.

The arrangement shown in figure 4-8 provides protection only against failure of the normal utility service. Continuity of power to critical loads can also be disrupted by either of the following:

— An open circuit within the building (load side of the incoming service)
— An overload or fault tripping out a circuit
— Electrical or mechanical failure of the electric power distribution system within the building

It may be desirable to locate transfer devices close to the load and have the operation of the transfer devices independent of overcurrent protection. Multiple transfer devices of lower current rating, each supplying a part of the load, may be used rather than one transfer device for the entire load.

Availability of multiple utility service systems can be improved by adding a standby engine-generator set capable of supplying the more critical load. Such an arrangement, using multiple automatic transfer switches, is shown in figure 4-9.

4.3.5 Overcurrent protection

 Caution should be exercised to assure that transfer control and operation do not in any way detract from overcurrent protection and vice versa. Furthermore, the transfer and overcurrent protective devices should be so arranged that means for disconnecting incoming service is conventional and readily accessible. Chapter 6 provides a more in-depth analysis of overcurrent protection.

4.3.6 Transfer device ratings and accessories

The required characteristics of transfer devices should include the capabilities of

— Closing against inrush currents without contact welding
— Carrying full rated current continuously without overheating
— Withstanding available short-circuit currents without contact separation
— Properly interrupting the loads to avoid flashover between the two utility services

In addition to considering each of the above individually, it is also necessary to consider the effect each has on the other. Particular consideration should be given to coordination between automatic transfer switches and overcurrent protection. High fault currents create electromagnet forces within the contact structure of circuit breakers, which help provide fast opening and therefore minimum clearing time; however, automatic transfer switches designed to withstand high fault currents utilize these electromagnetic forces in a reverse manner to assure that the transfer switch contacts remain closed unit the fault has been cleared. Contact separation, while carrying fault level current, results in arcing, melting of contact surface, and

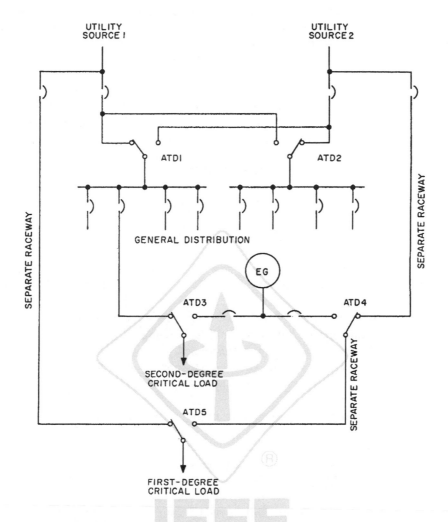

Figure 4-9—Two utility sources combined with an engine-generator set to provide varying degrees of emergency power

possible contact welding upon reclosure and cooling of molten metal. ANSI/UL 1008-1988 does not permit contact welding after the transfer switch has been subjected to the withstand current test, which is the recommended means of verifying this capability. For these reasons, transfer switching devices should be selected from those designed and approved for the purpose.

Most transfer switches are capable of carrying 100% rated current at an ambient temperature of 40 °C. However, transfer switches incorporating integral overcurrent protective devices may be limited to a continuous load current not to exceed 80% of the switch rating. The manufacturer's specification sheets indicate whether the device is 80% or 100% rated.

Transfer switches differ from other emergency equipment in that they continuously monitor the utility source and continuously carry current to critical loads. Fault currents, repetitive switching of all types of loads, and adverse environmental conditions should not cause excessive temperature rise or detract from reliable operation.

Most transfer switches are rated for total system transfer and thus are suitable for continuous duty control of motors, electric discharge lamps, tungsten filament lamps, and electric heating equipment, provided that the tungsten lamp load does not exceed 30% of the switch rating. Some manufacturers also provide transfer switches for 100% tungsten lamp load. There are cases where transfer switches are limited to specific loads, such as resistance loads only. For these reasons, the load classification should be determined when selecting transfer switches.

Load transfer devices are available in the following forms:

— Automatic transfer switches are available in ratings from 30 to 4000 A, to 600 V (figure 4-10).
— Automatic power circuit breakers consisting of two or more power circuit breakers that are mechanically or electrically interlocked, or both, rated from 600 to 3000 A, to 15 kV.
— Manual transfer switches (600 V) available in current ratings from 30 to 200 A.
— Nonautomatic transfer switches available in ratings from 30 to 4000 A, to 600 V, manually controlled and electrically operated.
— Manual or electrically operated bolted pressure switches (600 V) fusible or nonfusible available in ratings from 800 to 6000 A.

Features and accessories depend upon the form of transfer device and may include the following:

— Voltage monitors that have adjustable settings for dropout (unacceptable voltage) and pickup (acceptable voltage). The dropout initiates transfer of the load to the alternate source; the pickup initiates retransfer of the load back to the normal source. The dropout range is typically 75-95% of the setting selected for pickup. The typical pickup setting range is 85-98% of nominal voltage. Usual setting for most types of load are 85% of nominal voltage for dropout and 90% for pickup. (Dropout is usually about 95% of pickup.) Lower dropout or additional time delay may be necessary if significant voltage drop is produced by starting large motors.
— Test switch to simulate a power failure to provide a periodic test of the emergency source and the transfer operation.
— Controls for closed transition if the utility will permit the two sources to be momentarily tied together and if the switch design permits. This will allow manual transfer from the normal to the emergency feeder and back without the momentary transfer interruption.
— Provisions for switching the neutral conductor and thereby minimizing ground currents and simplifying ground-fault sensing. For further discussion, see Chapter 7.
— Controls for motor load transfer so as to avoid abnormal currents caused by the motor's residual voltage being out of phase with the voltage source to which the motor is being transferred.

**Figure 4-10—Modular-type automatic transfer switch
suitable for all classes of load**

— Circuitry to initiate starting and stopping of the engine-generator set(s) depending upon availability of the normal source of power.
— Time delays in the transfer switch to permit proper programming of transfer switch operation. A time-delay relay, usually adjustable from 0–6 s, is used to provide override of momentary interruptions and to initiate engine start and power transfer if the outage or voltage reduction is sustained. This feature is necessary to minimize wear on the engine-starting motor, ring gear, and other system equipment and to prevent unnecessary drain on the engine-cranking battery.

This time delay is usually set at about 1 s, but can be set for longer if circumstances warrant. If delay settings are longer, care needs to be taken to ensure that sufficient time remains to get the alternate power source on line within the time prescribed by applicable codes if the system is a required system.

After the engine has started and generator output is at proper voltage and frequency, another time-delay relay is activated to permit the generator output to stabilize under no load; this time delay is typically set for less than 1 min. Upon time-out, the load is transferred to the standby source.

99

Activation of another timer coincides with restoration of the normal source; this timer is typically adjustable from 0–30 min. The function of this time-delay relay is to provide an established minimum running time for the engine-generator any time that the unit is activated and to maintain the transfer switch in the standby mode, even if the normal source has been restored.

The purpose of this time delay is twofold. It is not uncommon for prolonged power outages to be preceded by a series of brief outages separated from each other by a matter of several seconds or a few minutes; the time delay prevents unnecessary cycling during such periods. It also ensures that the engine-generator will get a good workout under load, preserving it in good operating condition.

The transfer switch should be designed so that this feature is automatically nullified if the engine-generator set fails and power is available from the normal source.

A fourth timing function is recommended to permit the engine-generator to run unloaded for a while after transfer back to the normal source; an interval of 5 min or less is usually applied. This function permits the units to cool down properly and permits fan action to prevent excessive heat from building up in the generator. This feature is especially recommended for diesel-driven units.

If the standby system comprises more than one automatic transfer switch, it is desirable to sequence the transfer of loads from normal to standby source. This function, also performed by timers, can reduce the starting kVA requirements of the engine-generator set—an especially important consideration when the load is predominantly motors.

4.3.7 Voltage tolerances

The basic standard for the voltage tolerance for utilization equipment is ANSI C84.1-1989. These limits are based on the T-frame motor with slightly reduced limits for equipment other than motors. In the case of special equipment, the manufacturer's tolerance limits should be obtained. Care should be taken in determining the minimum voltage for transfer switch operation to distinguish between equipment that is not damaged by low voltage, even though operation is unsatisfactory, such as incandescent lamps and resistance heaters, and equipment that may be damaged by low voltage or that may cause damage or unsafe conditions at low voltage.

4.3.8 Transferring motor loads

Transferring motor loads between two sources requires special consideration. Although the two sources may be synchronized, the motor will tend to slow down upon loss of power and during transfer, thus causing the residual voltage of the motor to be out of phase with the oncoming source. The speed of transfer, total inertia, and motor and system characteristics are involved. On transfer, the vector difference and resulting high abnormal inrush current could cause serious damage to the motor, and the excessive current drawn by the motor may trip the overcurrent protective device. Both motor loads with relatively low load inertia in relation to torque requirements, such as pumps and compressors, and large inertia loads, such as induced draft fans, etc., that keep turning near synchronous speed for a longer time after loss of power, are subject to the hazard of out-of-phase switching. Automatic transfer switches can be provided with various accessory controls to overcome this problem, including the following:

— In-phase transfer
— Motor load disconnect control circuit
— Transfer switch with a timed center off position
— Overlap transfer to momentarily parallel the power sources

In-phase transfer as shown in figure 4-11 is commonly used for transferring low-slip motors driving high-inertia loads, provided that the transfer switch has a fast operating time. A primary advantage of in-phase transfer is that it can permit the motor to continue to run with little disturbance to the electrical system and the process that is being controlled by the motor. Another advantage is that a standard double-throw transfer switch can be used with the simple addition of an in-phase monitor. The monitor samples the relative phase angle that exists between the two sources between which the motor is transferred. When the two voltages are within the desired phase angle and approaching zero phase angle, the in-phase monitor signals the transfer switch to operate and reconnection takes place within acceptable limits.

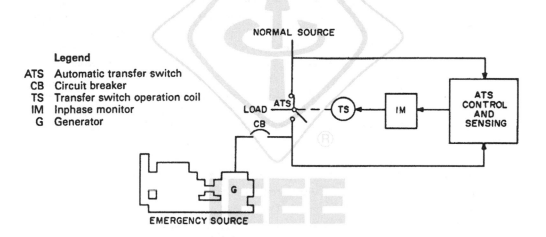

Figure 4-11—In-phase motor load transfer

Motor load disconnect control circuits, such as shown in figure 4-12 and similar relay schemes, are also a common means of transferring motor loads.

As figure 4-12 indicates, the motor load disconnect control circuit is a pilot contact on the transfer switch that opens to de-energize the contactor coil circuit of the motor controller. After transfer, the transfer switch pilot contact closes to permit the motor controller to reclose. For these applications, the controller must reset automatically. The disconnect circuit should be arranged to open the pilot contact for approximately 0.5–3 s before transfer to the alternate power source is initiated.

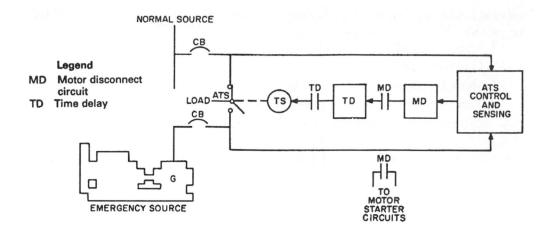

Figure 4-12—Motor load disconnect circuit

Transfer switches with timed center off (neutral) position are also used for switching motor loads; figure 4-13 shows a typical arrangement. Interconnections between the transfer switch and motor controller are not required. Because there is no direct control of the motor controller, the motor controller may not drop out if it sees the residual voltage from the spinning motor. The off-time must be long enough to permit the residual voltage to reduce to a value (typically 25% of rated motor voltage) at which reconnection will not harm the motor, the driven load, or trip the breaker. ANSI/NEMA MG 1-1993 outlines a method of calculating safe values. The open-circuit voltage decay times for a series of motors are shown in figure 4-14. The center hold time should not be additive to the generator start-up time, so that the power outage is not needlessly lengthened by the center hold time of the transfer switch. Only when switching between two live power sources should the center hold function be in operation.

Overlap (closed transition) transfer with momentary paralleling of two power sources is shown in figure 4-15. An uninterrupted load transfer provides the least amount of system and process disturbance. However, overlap can only be achieved when both power sources are present and properly synchronized by voltage, frequency, and phase angle.

In resent years there has been an increasing use of closed transitions in emergency and standby power systems. This eliminates the problems associated with out-of-phase transfers of motors, such as transient inrush or loss of speed. This also reduces the number of undesireable interruptions of critical loads, such as computer systems. Permission from the utility, and compliance with their requirements, may be required when local generation is to be paralleled with the utility system, even for a short period.

4.3.9 Typical systems

Figure 4-16 illustrates a typical system supplying electric power to a manufacturing plant. The system is designed for initial operation with Utility Line 1 utilized as the normal source and Utility Line 2 utilized as a normally open auxiliary source. The two utility lines are syn-

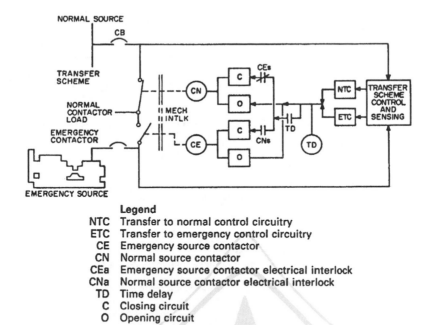

Legend

NTC	Transfer to normal control circuitry
ETC	Transfer to emergency control circuitry
CE	Emergency source contactor
CN	Normal source contactor
CEa	Emergency source contactor electrical interlock
CNa	Normal source contactor electrical interlock
TD	Time delay
C	Closing circuit
O	Opening circuit

Figure 4-13—Neutral off position

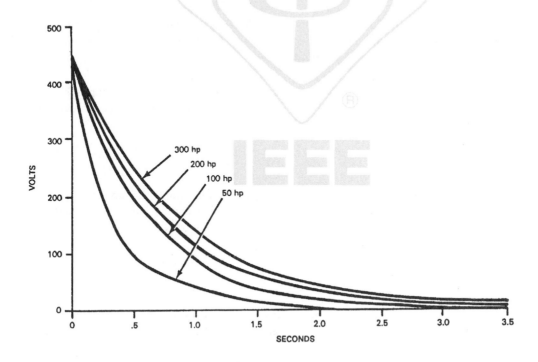

**Figure 4-14—Induction motor open-circuit voltage decay
(based on constant speed)**

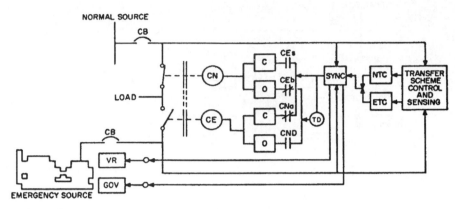

Legend

CEb Emergency source contactor electrical interlock
CNb Normal source contactor electrical interlock
TD Time delay to open alternate contactor if proper contactor does not operate to terminate parallel operation
SYNC Automatic synchronizer to synchronize emergency source in voltage frequency and phase angle with normal source

Figure 4-15—Closed transition transfer

chronized with each other so that they can be paralleled, but are not normally operated in this manner. However, unless the relaying is designed for it, the operation of the two incoming lines in parallel should be kept to a minimum—that is, the switching time.

Utility Lines 1 and 2 enter the plant from a substation some distance away through underground conduits separated by about 1 ft and encased in the center of a 3×3 ft concrete enclosure 7 ft below the surface for protection.

Operation is as follows:

a) If voltage on the normal source (Line 1) drops appreciably for several cycles, the undervoltage relay will deactivate, trip the circuit breaker in Line 1, and close the circuit breaker in Line 2 (if acceptable voltage is present on Line 2).

b) When voltage is restored to Line 1, the undervoltage relay is activated and initiates a timer. After the voltage has been present on Line 1 for a predetermined time (usually 1–10 min), the circuit breaker in Line 1 closes, after which the circuit breaker in Line 2 opens.

c) If there is no voltage present on Line 2 when Line 1 loses voltage, the circuit breaker in Line 2 will not close. When voltage is restored to Line 1, the circuit breaker in Line 1 will immediately close.

d) If a fault or overload occurs on the load side of either incoming circuit breaker, a lockout relay keeps both circuit breakers open, disabling the automatic transfer system until manually reset.

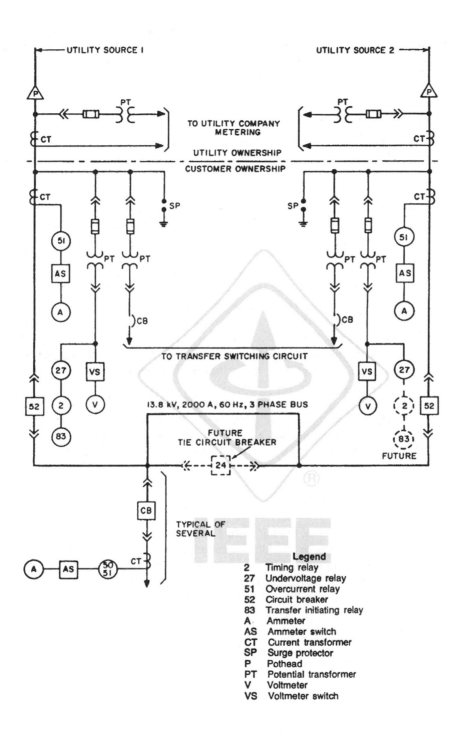

Figure 4-16—Typical system supplying electric power to manufacturing plant

As power demands increase, this system can be expanded by inserting a tie circuit breaker in the 13.8 kV bus and additional relaying. Part of the load would then be supplied by each utility line with transfer of the entire load to the line feeder, should power be lost to one line. Load shedding of noncritical loads could be incorporated if necessary.

Operation would then be as follows:

a) A loss of voltage or appreciable decrease of voltage on either utility line will cause that normally closed circuit breaker to open and the normally open tie circuit breaker to close. When normal voltage returns, the open utility line circuit breaker will close in a preset time (1–10 min), after which the tie circuit breaker will open.

b) A simultaneous loss of voltage on both utility lines will cause both normally closed utility line circuit breakers to open and the normally open tie circuit breaker to close. A return to normal voltage on either utility line will cause that utility line circuit breaker to close in its preset time and the tie circuit breaker to remain closed. When normal voltage is established on the second utility line, that utility line circuit breaker will close in its preset time after which the tie circuit breaker will open.

c) Fault current or overload current causing either utility line circuit breaker to open will also make the automatic closing feature of the tie circuit breaker inoperative until manually reset.

d) If the utility company needs to take one line out of service, they notify the customer who then manually closes the tie circuit breaker and opens the line to be affected.

The arrangement shown in figure 4-15 only provides protection against failure of the utility source. To provide protection against disruption of power within the building areas, it may be desirable to locate additional automatic transfer switches downstream and close to the load. A combination of circuit breakers and downstream automatic transfer switches is shown in figure 4-9.

4.3.10 Bypass isolation switches

In many installations, performing regular testing or detailed inspections on the emergency system is difficult because some or all of the loads connected to the system are vital to human life or are critical in the operation of continuous processes. De-energizing these loads for any length of time is also difficult. This situation often results in a lack of maintenance. For such installations, a means can be provided to bypass the critical loads directly to a reliable source of power without downtime of the loads. The transfer switch can then be isolated for safe inspection and maintenance.

Two-way bypass isolation switches are available to meet this need. These switches perform three functions:

a) *Shunt the service around the transfer switch without interrupting power to the load.* When the bypass (BP) handle (upper handle) is moved to the bypass-to-normal (BP-NORM) position (figure 4-17), the closed transfer switch contacts are shunted by the right-hand BP contacts. The flow of current then divides between the bypass and transfer contacts. This assures there will not be even a momentary interruption of

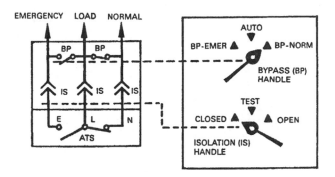

Figure 4-17—Bypass to normal

power to the load should current no longer flow through the transfer switch, in which case the full current is immediately carried by the bypass contacts.

b) *Allow the transfer switch to be electrically tested and operated without interrupting power to the load.* This can be done as shown in figure 4-18. With the isolation (IS) handle (lower handle) moved to the test position, the load terminals of the transfer switch are disconnected from the power source. The transfer switch is still energized from the normal and emergency sources and can be electrically tested without interrupting the load. The closed right-hand BP contacts carry the full load.

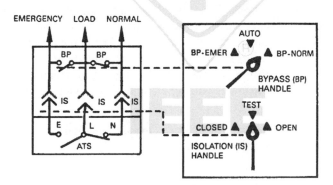

Figure 4-18—Test position

c) *Electrically isolate the transfer switch from both sources of power and load conductors to permit inspections and maintenance of the transfer switch.* (See figure 4-19.) With the isolation handle moved to the open position, the automatic transfer switch (ATS) is completely isolated. The load continues to be fed through the BP contact. With drawout capability, the transfer switch can now be completely removed without interrupting the load. In this mode, the bypass switch has a dual function. In addition to bypass, it also operates as a manual backup transfer switch.

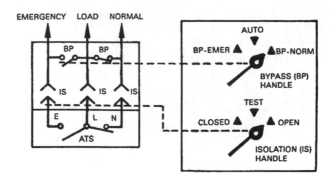

Figure 4-19—Complete isolation

Although the foregoing illustrations show bypass to the normal source, the transfer switch can also be bypassed to the emergency source without interrupting power to the load, provided bypass is made to the source feeding the critical load. When bypassing to the emergency source, the same three functions can be performed after the transfer switch has transferred to emergency. While two-way bypass isolation switch arrangements have been available for many years, only recently has it become possible to combine a two-way, noninterruption bypass function with the automatic transfer function all in one interconnected assembly.

The bypass and isolation portions of the switch assembly should incorporate zero maintenance design. This design concept avoids system shutdown during maintenance or repair. To achieve zero maintenance design, bypass contacts should be in the power circuit only during the actual bypass period. The objection to retaining the bypass contacts in the circuit at all times is that they, along with the bus bars, are also subject to damage from fault currents. While the transfer switch is repairable without disruption of service, the bypass switch is not.

Providing a combination automatic transfer and bypass isolation switch in lieu of an automatic transfer switch more than doubles the cost.

4.3.11 Nonautomatic transfer switches

Nonautomatic transfer switches are used in applications where operating personnel are available and the load is such that immediate automatic restoration of power is not mandatory.

Some typical applications are found in health care facility equipment systems, industrial plants, sewage plants, civil defense control centers, farms, residences, communication facilities, and other installations where codes require approved devices. A typical installation of a nonautomatic transfer switch combined with several automatic transfer switches is shown in figure 4-20.

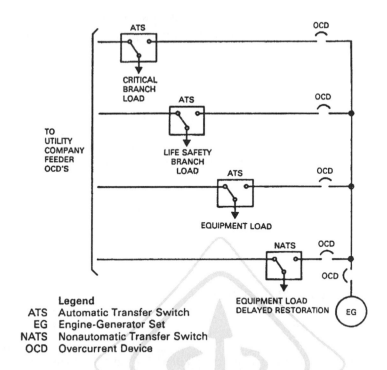

Legend

ATS	Automatic Transfer Switch
EG	Engine-Generator Set
NATS	Nonautomatic Transfer Switch
OCD	Overcurrent Device

Figure 4-20—Typical hospital installation with a nonautomatic transfer switch and several automatic transfer switches

Double-throw knife switches and safety switches are often not suitable for these applications. Many of these devices have limited capacity when switching between two unsynchronized power sources. Nonautomatic transfer switches generally have the same type of contacts and arc-quenching means as automatic transfer switches and meet ANSI/UL 1008-1988.

Both electrically operated and nonelectrically operated switches are available. Electrically operated units are arranged for local or remote control station operation. Accessibility to the transfer switch is not necessary when it is remotely controlled by remote control stations. This may be an advantage in a large facility where the devices can be controlled from the plant engineer's operations room.

Two interlocked control relays are often included with the electrically operated switch to permit

— Line runs over small-gauge wire
— Low operating current through control station switch
— Partial voltage check before operating

Nonelectrically operated units are similar to the electrically operated type except for omission of electrical operation and inclusion of a quick-make/quick-break operator that can be manually operated from outside the enclosure. The speed of operation is similar to the electri-

109

cally operated arrangement owing to the preloading of the main operating springs, thereby providing appropriate current make, break, and carry capabilities.

4.3.12 Conclusion

Approximately 90% of transfer schemes designed to switch from the prime power source to the emergency source for commercial installations utilize conventional double-throw transfer switches. For maximum system reliability, the transfer switches are usually located close to the load rather than at the incoming prime power source. The use of interlocked service entrance circuit breakers for transfer schemes is usually limited to medium-voltage primary switching.

Two parallel in-phase separate utility sources on line continuously with proper relaying on a normally closed tie circuit breaker provide increased reliability of electric power in some applications. This possibility should be investigated with the utility company representatives.

4.4 Turbine-driven generators

4.4.1 Introduction

Two general types of turbine prime movers for electrical generators are available: steam and gas/oil.

4.4.2 Steam turbine generators

Steam is usually not available if all electric power has been lost, although there are independent steam supply systems that may themselves have uninterruptible electrical systems. In this case steam might be considered. There are compact steam turbines that could bring power onto the line in about 5 min. This is a rather special source of supply, and details are not presented.

Steam turbines are used to drive generators that are larger than those that can be driven by diesel engines. However, steam turbines are designed for continuous operation and require a boiler with fuel supply and a source of water. Thus, they are expensive for use as an emergency or standby power supply and may have environmental problems involving fuel supply, noise, combustion product output, and heating of the condensing water.

Figure 4-21 shows an on-line steam turbine generator supplying a critical bus in parallel with one source of utility power. An alternate utility source can be manually switched on in a minute or so should there be a failure of the on-line utility source. The normal utility supply system should be large enough to supply the entire critical bus if the turbine is off. Relaying for such a system should be worked out with the utility. A contract is required with the utility to establish the right to parallel and the disposition of power purposely or inadvertently shipped to the utility. The system should function to interrupt generator input to utility faults, avoid out-of-synchronism, and detect is landing of the generator with a portion of the utility load.

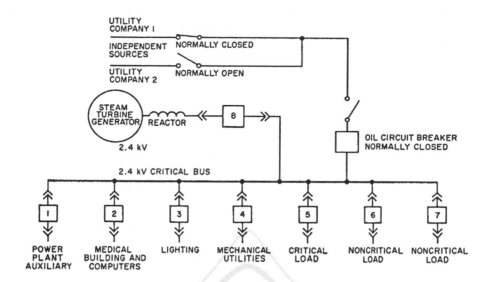

Figure 4-21—Emergency and standby power system using steam-turbine and dual-utility supply

4.4.3 Gas and oil turbine generators

The most common turbine-driven electric generator units employed today for emergency or standby power use gas or oil for fuel. Various grades of oil and both natural and propane gas may be used. Other less common sources of fuel are kerosene or gasoline. Service can be restored from about a 10 s minimum to several minutes, depending upon the turbine used.

Aircraft-type turbines driving generators have been commonly used where electric power may be needed for a few hours to days. Small industrial units have been developed. A small fuel storage facility for safety may be adequate, provided plans have been made by which additional fuel will be delivered when needed. Care should be taken to assure an adequate gas supply, should this be the source of energy, since an uninterruptible supply from a public utility company may be very expensive or unavailable. An interruptible supply may not be available when needed during cold weather. Earthquakes may destroy extensive underground utility distribution systems, but local storage may be intact. Environmental considerations may require the use of low-sulfur oil, which may be difficult to obtain.

Savings are possible by the installation of a turbine for emergency and standby power when used as a peak clipping unit to reduce the demand charge. This has the operating advantage of checking the unit often enough under load so that the operating personnel are familiar with the equipment and the unit is known to be ready for an emergency.

Turbine designs fall between two extreme categories. Aircraft-type engines embody highly sophisticated techniques for very light weight in relation to horsepower (0.25–0.50 lb/hp).

This shortens life. Figure 4-22 shows a typical generator of this type with a riser diagram of typical loads served. Figure 4-23 shows a modular packaged gas turbine. The opposite philosophy employs the massive, bulky design techniques of steam turbines in an effort to assure long life, but with 10 lb/hp. Both have their place depending on the cost justification and hours of usage per year. Reliable industrial units are available within these ranges.

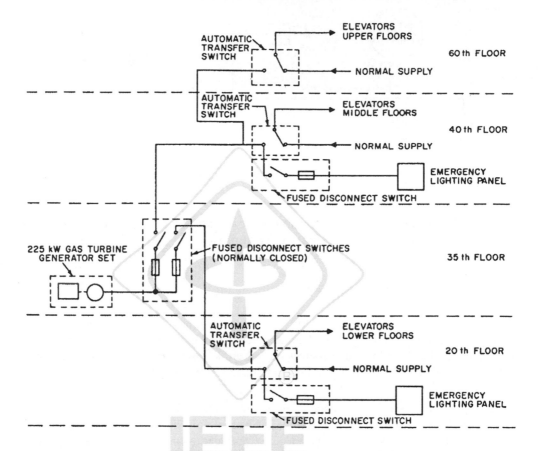

Figure 4-22—Typical gas-turbine-generator and riser diagram of auxiliary power system

Accessory equipment for a gas turbine, such as filtering, silencing apparatus, and vibration mounts, may be required when climate conditions indicate contaminated dust-laden air or areas where noise and vibration level attenuation are required. Bands of noise from 75–9600 Hz are common and attenuation from 5–60 dB or more may be necessary in various bands.

A complete 750 kW gas turbine generator unit weighs approximately 13 000 lb and occupies less than 80 ft^2 of floor area. This factor of compact size and light weight can considerably reduce building costs and allow more efficient economic utilization of building space. Rooftop installations are both feasible and practicable.

Figure 4-23—Modular packaged gas-turbine-generator set mounted on trailer

Combustion turbines starting and loading are accomplished either automatically or manually. Warmup is not necessary.

There are four basic starting systems available for turbines:

— Electric motor supplied from batteries
— A small steam turbine
— A compressed air or gas system
— A small diesel engine

The controls for multiple-unit installations generally involve some interconnection considerations in a master control panel or synchronizing panel. The turbines may be programmed for automatic or manual operation, start sequence, and synchronizing, if desired.

Figure 4-24 shows the reduction in output capacity as gas- or oil-fired combustion turbines are installed at increasing altitudes. High air-input temperatures with the associated lower air density and low barometric pressures also reduce the available output. These limitations must be taken into account or the anticipated reliability and capacity may not be obtained.

Fuel consumption at sea level will be about 10 000–17 000 Btu/kWh output, depending upon size and variable factors. Thermal efficiency may be raised considerably if waste heat or recuperation can be used.

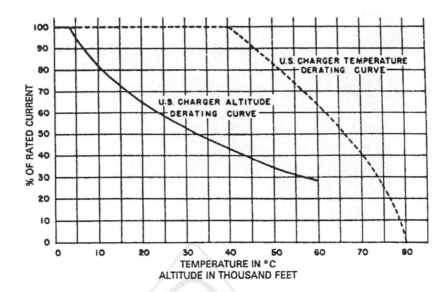

Figure 4-24—Typical performance correction factor for altitude

4.4.4 Advantages and disadvantages

See 4.2.23 for merits of diesel engines versus gas-turbine prime movers.

4.5 Mobile equipment

4.5.1 Introduction

An important, and yet often overlooked, source of emergency or standby power is mobile equipment. For some industrial and commercial applications, it can be the simplest, most economical, and most convenient solution for emergency or standby needs. Mobile equipment, in the broadest context of emergency and standby equipment, embraces portable transformers and even substations with switching and protective devices as are available and used by most utility companies. Some utility companies' generating equipment is located on barges and transported on waterways as needed. This discussion, however, is limited to land-based mobile equipment.

The widest usage, by far, for most industrial and commercial applications, are engine-driven and turbine-driven generating equipment. Characteristics of both of these prime movers as stationary installations are discussed in detail in 4.2 and 4.4. It is the intention of this sub-clause to pinpoint the special requirements of those prime movers when they are adapted for mobility. Some special precautions that should be followed for mobile equipment are also outlined. The decision to have mobile equipment is generally based on having multiple usages. Thus, transportability to serve several load groups, with their varying needs and electrical characteristics, will place restraints on the design/selection process of such equipment.

4.5.2 Special requirements

Mobile generating units can take almost any form from only a prime mover and generator assembly to a complete self-contained plant having its own transporting power. Smaller units can be considered mobile even if they are skid-mounted and have to be transported by loading on and unloading from another vehicle. Obviously, there is some limit beyond which it is not practical, either because of weight or physical size, to load and unload a unit for transporting to achieve the necessary mobility. It is also obvious that a point can be reached whereby generating equipment, because of its physical size and weight, should not be considered for mobile application, even if permanently installed on a truck-bed or a trailer assembly. In terms of capacity, the size break of practicality will vary with engine or turbine drives as prime movers, equipment handling facilities, and also with how much auxiliary equipment, for support of the unit, needs to be transported. Based on these premises, the following is an attempt to describe the several special requirements or needs of generating equipment when it is adapted for mobile applications.

Since mobile equipment may be required to be used outdoors or, when not in use, stored outdoors, it can be desirable to house it in a weather-proof enclosure. If its use may be in a sound-sensitive area, provisions for noise attenuation may be necessary. Whatever type of enclosure is employed, special precautions may be necessary to assure that the unit will have sufficient combustion and cooling air to operate within its rating. It may be necessary to equip the unit with louvers that are arranged to open automatically when the unit is running. For units where soundproofing is required, a well-designed forced-air ventilating system will probably be needed. For application in sound-critical areas, such as residential, an appropriate high sound attenuating exhaust silencer or muffler may be warranted.

To avoid possible duplication of fuel-storage facilities in all locations where the unit will find use, it may be desirable to provide fuel storage with the unit. Storage capacity will depend on each need; however, an 8 h supply as a minimum would seem to be a reasonable period within which a portable fuel transport vehicle could be dispatched to replenish the fuel supply. Fuel oil for a diesel engine is a good fuel choice because of its availability, transportability, and storability during periods of disuse and because it presents less hazard than gasoline or natural and bottled gases. Tank capacity should be based on the unit's consumption when operating at full load.

If the mobile unit is to be a towed vehicle, it will probably be required to meet all of the state's (and possibly Interstate Commerce Commission's) requirements for such items as lights and markings. The vehicle should be designed for a realistic road speed, have stop lights, and probably a braking system. Thus, the plug receptacle wiring connections and the hitch assembly need to be compatible with similar mating equipment of the towing vehicle. Figure 4-25 shows a typical trailer-mounted unit in the range of 15–45 kW. Figure 4-26 shows a 2800 kW turbine-generator unit with self-contained switchgear.

Figure 4-25—Typical trailer-mounted model (15–45 kW capacity)

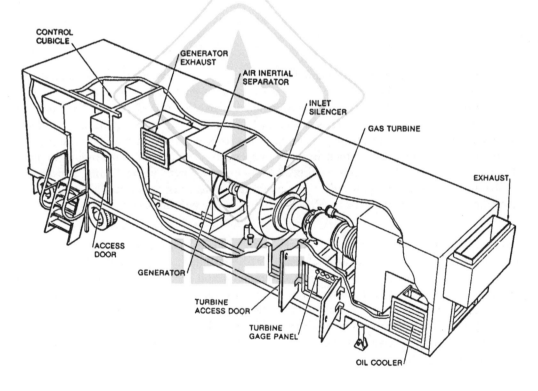

Figure 4-26—Typical 2800 kW mobile turbine-driven generator set

A careful selection of the generator output voltage, or voltages, phases, and frequency should be made to be compatible with all envisioned load requirements. Multiwinding generators can be specified to enable field connection and selection of voltages. Most mobile rental units have multiple windings and are reconnectable for common utilization voltages.

Often with smaller mobile units it is advantageous to transport the cable connection with the generating equipment. If connection time is critical in restoring electrical service, the cable connection can be hard-wired at the generator terminals, transported on an integral reel, and equipped with a plug to mate with the loadend receptacle. That receptacle could, in turn, be hard-wired into the load facility's electrical system. Many telephone building facilities and switching centers are arranged for such a plug-in connection of a mobile standby unit. The cable length should be determined for the extreme location where the equipment will be used. If a cable reel is used, the diameter should be selected after consideration of the manufacturer's recommended minimum bending radius for the cable. The cable should be of a portable variety as recognized by the NEC.

A disconnect switch or a circuit breaker is often installed at the generator. See Chapter 6 for information on generator protection.

Speed control through governor and fuel supply systems selection for prime movers can be a critical choice for a mobile unit if no consideration of the demands of the connected load is made. The same is true in a choice of voltage-regulating methods in combination with excitation systems for the generator. Suffice it to say that a more extensive analysis, before selection, should be made for a mobile unit in comparison with a stationary installation. This is because of the several different possible demands that may be placed on a mobile unit through the more diversified demands of the loads. Improper selection of speed control or voltage control, or both, could mean either money spent wastefully or could cause the unit to be unresponsive to the more critical demands of some loads.

It is generally advantageous to arrange mobile units for starting with self-contained electric storage batteries because of their transportability. A compressed-air start unit would require a fairly large volume air receiver that would usually reach such large size and high weight proportions that its transportability would be difficult. If batteries are used, the permanent storage location, used when the mobile unit is not in service, should be arranged with a battery-charging unit.

If a reciprocating engine unit is to be used or stored outdoors, an ethylene glycol solution and an immersion heater should be used in the cooling system.

4.5.3 Special precautions

Mobile equipment, when compared with stationary equipment, will have some precautions that should be planned for and followed. Many of the items listed below are somewhat obvious but nevertheless often overlooked, especially in the early stages of planning for the mobile unit's utilization and its related storage area.

If a single area is used for storing the unit when not in service, it should be equipped with a means of heating the coolant and charging the unit's batteries through a battery charger and a flexible plug and receptacle connection. If an air start is planned, an air compressor with flexible high-pressure lines and connectors should be used. If the storage space is unheated and outdoors, in colder climates it may be advantageous to provide branch circuit wiring for connection of a unit's immersion-type heater located in the unit's cooling water jacket. If there are extended periods when the unit is not used, it may be advantageous to have a dummy load bank for maintenance testing of the unit under load. Other additional features that could prove valuable for installation at the storage facility are an annunciator unit, which monitors generator set key functions, and an automatic exercising unit.

If a plug-in unit is to be planned, it is important that each load facility, where a mobile unit is to be used, be wired with a receptacle that mates with, and is rated for, the plug on the unit. It should be connected to the load through a transfer switch. Because of inherent characteristics of a mobile generating unit, when compared with a facility's normal source (often a utility company), staged sequencing of returning the facility's loads to service may be in order. Rarely will automatic load sequencing be preferred over manual sequencing through a well-planned start-up procedure.

Assuming that, in initial planning, it may be possible at the load facility to anticipate the operating location of mobile equipment, the fresh air intakes for an adjacent or adjunct building should be physically well-separated from the operating location for the unit.

4.5.4 Maintenance

Since mobile equipment's usage is often unscheduled, necessary maintenance and testing procedures can become sloppy with important items neglected. The unit should be kept ready to go at all times. If the unit is for backup of life safety equipment, it should be treated as similar, stationary, permanently installed equipment employed for the same function. As such, a regularly scheduled operating run of the unit for some representative duration under load will enable checking of such important functions as prime mover lubrication and cooling, charged batteries, and starting systems. This testing can often be accomplished through automatic exercising and alarm annunciation equipment installed at the storage location.

4.5.5 Application

Mobile equipment finds widespread application on multifaceted and physically scattered facilities such as might be operated by a municipality. Many municipalities will have such diversified operations, all of which will, on occasion, require emergency and standby power, such as sewage and waste water treatment and pumping plants, garbage and refuse collection and disposal, central fire-alarm stations, centralized traffic-control facilities, convention, sports, and recreational complexes, and power and steam generating plants. Other users of mobile equipment might include college and educational facilities, military bases, and large governmental, institutional, and industrial complexes, all typified by scattered individual buildings, most having their own electrical service and, in many cases, privately owned electrical distribution facilities between buildings.

4.5.6 Rental

Often the expenses of purchase of a mobile unit cannot be justified when measured against how often the equipment is needed and used. There are several sources for the rental of mobile generating equipment, namely, equipment manufacturers' distributors and service organizations, some utility companies, and large construction contracting firms. Rental houses generally charge approximately 10% of the list price of the equipment per month based on an 8 h day. The weekly rate is generally 1/3 the monthly rate and the daily rate, 1/3 the weekly rate. For more than 8 h per day, the rate is 1-1/2 to 2 times the 8 h rate.

Sometimes power is lost from the normal utility supply source, but a lower or higher voltage is available close by. A mobile transformer can be used for emergency power secured in time to prevent damage from freezing or in a quantity sufficient for partial production.

4.5.7 Fuel systems

Growing shortages of gas and liquid fuel sources require advanced planning for a firm. A dependable source of fuel supply, readily available under any foreseeable emergency condition, should exist. When natural gas is planned, a firm source should be available; a back-up source of propane should be considered. Where liquid fuels are planned, ready available storage at the point of usage should be considered. Since liquid fuels deteriorate during long storage, a system of use and replacement to assure a fresh supply should be planned.

4.5.8 Agricultural applications

Farm standby tractor-driven generators are available, practical, and usually reasonable in cost, since the prime mover is serving a dual purpose and is usually on hand for other uses.

4.6 References

This chapter shall be used in conjunction with the following publications:

ANSI C84.1-1989, American National Standard Voltage Ratings for Electric Power Systems and Equipment (60 Hz).[3]

ANSI/NEMA ICS 2-1993, Industrial Control and Systems Controllers, Contractors, and Overload Relays Rated Not More Than 2000 Volts AC or 750 Volts DC.[4]

ANSI/NEMA MG I-1993, Motors and Generators.

ANSI/NFPA 101-1994, Code for Safety to Life from Fire in Buildings and Structures.[5]

ANSI/UL 1008-1988, Safety Standard for Automatic Transfer Switches.[6]

---

[3]ANSI publications are available from the Sales Department, American National Standards Institute, 11 West 42nd Street, 13th Floor, New York, NY 10036, USA.

[4]NEMA publications are available from the National Electrical Manufacturers Association, 2101 L Street NW, Washington, DC 20037, USA.

[5]NFPA publications are available from from the Sales Department, American National Standards Institute, 11 West 42nd Street, 13th Floor, New York, NY 10036, USA.

[6]UL publications are available from Underwriters Laboratories, Inc., 333 Pfingsten Road, Northbrook, IL 60062-2096, USA.

EGSA 101G-1995, Glossary of Electrical and Mechanical Terminology and Definitions.[7]

EGSA 101P-1995, Performance Standard: For Engine Driven Generator Sets.

EGSA 101S-1995, Guideline Specifications: For Engine Driven Generator Sets, Emergency or Standby.

IEEE C37.95-1989, IEEE Guide for Protective Relaying of Utility-Consumer Interconnections (ANSI).[8]

IEEE Std 100-1992, The New IEEE Standard Dictionary of Electrical and Electronics Terms (ANSI).

IEEE Std 141-1993, IEEE Recommended Practice for Electric Power Distribution for Industrial Plants (IEEE Red Book) (ANSI).

IEEE Std 142-1991, IEEE Recommended Practice for Grounding of Industrial and Commecial Power Systems (IEEE Green Book) (ANSI).

IEEE Std 241-1990, IEEE Recommended Practice for Electric Power Systems in Commercial Buildings (IEEE Gray Book) (ANSI).

IEEE Std 387-1984, IEEE Standard Criteria for Diesel-Generator Units Applied as Standby Power Supplies for Nuclear Power Generating Stations.[9]

NFPA 70-1996, National Electrical Code®.

4.7 Bibliography

Additional information may be found in the following sources:

[B1] Castenschiold, R., "Closed-Transition Switching of Essential Loads" *IEEE Transactions on Industry Applications*, vol. 25, no. 3, May/June 1989.

[B2] Daugherty, R. H., "Analysis of Transient Electrical Torques and Shaft Torques in Induction Motors as a Result of Power Supply Disturbances," *IEEE Transactions on Power Apparatus and Systems*, vol. PAS-101, no. 8, Aug. 1982.

[B3] *Engineer's Guidebook to Power Systems*, Kohler Company, Kohler, WI.

[7]EGSA publications are available from the Electrical Generating Systems Association, 10251 W. Sample Rd., Suite B, Coral Springs, FL 33065.

[8]IEEE publications are available from the Institute of Electrical and Electronics Engineers, 445 Hoes Lane, P.O. Box 1331, Piscataway, NJ 08855-1331, USA.

[9]This standard has been withdrawn; however, copies can be obtained from the IEEE Standards Department, 445 Hoes Lane, P.O. Box 1331, Piscataway, NJ 08855-1331, USA.

[B4] Gill, J. D., "Transfer of Motor Loads Between Out of Phase Sources," *IEEE Transactions on Industry Applications*, vol. IA-15, no. 4, pp. 376–381, Jul./Aug. 1979.

[B5] Heising, C. R. and Johnston, Jr, J. F., "Reliability Considerations in Systems Applications of Uninterruptible Power Supplies," *IEEE Transactions on Industry Applications*, vol. IA-8, pp. 104–107, Mar./Apr. 1972.

[B6] IEEE Committee Report. "Report on Reliability Survey of Industrial Plants, Part 1: Reliability of Electrical Equipment," *IEEE Transactions on Industry Application*, vol IA-10, pp. 213-235, Mar./Apr. 1974.

[B7] Johnson, G. S., "Rethinking Motor Transfer," Conference Record. IEEE Industry Applications Society, Toronto, Ontario, Oct. 1985.

[B8] McFadden, R. H., "Re-energizing Large Motors After Brief Interruptions—Problems and Solutions," 1976 Pulp and Paper Conference, San Francisco, CA.

[B9] *Onan Power Systems Manual*, Onan Corporation, 1400 73rd Avenue, NE, Minneapolis, MN.

[B10] Sawyer, J. W., *Gas Turbine Emergency/Standby Power Plants*. Gas Turbine International, Jan./Feb. 1972.

Chapter 5
Stored energy systems

5.1 Introduction

Energy usable for electrical power generation may be stored in many ways. For example, liquid and gaseous fuels are a form of energy stored for use in engines and turbines to turn generators. In this chapter, the two most prevalent stored energy systems, i.e., battery systems and mechanical stored energy systems, will be examined.

Battery systems store energy in electrochemical cells that convert chemical energy into electrical energy (figure 5-1). These cells are of the rechargeable storage type, designed for standby application. They are also known as stationary cells. The name "stationary" is derived from the fact that these cells are designed for service in a permanent location. A battery is made up of two or more cells connected together electrically, in series, parallel, or a combination of both, to obtain the desired battery voltage and capacity (in amperehours or watthours) required for the application. This energy may be used directly to power dc equipment or may be converted to useful ac power by one of two means, either by a dc motor used to drive an ac generator or by a static dc-ac converter (e.g., a static inverter).

Mechanical systems store energy in the form of kinetic energy in a rotating mass. This energy is converted to useful power by using the kinetic energy to turn an ac generator.

This chapter also discusses methods by which motor generator sets and static inverters have been configured into power conditioning systems and uninterruptible power supply (UPS) systems. Each system is designed to meet one or more of the following goals:

— To filter, regulate, and condition power for sensitive computers and other electronic equipment;
— To isolate the load from the power source;
— To permit orderly, controlled shutdown of equipment in the event of a power failure;
— To bridge the interval from the occurrence of a power failure until an emergency standby generator can start and assume the load;
— To provide continuous power uninterrupted by power failures.

Note that power conditioning and isolation are important benefits of energy storage systems. In fact, more UPS systems are installed for power conditioning purposes than for backup power purposes since many power-related problems do not require the battery to come on-line. So, in selecting a system, careful attention should be paid to the quality of output power in terms of harmonic distortion, stability, overload capacity, overload protection, and reliability.

The primary difference in the two energy storage systems is that a battery can be selected to provide minutes or hours of backup time, while the mechanical stored energy system has a practical time limit of less than 10 s. Batteries used with UPS systems are most often sized to

(a) Vented battery

(b) VRLA battery

Figure 5-1—Stationary battery installation

provide 15 min of backup, during which time an emergency generator can be brought on-line if the normal power has not been restored.

For this reason, most UPS systems (whether rotating or static) use batteries as their primary backup power source. One notable exception is the engine/motor-generator (MG) system described in 5.6.8. The other exception is the engine-generator/motor-generator described in 5.6.9. All other systems available today convert dc power provided by the battery to ac power through an inverter, an ac generator, or some combination of the two.

This chapter addresses these systems by first discussing the two energy storage systems, i.e., electrochemical (battery) and inertia (mechanical). Once this is done, the two basic methods available for conversion of the stored energy to ac power, i.e., the ac generator and the static inverter, are discussed for those instances where the dc power available from the battery will not be used directly to power dc-rated devices. Static UPS systems are discussed in 5.5. Motor-generators and rotating UPS systems are discussed in 5.6. Both types of UPS systems accomplish one or more of the goals listed previously in 5.1.

5.2 Definitions

For definitions used in this chapter, see Chapter 2 of this publication, IEEE Std 100-1992,[1] and other standards listed in 5.7.

5.3 Battery systems

5.3.1 Introduction

A battery is the most dependable source available for emergency or standby power and can also be one of the most versatile when applied with other devices. There are various battery designs available, each of which is tailored to meet the specific needs of a particular application. For example, batteries may be characterized as either *starting, lighting, and ignition* (SLI) or *industrial*. The SLI batteries include those used in automobiles, marine application, golf carts, trucks, etc. SLI batteries are outside the scope of this standard. Industrial batteries include motive power, railroad, and standby (including stationary) types. Motive power batteries are used for applications such as forklift trucks, mining equipment, airline ground equipment, and electric vehicles. Railroad batteries, as the name implies, are used for locomotives, railway signaling, railcar air conditioning/lighting, and people movers. Batteries of the standby type are of interest in this chapter because of their relevance to the purpose of this recommended practice. They are used in the following applications:

— Telecommunication systems
— Electric substations
— Electric generating stations
— UPS systems

---

[1]Information on references can be found in 5.7.

— Industrial control
— Emergency lighting
— Security/alarm systems
— Solar photovoltaic systems

A standby battery system comprises three basic components: the battery, the charger, and the load. When a battery is used in conjunction with a UPS, the battery is considered a component of the UPS system. The stationary battery, designed for standby service, is most often operated in what is termed *full-float,* with infrequent cycling (i.e., a discharge followed by a recharge) expected over its service life. Full-float operation is characterized by the battery, the charger, and the load all being connected together in parallel (figure 5-2). In normal operation, the charger supplies the load while supplying a small amount of charging current to the battery to keep it fully charged. The only times the battery supplies the load are when the

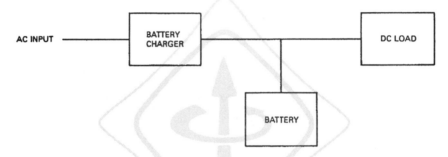

Figure 5-2—Stationary battery in float operation

charger becomes unavailable or when the current required by the load exceeds the output rating of the charger (e.g., inrush currents).

5.3.2 Stationary batteries In standby service

There are two types of stationary batteries used in standby applications: the lead-acid type (figure 5-3), and the nickel-cadmium (NiCd) type (figure 5-4). Of these two types, lead-acid is the most often used. (Within the USA, lead-acid batteries are used almost exclusively, while in Europe, nickel-cadmium batteries are used more often, particularly for switchgear tripping.) The lead-acid battery is less costly than the equivalent nickel-cadmium cell, requires less cells to make up a battery of any specific voltage, and is available in larger capacities than nickel-cadmium cells. More recently, the requirements within the USA for disposal of nickel-cadmium cells under federal, state, and local environmental guidelines has also limited their use. Under these guidelines, spent nickel-cadmium cell are considered hazardous *waste*, while spent lead-acid cells are considered hazardous *material*. In the USA, the owner of the battery is responsible for the battery "from cradle to grave," including the beneficial recycling of the battery (Migliaro 1993 [B19]).[2] (Many other countries have similar requirements for recycling, and others are in the process of adopting such requirements.)

---

[2]The numbers in brackets preceded by the letter B correspond to those in the bibliography in 5.8.

Figure 5-3—A stationary lead-acid cell (vented type)

Figure 5-4—A Stationary nickel-cadmium cell

Both types of batteries are available in a number of designs that can cause one type to be favored over another for a specific application. Although a brief discussion will be included in this chapter, the battery manufacturers can provide additional detail for each design.

5.3.2.1 Lead-acid cells

The lead-acid cell is the oldest of the secondary (i.e., rechargeable) batteries. The first commercial lead-acid battery was developed by Gaston Planté in 1886. The plates of this battery were made from pure lead and, to this day, solid pure lead plates are identified as Planté type. (This type of plate is no longer manufactured in some countries, e.g., the USA.) Lead-acid cells have a nominal open-circuit voltage of 2.0 Vdc, so that a 24, 48, 120, or 240 Vdc battery would normally be made by connecting 12, 24, 60 or 120 cells, respectively, in series. (When the cells are connected in series, they are often referred to as a *string*.) This is shown in table 5-1; however, the actual number of cells (and similarly the float and equalize voltages)

Table 5-1—Typical number of cells in batteries

Nominal battery voltage	120	48	32	24	12
Number of lead-acid cells	60	24	16	12	6
Number of nickel-cadmium cells	92	37	24	19	9
Equalize-recharge voltage	140	56	37	28	14
Float voltage	133	53	36	26.6	13.3
End voltage	105	42	28	21	10.5
Voltage window	140–105	56–42	37–28	28–21	14–10.5

NOTES

1—It is not uncommon to vary the number of cells for a specific application.

2—This table is meant to provide general information. The numbers in the table have been rounded for convenient presentation of the data. The user should refer to Chapter 6, IEEE Std 485-1983, IEEE Std 1184-1994, and IEEE Std 1115-1992 for guidance on the criteria for selecting the number of cells required for a battery installation, as well as the float and equalize voltages.

used for a particular installation is a function of the system design. When dc equipment (e.g., switchgear controls, relays, timers, etc.) is supplied from the battery and dependent upon the system voltage limits, a battery with one to four less cells can be used to reduce the required applied potential of the charger without exceeding the maximum voltage rating of the connected equipment. For example, if voltage-sensitive components (rated 125 Vdc ± 10%) are loads on a dc bus supplied directly by the battery, a nominal 125 Vdc battery comprising 58 cells as compared to 60 cells will enable the equalize voltage to be limited to 135 Vdc rather than 140 Vdc when charging the cells at 2.33 V per cell, thus keeping the bus voltage within the rating of the component. When an installation uses a reduced number of cells, a larger capacity cell is required to serve the load, since a higher end-of-discharge voltage will be required to meet the system minimum voltage requirements. Information on selecting the number of cells for a battery (as well as information on sizing a battery) can be found in IEEE Std 485-1983. Additionally, in industry, 120 V and 240 V batteries are often referred to as 125 V and 250 V, respectively.

Lead-acid cells may be either the vented or valve-regulated type. They may be supplied as individual units (i.e., single cells) or as multi-cell units (also referred to as *monoblocs*). Where more capacity is required than is available from a single battery string, individual battery strings may be paralleled to provide the required capacity.

5.3.2.1.1 Vented cells (*flooded cells*)

Although the term *vented cells* is being used in the latest standards related to these cells to distinguish them from valve-regulated cells, much of the literature in the industry, including many battery manufacturers' instruction manuals still uses the term *flooded cells*. Based upon this, both terms are included in this recommended practice. The vented (flooded) cell is one in which the plates are flooded with electrolyte (figure 5-3). The electrolyte, which is dilute sulfuric acid in water, may spill from the cell if it is tilted or otherwise upset. Traditionally, the nominal full-charge specific gravity (SG) of the electrolyte for stationary-type vented cells was 1.215 ± 0.010; however, cells that are currently available often use nominal SGs of 1.250 and 1.300, particularly when they are applied in UPS systems. (Higher specific-gravity electrolyte results in a cell with increased capacity; however, its expected life will be somewhat reduced and its float voltage must be increased to compensate for higher internal losses within the cell.) In addition, when the battery is installed in a location where the average ambient temperature is 85 °F, a nominal SG of 1.170 may be supplied. (This is termed a *tropical gravity cell*.) The cell is vented and allows the escape of gases generated during charging (e.g., hydrogen and oxygen). To prevent the accidental ignition of these gases, the cell should be fitted with a flame-arrestor-type vent (figure 5-5).

Assuming the battery is properly sized, installed, and maintained, the normal failure mechanism for the vented lead-acid cell is the corrosion of the positive plate. Because of this, a number of positive plate designs are available:

— *Rectangular flat plate.* This plate is also known as a *rectangular pasted plate* or *Fauré plate.* (The word *rectangular* is usually omitted when describing this plate.) This type of plate has two components: The first component is a support structure called a *grid;* the second component is the active material, which is applied to the grid in the form of a paste. The grid is made of a lead alloy (which provides mechanical strength) and functions to support the active material and to carry current to and from the active material. The active material react chemically to produce or absorb energy during the discharge or charge of the cell. (See figure 5-6.)
— *Round pasted plate.* This plate is also known as a *round plate.* It uses a grid made from pure lead, which is pasted with active material. When fabricated, these plates are positioned horizontally and have a slightly conical shape. (See figure 5-7.)

Figure 5-5—Flame arrestor vents with dust covers

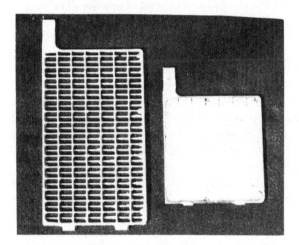

Figure 5-6—Flat plate (right) and grid (left)

— *Tubular plate.* This plate has four components. The first component is a lead alloy casting that has a top bar from which a number of spines extend. A porous fiber tube is then fitted over each spine and the area between the spine and the tube is filled with lead oxide powder. The ends of the tubes are then closed with a plastic cap that holds the powder in the tubes. (See figure 5-8.)

— *Modified Planté plate.* This plate uses a lead alloy grid in which circular holes have been cast. Pure lead strips are corrugated and rolled into buttons called *rosettes*. The rosettes are then pressed into the grid. (See figure 5-9.)

The negative plate used with each type of positive plate is a pasted plate. In each case, the shape of the negative plate, i.e., round or rectangular, matches that of the positive plate.

Figure 5-7—Round plate (right) and grid (left)

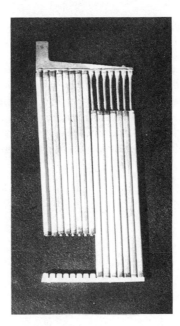

Figure 5-8—Tubular plate

Lead alloys used to cast a flat plate grid are lead-antimony (Pb-Sb) or lead-calcium (Pb-Ca). Another alloy sometimes mentioned is lead-selenium (Pb-Se), which is actually, however, a low-antimony alloy with selenium added to improve its ability to be cast. Pasted plates are available in all alloys, while the tubular and modified Planté are only available as lead-antimony. The predominant cell used today is the pasted plate lead-calcium type because it pro-

Figure 5-9—Modified Planté plate

vides the best short time (i.e., less than 1 h) discharge rates. It is also considered a low maintenance cell; however, it may not be suitable for applications where it will be cycled frequently or where high temperatures will be the norm. Lead-antimony on the other hand, can be cycled approximately six times as much as a lead-calcium cell; however, it has the disadvantage of requiring more frequent addition of water and frequent equalizing charges as the cell ages. The lead-calcium cell requires little watering throughout its lifetime.

5.3.2.1.2 Valve-regulated cells

A valve-regulated lead-acid (VRLA) cell (figure 5-10) is one in which

a)   The electrolyte is immobilized;
b)   The cell is essentially sealed, except for a relief valve that opens when the internal pressure exceeds a predetermined value; and
c)   Recombination of oxygen generated within the cell occurs, essentially suppressing hydrogen evolution and limiting water consumption.

These cells are sometimes referred to as *maintenance-free* or *sealed,* but they are, in fact, neither [see item b)]. Actually, these cells are somewhat more sensitive to voltage (this is particularly true for equalize charging, see 5.3.6.1) and temperature variations during operation than are their vented counterparts. Additionally, the cells are also more sensitive to deep discharges. The cells themselves operate on what is called the oxygen recombination cycle. When a cell is on charge, oxygen is generated at the positive plate (just as in a vented cell); however, because the cell is sealed (i.e., the relief valve is normally closed), the oxygen does not leave the cell but is transported through the separator to the negative plate. Once at the

Figure 5-10—Cutaway of a VRLA cell (absorbed electrolyte type)

negative plate, the oxygen oxidizes the lead on the plate. The lead oxide formed reacts with sulfuric acid present in the electrolyte to form lead-sulfate and water. Then, since the negative plate is on charge, the lead-sulfate is converted to lead and sulfuric acid. These reactions essentially eliminate the loss of water from the cell, so that under normal operation, water additions to the cell are not needed over its lifetime. If the VRLA cell is not operated properly it will lose water, which cannot be replaced. This can lead to "dry out" of the cell or, in the worst case, can result in thermal runaway of the cell. Both of these conditions will cause the cell to lose capacity with the cell eventually failing prematurely. (Refer to Harrison 1992 [B10] and Misra et al. 1992 [B22].)

The electrolyte within the cell is immobilized by using a separator (i.e., a glass or polymeric fiber mat) to absorb the electrolyte, or a gelling agent to gel it. The electrolyte itself has a specific gravity between 1.260 and 1.310, depending upon manufacturer and the cell design.

5.3.2.2 Nickel-cadmium cells

The nickel-cadmium stationary cell is a secondary cell that uses an alkaline electrolyte. It has a nominal voltage of 1.2 Vdc. However, unlike the lead-acid cell, its electrolyte, a dilute solution of potassium hydroxide in water, does not take part in the cell reactions.

In general, nickel-cadmium cells have long cycle life and are rugged in construction. They are relatively insensitive to overcharging and undercharging, although excessive overcharging can result in loss of water in the electrolyte solution by dissociation of the water in the electrolyte into hydrogen and oxygen. These batteries are suitable for long-term storage, are considered to have low maintenance requirements, and have good short-time discharge rates. They are particularly well-suited for applications in which the battery will be subjected to temperature extremes.

Two nickel-cadmium cell designs are used for stationary batteries in standby applications: the *pocket-plate* design and the *fiber-plate* design. Cells of either design are of the vented type, i.e., they have free electrolyte and long cycle life when compared to lead-acid stationary batteries.

Another design, called a *sintered-plate,* has an undesirable characteristic referred to as "memory effect." This characteristic is not observed in either the pocket-plate or fiber-plate designs; however, it is often mistakenly thought to apply to any nickel-cadmium cell. The sintered-plate design is available in vented or sealed types. This design is used in some emergency lighting units, particularly the fluorescent or decorator types.

5.3.2.2.1 Pocket-plate cells

This design derives its name from the fact that the active materials in the plates are held in "pockets" (figure 5-4). The pockets are fabricated from finely perforated steel strips. Two of these strips, formed into troughs, are used to sandwich the active material in the pocket.

5.3.2.2.2 Fiber-plate cells

The fiber-plate cell is the most recently introduced design for stationary applications. The plate itself is a very porous fiber mat. The fibers are nickel-plated and then are impregnated with the active materials. This type of cell has a high power-to-weight ratio.

5.3.3 Installation design

IEEE Std 484-1996 provides guidance for the installation design for vented lead-acid batteries. A similar document, IEEE Std 1187-1996, was developed for VRLA batteries. ANSI/ NFPA 111-1993 [B5] provides performance requirements for UPS systems, including limited information on batteries.

Installation design should consider, but not be limited to, the following:

— Safety
— Location
— Mounting
— Heating, ventilation, and air-conditioning
— Seismic requirements
— Maintenance requirements
— Illumination
— Instrumentation (including monitoring/alarms)
— Overcurrent protection (see Chapter 6)

5.3.4 Battery sizing

Proper sizing of a battery will ensure that it meets its design function. Battery size can be calculated using methods that assume either constant current or constant power loads (i.e., UPS systems). IEEE Std 485-1983 and IEEE Std 1115-1992 show straightforward calculating techniques for constant-current sizing of lead-acid and nickel-cadmium batteries, respectively. Sizing of lead-acid or nickel-cadmium batteries (using the constant power method) used in UPS systems is included in IEEE Std 1184-1994. Included in IEEE Std 485-1983 and IEEE Std 1115-1992 are cell sizing worksheets, which take the user step-by-step through the calculation. Although the methods presented in these standards are valid for all stationary batteries, a document is being developed to highlight additional selection criteria for VRLA cells (IEEE P1189). To properly size any battery one of the first steps is to define the loads that the battery must serve and develop a duty cycle (figure 5-11). The duty cycle, as well as the various types of loads (figure 5-12), e.g., continuous, noncontinuous, momentary, and random, are discussed in IEEE Std 485-1983 and IEEE Std 1115-1992.

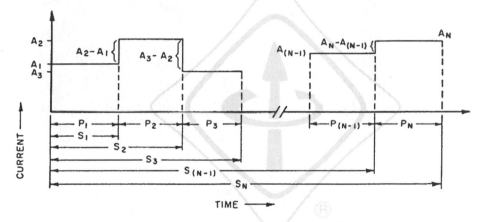

Source: Reprinted from IEEE Std 485-1983.

Figure 5-11—Generalized duty cycle diagram

The size of the battery required depends not only on the size and duration of each load, but also on the sequence in which the loads occur. For example, a larger capacity battery will be required if the load requirements it has to serve are larger near the end of its duty cycle than at the beginning of its duty cycle. It also depends upon the factors selected for design margin (e.g., spare capacity for future load growth), lowest expected battery operating temperature, and aging. It is important to consider the lowest expected cell temperature during operation, since the capacity of a battery decreases if temperatures drop below 25 °C, which is the rating basis for all batteries in the USA. (Note that for cell temperatures above 25 °C the capacity of the battery will increase, although credit for this is not usually taken in determining battery size. High temperatures, however, do reduce battery service life.) Similarly, an aging factor is used to ensure that the battery is able to continue to serve its design basis load, even as the battery nears its end-of-life. Each of these factors are discussed in IEEE Std 485-1983 and IEEE 1115-1992, as well as in Migliaro 1987 [B18] and Migliaro and Albér 1991 [B20].

A typical duty cycle (see figure 5-11) and the formulas for sizing both lead-acid and nickel-cadmium batteries [see equations (1) through (3)] were taken from IEEE Std 485-1983 and IEEE Std 1115-1992. The duration of the duty cycle is user-selected based upon the specific requirements for the installation, although some backup times have evolved as "standards" over time. For instance, 8 or 10 h is often used for substation batteries; 5 h for telecommunication batteries; 2, 3, or 8 h for generating units; and 5 or 15 min for UPS systems.

(a) Switchgear

(b) Inverter

Figure 5-12—Examples of battery loads

(c) Emergency motor

(d) Security systems

Figure 5-12—Examples of battery loads *(Continued)*

Lead-acid cell sizing (positive plate method):

$$\max_{S=1}^{S=N} F_S = \max_{S=1}^{S=N} = \sum_{P=1}^{P=S} \frac{A_P - A_{(P-1)}}{R_T} \tag{1}$$

Lead-acid cell sizing (ampere-hour method):

$$\max_{S=1}^{S=N} F_S = \max_{S=1}^{S=N} = \sum_{P=1}^{P=S} \left[A_P - A_{(P-1)}\right] K_T \tag{2}$$

Nickel-cadmium cell sizing:

$$\max_{S=1}^{S=N} F_S = \max_{S=1}^{S=N} = \sum_{P=1}^{P=S} \left[A_P - A_{(P-1)}\right] K_t T_t \tag{3}$$

where

A_P are the amperes required for period (see Note 3).

F_S is the capacity required by each section S.

K_T is the ratio of rated ampere-hour capacity (at a standard time rate, at 25 °C, and to a standard end-of-discharge voltage) of a lead-acid cell, to the amperes that can be supplied for T minutes at 25 °C, and to a given end-of-discharge voltage.

K_t is the capacity rating factor for a given nickel-cadmium cell type, at the t minute discharge rate at 25 °C, to a definite end-of-discharge voltage (see Note 4).

N is the number of periods in the duty cycle.

P is the period being analyzed.

R_T is the number of amperes that each positive plate can supply for T minutes, at 25 °C, to a definite end-of-discharge voltage for a lead-acid cell.

S is the section of the duty cycle being analyzed. Section S contains the first S periods of the duty cycle; for example, section S_5 contains periods 1 through 5. (See figure 5-11 for a graphical representation.)

T_t is the temperature derating factor for a nickel-cadmium cell at t minutes, based on the electrolyte temperature at the start of the duty cycle.

T, t the time in minutes from the beginning of period P through the end of section S for lead-acid and nickel-cadmium cells, respectively.

NOTES

1—The final cell selected should include factors for design margin, temperature correction, and aging (refer to the cell sizing worksheet included in IEEE Std 485-1983).

2—The final cell selected should include factors for design margin, and aging (refer to the cell sizing worksheet included in IEEE Std 1115-1992).

3—If the current for period $P+1$ is greater than the current for period P, then section $S = P+1$ will require a larger cell than section $S = P$. Consequently, the calculations for section $S = P$ can be omitted.

4—If the nickel-cadmium cell will be constant potential charged, the capacity rating factor used shall be based upon constant potential charging.

In order to choose the appropriate size nickel-cadmium cell, the method to be used for charging the cell must be considered. Nickel-cadmium ratings are based on constant current charging; however, most standby batteries use constant potential charging. Prolonged constant potential (i.e., float) charging of a nickel-cadmium battery may reduce its capacity from rated, dependent upon the discharge rate. As a result, voltage decay upon discharge will occur faster than that of a full-capacity battery. The effects of constant potential charging can be accounted for during battery sizing by using capacity rating factors based upon this method of charging (see IEEE Std 1115-1992). These factors should be obtained from the battery manufacturer, as they vary between manufacturers. *Caution: A sealed nickel-cadmium cell should be charged with a constant-current charger only.*

Once the loads are defined, a cell type must be selected as well as the number of cells that will make up the string. The predominant type of cell used for stationary batteries is the lead-calcium flat plate in either a vented or VRLA design. A few other types of cells, or different numbers of cells, can be evaluated to optimize the selection. The number of cells in a battery for any specific system is determined by considering any of the following as a limiting condition: minimum system voltage, maximum system voltage, float voltage, and charging voltage. The maximum and minimum voltages may not be as critical for UPS systems, since the inverter design can usually accommodate a large voltage variation (i.e., voltage window).

The battery is sized to support the critical load for the worst-case conditions until either the critical load can be shut down in an orderly manner, the normal power source returns, or an alternate standby ac source can be started and connected. Battery support times might be in minutes (e.g., 5, 10, 15 or 30 min) or in hours (e.g., 1.5, 2, 5, or 8 h). The shorter backup times are consistent with UPS system design, while the longer backup times are used for telecommunications, electric power, and emergency lighting systems. The longer the battery supply time, the larger the battery capacity required to serve the load. Rather than purchasing larger battery capacity (i.e., when a longer backup time is not a requirement of a code or standard), the installation of an engine or combustion-turbine generator standby power source should be evaluated.

5.3.5 Battery maintenance and testing

Requirements for maintenance and testing are discussed in Chapter 8. In addition, IEEE Std 450-1995 and IEEE Std 1106-1995 provide guidance for the maintenance and testing of vented lead-acid and nickel-cadmium batteries, respectively. A similar document is being developed for VRLA batteries (IEEE P1188); until it is approved and published, the guidance in IEEE Std 450-1995, in conjunction with the battery manufacturer's maintenance instructions for the VRLA battery, may be used. ANSI/NFPA 111-1993 [B5] provides requirements for maintenance and testing for batteries in certain legally required emergency and standby systems.

5.3.6 Recharge/equalize charging

5.3.6.1 Lead-acid batteries

Lead-acid stationary batteries are charged using a constant potential charger. Two values of charge voltage are usually specified. These are float and equalize voltage (also refer to Chapter 6). (The equalize voltage specified by the battery manufacturer is also the value used to recharge a battery after a discharge.) For each battery, the manufacturer's instructions will specify the voltage, or range of voltage, for float and equalize. In the case of a VRLA battery, the manufacturer may also provide a range of cell float voltages based upon cell temperature (i.e., temperature-compensated float voltage), or may simply provide a temperature correction factor to be applied to the float voltage. It is important that the battery manufacturer's instructions for float voltage, equalize voltage, and charging be followed. For example, the battery manufacturer may not specify an equalize voltage for a VRLA battery. The application of an improper (i.e., too high) voltage during charging for a VRLA battery can lead to dry out of the cells or can result in thermal runaway. This can occur in either float or equalize operation if the VRLA battery's charging voltage is improperly set.

Lead-calcium cells placed on float charge at the high end of their voltage range may not require equalize charges to be applied. An equalize charge may be required if the individual cell voltages or specific gravities drift too far apart (i.e., have too great a spread.) The reason for requiring an equalize charge is that some of the individual cells in the series string may not get enough current to keep them fully charged while on float charge. This loss of charge is related to the self-discharge of the individual cell, which results in its voltage dropping over time. When the battery is placed on equalize, the higher charge voltage causes an increased current to flow through the string. This higher current is sufficient to overcome the self-discharge of all the cells in the string, restoring each of them to full charge. Equalize charges should be given only when necessary and should be applied in accordance with the battery manufacturer's instructions. At one time equalize charges were considered to be part of periodic maintenance; however, today they are considered a maintenance corrective action. Lead-antimony alloy cells require more equalize charges than do other lead acid cells. This is due to their increased self-discharge rate as they age.

While it is always best to have both float and equalize functions, some UPS system battery chargers do not have an equalize function. It may have been omitted from the specification through oversight or because it was thought that setting the float voltage high enough would eliminate the need for equalize charges. If an equalize setting is not available, any charging of the battery (e.g., initial charge, recharge following a test, or a discharge) must be accomplished at the float-voltage setting. This can result in extremely long charge times and may even require the use of supplemental chargers (e.g., single-cell chargers) to ensure that the battery is maintained in good health. *Caution: Charging of VRLA cells should be done in strict conformance with the battery manufacturer's instructions.*

5.3.6.2 Nickel-cadmium batteries

Nickel-cadmium vented-type batteries may be constant-potential charged but are more suited to constant-current charging, if this type of charging can be tolerated by the load on the battery. When a constant-current charge is used, recharge may be accomplished using a two-rate charge, i.e., an initial (high-current) rate followed by a finish (low-current) rate that is begun once the charge is approximately 80% complete. If constant-potential charging is used, a nickel-cadmium battery may not be able to develop its rated capacity, depending upon the rate at which it is discharged and the required minimum battery voltage (refer to 5.3.4 and IEEE Std 1115-1992). *Caution: A sealed nickel-cadmium battery should only be applied with a constant-current charger.*

5.3.6.3 Operation

Standby batteries are normally applied in float operation; the battery, battery charger, and load are connected in parallel (see figure 5-2). The charging equipment should be sized to provide all of the power normally required by relatively steady loads, such as indicating lamps and relay coils, and minor intermittent loads, plus enough additional power to keep the battery at full charge. Relatively large intermittent loads will draw power from the battery; this power will be restored to the battery by the charger when the intermittent load ceases. Battery charger sizing is discussed in IEEE Std 946-1992.

When ac input power to the system is lost, the battery instantly assumes all of the connected load. If the battery and charger are properly matched to the load and to each other, there will be no discernible voltage dip when the system reverts to full battery operation.

When an emergency load on the system ends and charging power is restored, a constant-potential charger will deliver more current than if the battery were fully charged. Some constant-potential chargers will automatically increase their output voltage to the equalize setting after power to the charger is restored. (Similarly, a constant-current charger may automatically increase its output to the high rate.) The charger must be properly sized to ensure that it can serve the load and restore the battery to full charge within an acceptable time. The increased current delivered by a constant-potential charger during this restoration period will taper off as the battery approaches full charge.

The charging rectifier, or battery charger, is an important part of the emergency power system, and consideration should be given to redundant chargers on critical systems. Refer to figure 5-13 for a typical redundant system. The charger should be operated *only* with the battery connected to the dc bus. Without this connection, excessive ripple on the system could occur, which could affect connected equipment (e.g., causing misoperation or failure). If a system must be able to operate without the battery connected, then a battery eliminator should be specified. The battery charger output must be derated for altitude, when it is installed in locations above 3300 ft (1000 m), and for temperature, when the ambient temperature exceeds 50 °C. The battery charger manufacturer can provide these derating factors and should account for them in the battery charger's design.

5.3.7 Battery system short-circuit calculation

The short-circuit capability of a dc system should not be overlooked. Chapter 6 discusses this; however, an in-depth discussion of the subject is included in IEEE Std 946-1992. This

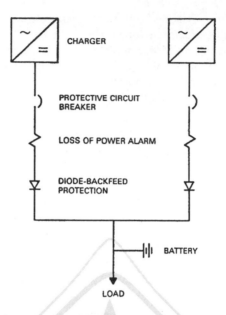

Figure 5-13—Typical redundant charger circuit

standard also illustrates the calculation method used for both battery and charger contribution to the fault in its annexes.

Recent testing (referenced in IEEE Std 946-1992) has demonstrated that the short-circuit current delivered by a battery is independent of the cell temperature or full-charge specific gravity. It is recommended that short-circuit calculations be performed using the battery open-circuit voltage at a temperature of 25 °C. A conservative rule-of-thumb is as follows: The short-circuit current delivered by a lead-acid battery is equal to ten times its 1 min discharge rate, in amperes, to an end voltage of 1.75 V per cell (Vpc), at 25 °C.

The short-circuit contribution from a static, constant-potential-type battery charger is its current-limit value in amperes. Motor-generator chargers, as well as dc motors on the system, will also contribute to a short circuit. Specific guidance is included in IEEE Std 946-1992; however, a typical range for this current is 7–10 times the machine's rated armature current.

5.3.8 Battery-powered emergency lighting

Emergency lighting systems are used to provide the required lighting to a facility for egress or other purposes (e.g., security), when the normal electrical supply is interrupted. The purpose of this lighting is to illuminate evacuation routes and exits so that the chance of personnel injury or loss of life can be minimized in the event of a fire or other emergency that can cause the illumination in an area to be lost or reduced to a level where evacuation may be difficult or impossible. Batteries are used in self-contained emergency lighting units (figure 5-14) and central emergency lighting systems (these may be dc, i.e., battery only or UPSs). Specific requirements for emergency lighting systems can be found in the National Electrical

Code (NEC) (NFPA 70-1996 [B2]), NFPA 99-1996 [B3], and ANSI/NFPA 101-1991 [B4]. The requirements for emergency lighting equipment (with the exception of UPSs) are included in ANSI/UL 924-1990 [B6]. The required backup time for batteries for emergency lighting is 90 min, although some systems may be designed to have a longer backup time. Also, if the emergency lighting depends upon the changing of sources (e.g., from the normal ac to dc), the change must occur automatically with no appreciable interruption (i.e., in less than 10 s). In areas that are normally lighted solely by high-intensity discharge (HID) systems, any battery-powered (i.e., self-contained or central battery) emergency lighting must continue to function, once power is restored, until the HID fixtures provide illumination. The system design also must consider a single failure of any individual lighting element (e.g., a lamp failure), such that any space requiring emergency lighting cannot be left in total darkness.

The emergency lighting fixtures may be incandescent (e.g., halogen or sealed-beam) or fluorescent. They vary in style from the industrial type suitable for use in classified areas, to the decorator type used in offices, convention centers, etc. Emergency lighting fixtures also include exit signs. The lamps illuminate stairs, stairway landings, aisles, corridors, ramps, passageways, exit doors, and any other areas requiring emergency lighting.

Figure 5-14—Self-contained emergency lighting unit

5.3.8.1 Emergency lighting units

Emergency lighting units (also referred to as unit equipment) are the most popular type of emergency lighting equipment used today (figure 5-14). The unit itself consists of a rechargeable battery, a battery charger, and one or more lamps or provision for remote lamps (or both). The unit will have the necessary controls to maintain the battery fully charged while the normal source of power is available and to automatically energize the lamps upon loss of the normal power supply. (Some units available today can also be supplied with capabilities for automatic testing and self-diagnostics.) The controls will de-energize the lamps immediately, or after a time delay (e.g., for areas normally illuminated solely by HID fixtures), upon restoration of the normal power supply. If the unit is used with a fluorescent fixture it will also have a high-frequency inverter and controls intended for that type of fixture.

These units can be supplied with any of the lead-acid or the pocket-plate nickel-cadmium batteries discussed previously in 5.3.2.1 and 5.3.2.2. This would include pure lead, lead-antimony, and lead-calcium cells and both vented and valve-regulated types. They may also be supplied with sintered-plate nickel-cadmium cells. In addition, the units may be supplied with chargers that have automatic temperature compensation of float/charge voltage. This feature should be considered a must when a VRLA battery is supplied in the unit. The selection of battery type depends upon the installation itself. For example, pocket-plate nickel-cadmium batteries may be used in high-temperature areas, such as near an industrial boiler, while VRLA or sealed sintered-plate batteries may be used in an office area. All of these batteries require periodic maintenance and testing with the vented types requiring the periodic addition of water as well.

The batteries in these types of units are either 6 Vdc or 12 Vdc. For the lead-acid cells, the electrolyte SG is normally 1.225 or greater (the upper limit of SG is 1.310) and the cell capacity is often expressed in ampere-hours (A-h) at the 10 h or 20 h discharge rate to 1.75 V per cell (Vpc), at 25 °C.

5.3.8.2 Central battery supplied emergency lighting systems

Building-wide systems may also be used to connect many lamps to a central battery and battery charger or dedicated emergency lighting UPS. These systems are generally 32, 48, or 120 Vdc, although some 12 and 24 Vdc are also available. When a UPS system is used, the battery voltage may be greater than 120 Vdc, depending up the size and design of the UPS.

The advantages of the central battery-supplied emergency lighting system are as follows:

— Centralized power source, eliminating the need for single units located throughout the building, use of less space (only lamps are in the areas to be protected), and remote location of the power source. This may result in a reduction in the time spent maintaining and testing the system.

— Availability of alarm and protection circuits, which increases the flexibility of the system.

— The ability to supply fixtures with a lower current, at a higher voltage, resulting in decreased losses.

The disadvantages of the central battery supplied emergency lighting system are as follows:

— The initial installation design is more complex, requiring raceways and cable to be installed.

— The failure of a single branch or feeder circuit may disable the emergency lighting to a large area.

5.3.8.3 Selecting emergency lighting systems

The selection of emergency lighting systems is based on the type of facility (e.g., offices, storage, laboratories, etc.) as well as the layout of the building, building areas, and their usage. The areas that need to be illuminated, as well as the light level necessary, must be identified. Guidance on determining the requirements for specific facilities, including illumination levels, can be found in ANSI/NFPA 101-1991 [B4] and NFPA 99-1996 [B3]. The NEC [B2] is applicable for the installation of the systems; however, it does not determine whether such systems are required, nor does the NEC determine the location of equipment. The minimum initial illumination level, required by ANSI/NFPA 101-1991 [B4], is an average of 1.0 fc (10 lx) and a minimum at any point of 0.1 fc (1 lx) measured along the path of egress at floor level. This may decline to 0.6 fc (6 lx) average and 0.06 fc (0.6 lx) minimum at any point at the end of the emergency period.

5.4 Mechanical energy storage

5.4.1 Introduction

Significant amounts of energy may be stored in the form of kinetic energy (inertia) in a rotating mass. This energy is created by an ac or dc motor imparting rotational energy to its rotor and the rotor of an ac generator (and flywheel, if used). The stored kinetic energy can be converted from inertia to useful ac power by the rotating ac generator.

5.4.2 Kinetic energy

The energy contained in a rotating mass is defined by the equation:

$$J = \frac{1}{2}(IA^2) \qquad\qquad (4)$$

where

I = the mass moment of inertia, in kg·m^2/rad^2
A = the angular velocity, in rad/s
J = energy, in Joules (N·m)

This energy is created by an ac or dc motor turning itself and the ac generator. The rotors and shaft(s) of the motor and generator make up the rotating mass. A flywheel may be added to increase the mass. The motor and generator may be coupled in a variety of ways. Couplings such as pulleys and belts increase the rotating mass.

The resulting stored kinetic energy (inertia) will continue turning the ac generator in the absence of power to the motor. The length of time that useful power is generated (called *ride-through time*) is determined by some key criteria:

— The inertia of the rotating mass

145

— The percentage of full-rated load placed on the ac generator
— The acceptable tolerance on the output frequency

For motor-generators under full load with a maximum under-frequency tolerance of –1 Hz and no flywheel, typical ride-through times range from 50–100 ms. The addition of a flywheel can raise the time to 0.5 s or more. Motor-generators with flywheels have been built with ride-through times of many minutes, using a constant r/min coupling; however, these have not proven commercially useful.

5.5 Battery/inverter systems

5.5.1 Introduction

Dc systems, particularly when they are large, may supply static inverters as loads; these inverters were, in the past, often referred to as uninterruptible power supplies. However, it is becoming more common to utilize a dedicated battery, charger, inverter, and accessories (e.g., a static transfer switch), when there is a need for an uninterruptible power source. This combination of battery, rectifier/charger, static inverter and accessories, represent today's static UPS system. The primary purpose of the UPS is to provide continuity and quality of power to the critical load(s) supplied by it. The batteries used with UPS systems are the stationary type discussed in 5.3.2.

These UPS systems are available in a number of designs and sizes, ranging from less than 100 W to several megawatts. UPS systems may provide single-phase or three-phase power at power frequencies (i.e., 50 or 60 Hz) or at higher frequencies (e.g., 400 Hz). In addition, static UPS systems, because of their wide range of design and application, may provide power of which the output purity may vary from a near-perfect sine wave (less than 1% total harmonic distortion [THD]) to essentially a square wave (greater than 25% THD).

5.5.2 Static UPS system description

The static UPS system is an electronically controlled solid-state system designed to provide an alternate source of conditioned, reliable, and break-free electrical power to a user's equipment. This equipment is often referred to as the "critical" or "protected" load. A UPS system maintains power to the critical load in the event of a partial or total failure of the normal source of power, typically, the power supplied by the electric utility.

There are a variety of UPS configurations available that provide for voltage regulation, line conditioning, lightning protection, redundancy, EMI management, extended run time, load transfer to other units, and other such features required to protect the critical load(s) against failure of the normal ac source, or against other power system disturbances.

Today, UPS technology continues to change making it more appropriate to describe a UPS system by its performance characteristics, rather than its electronic components, which may vary from system to system or change with time and technology. Therefore, a UPS system should have the following primary attributes as a minimum:

— The UPS must provide uninterruptible power. As the normal source falls outside of voltage limits, becomes excessively noisy, threatens to be disrupted in any manner, disappears, or becomes incapable of performing acceptably, the UPS should continue to provide continuous, break-free power to the critical load(s) it supplies for at least a minimum period of time (i.e., backup time).

The minimum backup time is generally specified by the user, but the actual operating time will be determined by the size of the energy storage device (i.e., the battery) associated with the UPS or by the load on the UPS at the time of failure of the normal power source.

— The UPS must provide its power at a stable frequency. The base frequency may be power frequencies such as 50 or 60 Hz, or other frequencies such as 400 or 1000 Hz. A typical requirement for 50 or 60 Hz UPS systems is to maintain the base frequency within ±0.5%.

— For most applications, the output waveform of a UPS system should be sinusoidal, with the THD of voltage 10% or less when tested on a linear load, with a single frequency component of 5% or less. It is recognized, however, that there are loads that can operate reliably with input waveforms having a higher harmonic content or as an extreme, with essentially square wave inputs (e.g., step function quasi-sine waves). Although some loads can function well with square wave input, the electrical interference that the square wave produces may affect other electrical equipment in the vicinity of the UPS.

— A system may include equipment that will provide transfers from line to battery or battery to line that are not continuous (i.e., containing breaks or discontinuities), depending upon the load or user requirements. These products that produce breaks during the transfer from line to battery or from battery to line are referred to as "standby power systems" (SPSs). They are sometimes incorrectly referred to as "standby UPS systems". Many SPSs are still applied today particularly for small UPS systems; e.g., for small computer systems in which a break in power flow is supported by the ride-through characteristics of the computer power supply, although the ride-through capability may be lost when the normal power source is lower than normal.

5.5.3 Types of UPS systems

There are two basic types of UPS systems used today. These are used in a variety of configurations. The types of UPS systems are discussed in this subclause, while the various configurations are discussed in 5.5.4. (The discussion that follows on UPS types and configurations, at times, refers to a single battery; however, this may be either a single or multiple strings of cells connected in parallel to obtain the required battery capacity.) In general, these two types of UPS systems have proven to be reliable when properly applied. The reliability of any UPS system can vary based upon a number of factors. Similarly, the availability of a UPS system can be increased by the addition of transfer switches, redundant equipment, and so forth. The topic of reliability is addressed in IEEE Std 493-1990 [B13]; reliability of emergency and standby power systems is addressed in Chapter 6 of that standard.

5.5.3.1 Double-conversion systems

Double-conversions systems are characterized by their topology. In these systems, the incoming line is first converted to dc. The dc then provides input power to a dc-to-ac converter (i.e., an inverter). The inverter output is ac, which is used to power the critical load. Many different types of inverters are used, each employing a variant of available technology. (Note that the recently revised NEMA PE 1-1993 [B23], identifies the double-conversion system as a "rectifier-inverter.")

Historically, the double-conversion UPS has found the most prominence in the industry. The double-conversion UPS system has been available for many years and has proven to be reliable when operated within its design limits. This type of system is the static electrical equivalent to the motor-generator set. The battery is connected in parallel with the dc input to the inverter, and provides continuous power to it any time the incoming line is outside of its specification or fails. Switching to the battery is automatic, with no break in either the input to the inverter or the output from it.

The double-conversion system has several advantages:

— It provides excellent frequency stability.
— There is a high degree of isolation from variations in incoming line voltage and frequency.
— A zero transfer time is possible.
— Operation is relatively quiet.
— Some systems can provide a sinusoidal output waveform with low distortion.

In the lower power UPS applications (0.1–20 kW), the double-conversion UPS has the following disadvantages. (Many of these disadvantages can be minimized if the system is carefully specified to use the latest topologies.)

— There is lower overall efficiency.
— A large dc power supply is required (typically, 1.5 times the full rated load rating of the UPS).
— Noise isolation line to load can be poor.
— There is greater heat dissipation, which may affect the service life of the UPS.

In addition, if the inverter is the pulse width modulated type, the high-frequency circuitry may produce electromagnetic interference (EMI). This may require special filtering and shielding to protect sensitive equipment from radiated and conducted interference. The double-conversion UPS may also produce excessive battery ripple current, possibly resulting in reduced battery life (see IEEE Std 1184-1994).

5.5.3.2 Single-conversion systems

Single-conversion UPS systems are those in which, during normal operation, the incoming line is used to provide power to the critical load either through a transformer or in conjunction with some series impedance. Some forms of single-conversion UPS products are classified as "line interactive" (see 5.5.3.2.1). The single-conversion UPS usually provides a higher operating efficiency at lower cost than the double-conversion UPS at a comparable system reliability. (Note that the recently revised NEMA PE 1-1993 [B23], identifies the single-conversion system as a "single-conversion converter.")

Unlike the double-conversion system, the incoming line to the single-conversion UPS is not rectified to produce dc power to provide input to the inverter. The normal ac power is supplied directly to the critical load through a series inductor or a linear or ferroresonant transformer. The normal ac also supplies a small charger used to maintain the UPS batteries in a fully charged condition. Thus the battery is only used when inverter requires the battery's output to supplement or replace the normal power source. Single-conversion UPSs include the ferroresonant type, some variants of the tri-port type, line interactive types, and some SPS designs. A discussion of some of these systems follows.

5.5.3.2.1 Line interactive systems

The line interactive UPS is rapidly achieving prominence in the industry. Lower cost, simplicity of design, and smaller "package" are some of the advantages of this design.

In the line interactive UPS, line power is not converted into dc but is fed directly to the critical load through a series inductor or transformer. Regulation and continuous power to the load is achieved through use of inverter switching elements in combination with inverter magnetic components such as inductors, linear transformers, or ferroresonant transformers.

The term "line interactive UPS" derives from the fact that the inverter interacts with the line to buck, boost, or replace incoming power as needed to maintain constant voltage to the critical load. In the absence of line power, the line interactive UPS provides the total power to the critical load. Some line interactive products exhibit a break in power to the critical load during line-to-battery or battery-to-line transfers (this type of system would be an SPS). Other designs are capable of producing true unbroken power to the critical load. Line interactive UPSs are available as single-phase or three-phase units.

5.5.3.2.2 Tri-port systems

The tri-port UPS provides line conditioning and good isolation from input to output by means of a multi-winding linear transformer combined with suitable filtering. In this arrangement, the inverter runs continuously, and shares the same transformer core as the ac input winding. Phasing is adjusted so that the inverter, although operating continuously, normally provides little or no power to the critical load. In some cases, the inverter may be configured to act as a battery charger when not called into service to deliver power to the load. When the ac input is outside of specification, or fails, the inverter responds and power to the inverter winding is magnetically coupled to the load through the transformer core, supplying the critical load. Since the inverter runs continuously, there is a true no-break power transfer to the critical load. In this arrangement power may be added or subtracted from the incoming line to maintain regulation and power flow to the critical load. This power correction is often referred to as "line interaction," and the tri-port UPS may be considered a form of line interactive UPS.

The advantages of the tri-port system are that a higher overall efficiency can be achieved compared to the double-conversion-type of UPS, and a separate battery charger may often be eliminated. A disadvantage of this type of system includes production of EMI due to the high-frequency inverter running continuously. This can require the addition of filtering and shielding to protect the critical load(s). Another disadvantage is that, because the transformer is linear, changes in input voltages may be transferred to the critical load and common-mode noise rejection may be low.

5.5.3.2.3 Ferroresonant systems

The ferroresonant transformer type of UPS is similar to the tri-port. It is also a form of line-interactive UPS. In this arrangement, a ferroresonant transformer magnetically couples the ac input to the critical load much like the linear tri-port transformer. The basic difference is that in the ferroresonant-based UPS, the inverter is not running continuously.

When the system line monitor detects that the line voltage either is outside of specification, has excessive noise imposed upon it, or has failed, the incoming line is automatically disconnected from the transformer primary and the inverter is simultaneously turned on. During the transfer to inverter power, the energy that is stored in the tank circuit of the ferroresonant transformer continues to provide power to the critical load, and since the inverter provides power to the core before this tank voltage can decay significantly, the load receives true, continuous, no-break power. This energy storage feature makes the ferroresonant type of UPS a true on-line UPS, even though the inverter is not running continuously.

While the ac input is present, the ferroresonant transformer provides line conditioning, lightning protection, noise isolation, ground isolation, and voltage regulation with the ferroresonant load winding operating in saturation. Magnetic compensation in the ferroresonant design provides a good sine-wave to the critical load without the need for complicated and expensive filtering elements. In the ferroresonant transformer, the windings are wound on different sections of the core. This construction provides physical and noise isolation between the primary and secondary winding. A Faraday shield provides additional noise isolation and enhanced lightning protection.

The ferroresonant transformer offers several advantages over the linear transformer in single-conversion UPS applications. For example, the ferroresonant transformer provides line regulation, typically ±3% for a 15% variation in the ac input. The ferroresonant transformer also provides approximately 120 dB (i.e., one million to one) attenuation of common-mode incoming noise, and about 70 dB rejection of transverse-mode noise. With the unit on-line, typical operating efficiencies are 91% or greater, and when "on-inverter," typical operating efficiencies are 89% at full load. Efficiencies are slightly less as the amount of load on a system is decreased from full-load. Additionally, good common-mode noise rejection and isolation are provided. The ferroresonant transformer tends to smooth out the input power factor, presenting a near-unity power factor to the line when the transformer is loaded with poor power factor loads. Typically, 0.7 pf (lagging) load is reflected back to the ferroresonant transformer primary as a 0.97 pf load.

The ferroresonant transformer can provide power to high crest factor loads. Excess energy stored in the magnetic tank circuit can provide high peak currents. Output frequency on-line can be as good as the power line grid (typically ±0.5%). Frequency stability on-inverter is computer-derived and is typically better than ±0.03 Hz (for a 60 Hz system). The ferroresonant transformer inverter operates at line frequency (50 or 60 Hz). Low-frequency inverter operation results in higher inverter efficiency, lower heat losses, reduced EMI, and lower cost.

There are also some disadvantages of the ferroresonant transformer including its weight when compared to an equivalent high frequency PWM inverter. In most installations, however, this has not proven to be a problem because a UPS is considered to be stationary equipment and is not moved once installed. Additionally, output harmonics tend to increase as the load level goes below 50%. In most cases, however, the THD is about 5%. Although the ferroresonant transformer is as efficient as a linear transformer when operated at or near rating, the efficiency of the ferroresonant transformer becomes lower when lightly loaded, typically 77% when the transformer is operated at 25% of rating. A comparison of the ferroresonant and linear transformers is presented in table 5-2.

Table 5-2—Comparison of a ferroresonant transformer and a linear transformer of the same power rating (220 V, 7500 VA, 60 Hz)

Load (%)	Efficiency of the ferroresonant transformer (%)	Efficiency of the linear transformer (%)
10	60.0	82.0
25	75.0	92.0
50	85.0	93.0
75	90.0	92.5
100	92.0	91.0

5.5.3.3 Other types

Other UPS types include dc-to-dc systems, which are often used for special applications. These are usually found on small computer systems, control systems, and alarm systems (e.g., annunciators).

5.5.4 Configurations

The following discussion is presented to familiarize the reader with various UPS configurations. In all of the examples illustrated double-conversion systems are shown; however, similar configurations with single-conversion systems are also possible.

The figures shown in the text are simplified for presentation and should not be assumed to cover all components of a UPS system. For example, in the case of switches, only transfer switches are shown, although an actual installation may make use of isolating switches, maintenance bypass switches, interrupters, tie switches, and so forth. (A detailed discussion of the various types of UPS switches and their application is included in NEMA PE 1-1993 [B23].)

The recent issue of NEMA PE 1-1993 [B23] identifies four major groups of single UPSs. These groups are as follows:

— Group 1: Double-conversion systems without bypass
— Group 2: Double-conversion systems with bypass
— Group 3: Single-conversion systems without bypass
— Group 4: Single-conversion systems with bypass

Each of the systems has a simplified symbol that is used to represent it (figure 5-15). Within each group, NEMA PE 1-1993 [B23] states that multiples of these single UPSs can be combined in parallel. It further identifies parallel configurations that are used for increased capacity and parallel configurations that are used for redundancy. In the discussion that follows, the description of the configuration itself is informative enough to enable the reader to determine whether the UPS is a single or parallel configuration. In the case of parallel configurations, the description includes the word "redundant" whenever the configuration is used for redundancy.

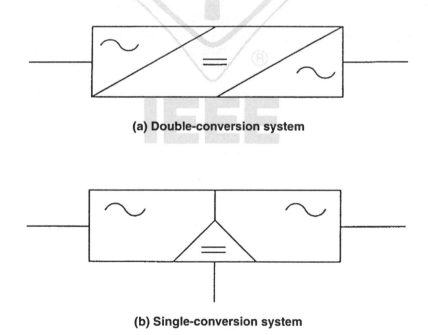

(a) Double-conversion system

(b) Single-conversion system

Figure 5-15—Simplified representation of a UPS system

5.5.4.1 Single UPS unit with rectifier/charger

The basic UPS configuration is a single UPS with rectifier/charger, consisting of a single rectifier/charger, battery, and inverter operating continuously. The normal ac input is supplied to the rectifier/charger and the critical load(s) are supplied from the inverter output. These are available in both single phase and three phase, with three-phase units available in sizes to over 500 kVA. A typical one-line diagram is shown in figure 5-16.

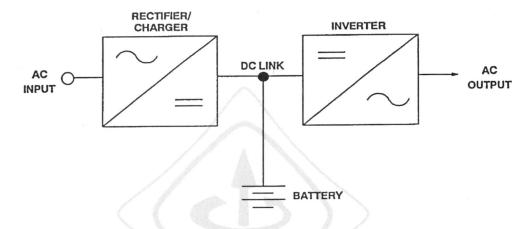

Figure 5-16—Single UPS unit with rectifier/charger

The single UPS is characterized by the inverter's ability to take its power supply from the rectifier/charger or battery. When the normal ac source or the rectifier/charger fail, the battery provides the input to the inverter to maintain the critical load(s). The capacity of the battery determines the period of time that the system can operate without the normal ac supply available. Backup times can vary from minutes to hours depending upon the user's requirements; however, the longer the backup time the larger in capacity the battery. Most systems today use a 15 minute backup time for the battery and rely on emergency diesel-generators or combustion-turbines to come on-line to provide emergency power for longer periods of time, should that be necessary.

5.5.4.2 Single UPS unit with separate battery charger

This configuration is similar to that in 5.5.4.1 except that the rectifier/charger is replaced by a separate rectifier and a separate battery charger. The rectifier provides the normal input to the inverter and the charger maintains the battery in a full-charged condition. A blocking device (e.g., a diode) is used between the battery and the dc link. Figure 5-17 is a typical representation of this configuration. Its operation is similar to the single UPS with rectifier/charger. The charger, however, need only be sized to charge the battery and maintain the battery in a fully charged condition.

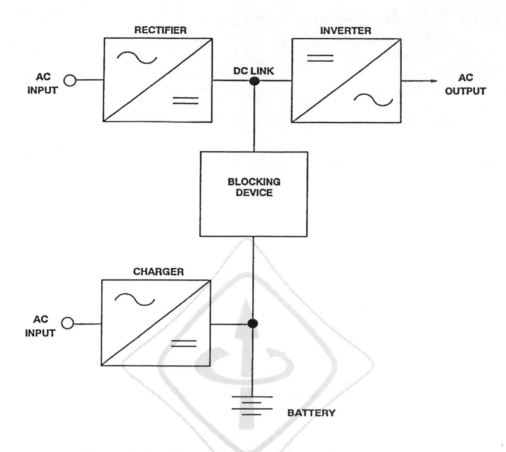

Figure 5-17—Single UPS unit separate battery charger

5.5.4.3 Single UPS unit with bypass and transfer switch

Either of the single UPS systems described in 5.5.4.1 and 5.5.4.2 can be combined with a bypass and transfer switch to enable operation from either the UPS or an alternate source. The characteristics of the alternate source should be compatible with that of the UPS ac output. This addition of a bypass and transfer switch provides a method of increasing the overall system reliability. For example, the addition of a static transfer switch may add about 10% to the cost of a single UPS unit, but its addition can make the system 8–10 times more reliable. This system is shown in figure 5-18.

When a bypass and transfer switch is used, the system may be operated as

— *UPS unit primary.* The primary state of the transfer switch selects the UPS to power the load. The alternate state of the transfer switch selects the bypass source. When an inverter failure is sensed, the critical load can be transferred to the bypass circuit in

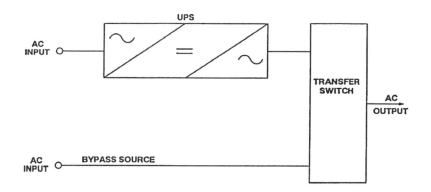

Figure 5-18—Single UPS unit with bypass and transfer switch

less than 4 ms, assuming a static switch is used. Figure 5-19 is an oscillogram of the load voltage as supplied during a transfer of the power source with a static switch.
— *Bypass primary.* The primary state of the transfer switch selects the bypass source to power the load. The alternate state of the transfer switch selects the UPS.

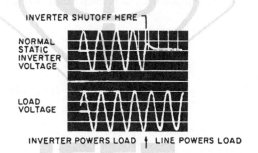

**Figure 5-19—Oscillogram of UPS output
during a transfer to the bypass source**

5.5.4.4 Parallel UPS with individual battery

Parallel UPS units are used when more power is required than can be supplied by an individual unit. The parallel units are treated as if they were one UPS with the output of the units connected to a common point. In this configuration, each parallel UPS has its own rectifier/charger and battery (figure 5-20).

5.5.4.5 Parallel UPS with a single battery

In this configuration, all of the UPS modules have their dc links connected to a single battery (figure 5-21).

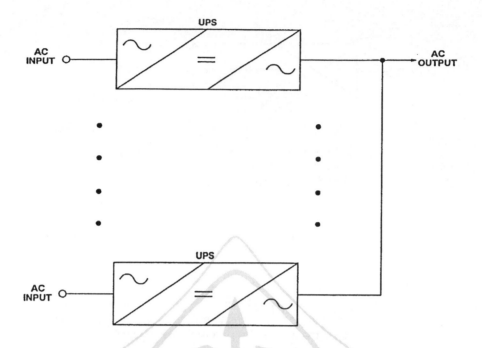

Figure 5-20—Parallel UPS with individual battery

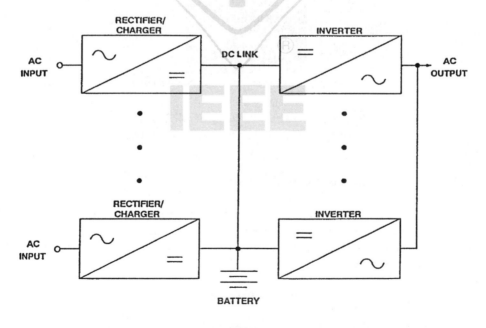

Figure 5-21—Parallel UPS with a single battery

5.5.4.6 Partial parallel UPS

This configuration consists of an unequal combination of one or more rectifier/chargers connected in parallel and one or more inverters connected in parallel with a common dc link and battery (figure 5-22).

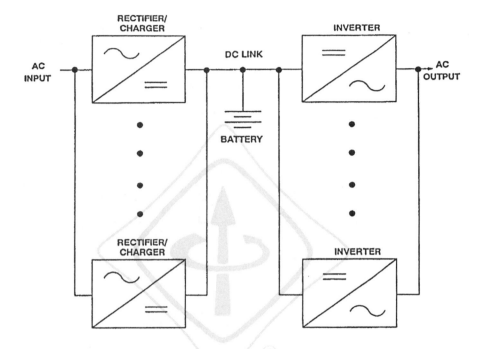

Figure 5-22—Partial parallel UPS

5.5.4.7 Parallel UPS with bypass and transfer switch

This configuration adds a bypass and transfer switch to any of the above parallel UPS configurations (figure 5-23). Functionally, the parallel UPS with bypass and transfer switch is equivalent to the single UPS with bypass and transfer switch (5.5.4.3).

5.5.4.8 Parallel redundant UPS

The need for redundancy is dependent on the user's and the system's requirements. Various levels of redundancy may be achieved by paralleling UPS modules. Redundant systems may have components that are common to all the modules (e.g., a single battery). Failure of such a common component may result in the loss of availability of power to the critical load. The parallel redundant configuration, shown in figure 5-24, uses a number of UPS modules connected in parallel to supply the load. If one UPS module is disconnected from the system, the remaining UPS module(s) maintains the continuity of power. If one UPS module fails, it is

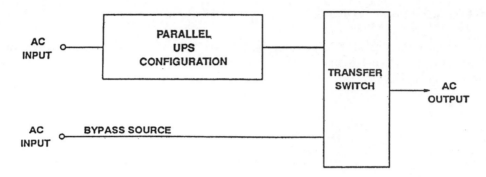

Figure 5-23—Parallel UPS with bypass and transfer switch

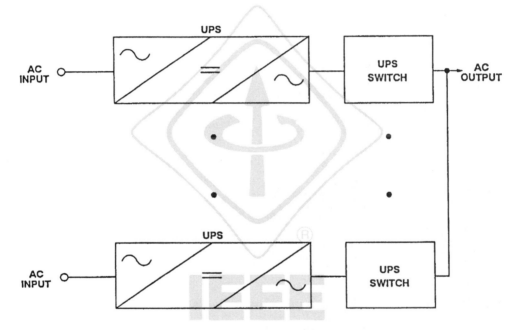

Figure 5-24—Parallel redundant UPS

isolated by the UPS switch to prevent it from interfering with the other UPS module(s) to maintain continuity of the load.

5.5.4.9 Parallel redundant UPS with common dc link (single battery)

In this configuration a number of rectifier/chargers and inverters are connected in parallel, with a single battery connected to their dc link. If one rectifier/charger or inverter is disconnected from the system, the remaining modules will maintain continuity of the load. If a module should fail it is isolated from the other modules which then maintain continuity of the load. (figure 5-25.)

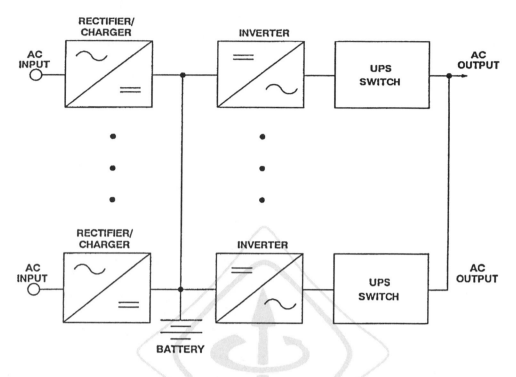

Figure 5-25—Parallel redundant UPS with common dc link (single battery)

5.5.4.10 Partial parallel redundant UPS

This configuration is characterized by an unequal combination of two or more rectifier/chargers connected in parallel and two or more inverters connected in parallel with a single battery. If one rectifier/charger or inverter is disconnected from the system, the remaining modules will maintain continuity of the load. If a module should fail, it is isolated from the other modules, which then maintain continuity of the load (figure 5-26).

5.5.4.11 Parallel redundant UPS with bypass and transfer switch

This configuration adds a bypass and transfer switch to any of the above parallel redundant UPS configurations (figure 5-27.) Functionally, the parallel redundant UPS with bypass and transfer switch is equivalent to the single UPS with bypass and transfer switch (5.5.4.3).

5.5.4.12 Standby redundant UPS

The standby redundant UPS, shown in figure 5-28, is made up of two UPSs and a transfer switch. Upon failure of the operating UPS the transfer switch will switch to the standby UPS.

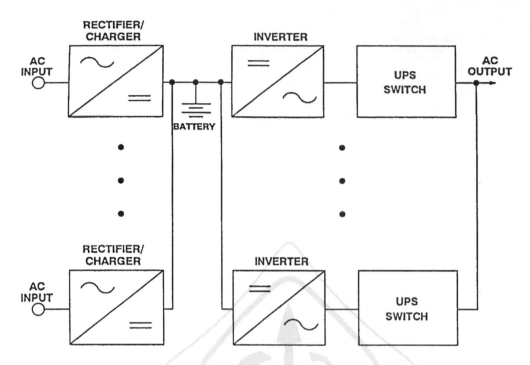

Figure 5-26—Partial parallel redundant UPS

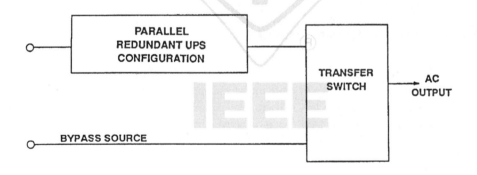

Figure 5-27—Parallel redundant UPS with bypass and transfer switch

5.5.4.13 Standby redundant UPS with common dc link (single battery) and transfer switch

This configuration is characterized by two rectifier/chargers and two inverters with a common battery connected to a transfer switch (figure 5-29).

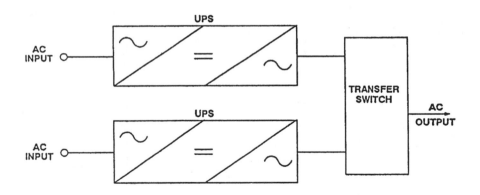

Figure 5-28—Standby redundant UPS with transfer switch

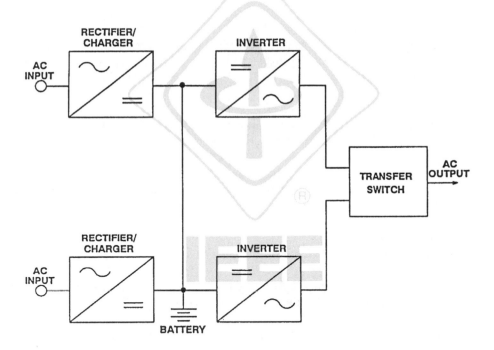

**Figure 5-29—Standby redundant UPS with common dc link (single battery)
and transfer switch**

5.5.4.14 Standby redundant UPS with bypass and transfer switch

This configuration adds a bypass and transfer switch to any of the above standby redundant UPS configurations (figure 5-30). Functionally, the standby redundant UPS with bypass and transfer switch is equivalent to the single UPS with bypass and transfer switch (5.5.4.3).

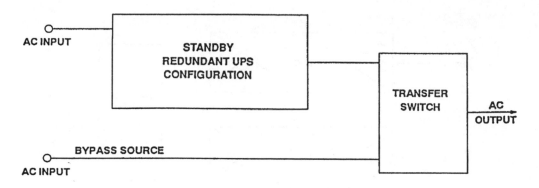

Figure 5-30—Standby redundant UPS with bypass and transfer switch

5.6 Motor-generators and rotating UPS systems

5.6.1 Introduction

Motor-generators are power systems that use a rotating ac generator to generate the usable output power. If batteries are added to enable the system to continue operation without utility power input, then the system becomes a UPS.

Motor-generators use ac or dc motors to drive ac generators. They use their rotating inertia to ride-through input voltages, sags, or total loss for periods up to 1/2 s (500 ms). When a flywheel is added, the ride-through time can be many seconds.

For protection against loss of power lasting longer than 1/2 s, batteries or other energy storage devices must be added. Conversion of battery power to rotating energy is accomplished by one of two ways:

— By use of a dc motor or
— By use of a dc-ac solid-state inverter feeding an ac motor.

To eliminate batteries, one system (5.6.8) uses a diesel generator and a flywheel motor-generator. These systems are described in the following subclauses of 5.6.

The ac generator is a versatile element, with a variety of means of driving it without interruption. Ac generators have low harmonic content and distortion. They are capable of operating reliably at high temperatures and under severe short-term overloads. They have a proven history of high reliability and predictable failure. The bearings can be tested at periodic intervals to detect deterioration and allow for planned replacement.

Three different motors may be used to drive the ac generator. They are ac induction (asynchronous), ac synchronous, and dc motors.

Induction motors offer the lowest cost per horsepower. Three-phase induction motors are most common. The output r/min is less than that from the ac synchronous motor because of slip. Torque increases as slip increases until the rotor stalls. Low-slip (0.4–0.7% slip) motors are recommended and available in sizes up to 100 hp. These motors have been designed to optimize slip, power factor, efficiency, and starting inrush. Typical slip is 0.4–0.7%, resulting in output of 1790 r/min under full load from a motor with a rated synchronous speed of 1800 r/min. Low-slip motors are sometimes built using oversize motors. These motors may have reduced efficiency.

Synchronous motors maintain a constant shaft speed independent of load and input voltage. They remain locked to the input frequency up to their pull-out torque. Their efficiencies are typically higher than induction motors.

Synchronous motors cannot develop torque at speeds lower than synchronous speed. For this reason these motors are usually started as induction motors or, alternately, under no-load conditions. Synchronous motors offer power factor correction as an advantage in some applications.

Dc motors offer the ability to regulate output frequency precisely. The speed of a dc motor may be varied by changing field excitation. For computer applications with tight frequency tolerance, a frequency regulator is used to adjust field excitation as input voltage and load vary. Dc motors have brushes that wear over time and need periodic replacement. Alarm systems are available that annunciate the need for their replacement. If brushes are regularly maintained, dc motors have the same life expectancy as induction or synchronous motors.

5.6.2 AC motor-generators

Nearly all ac motor-generators built today use brushless synchronous generators. The motor may be either induction or synchronous. Induction motors have an inherent slip that causes the output frequency of the system to be less than the input by a fraction of a cycle. Synchronous motors duplicate the incoming frequency precisely and track it. Most computer grade motor-generator sets utilize synchronous motors.

Several methods of construction are available, with the differences affecting ride-through time, isolation, and physical size (footprint). The smallest footprint is achieved by stacking the motor and generator and coupling their horizontal shafts using toothed pulleys and a belt (figure 5-31), or by mounting the motor and generator on a common vertical shaft. The stacked horizontal units get added ride-through from the mass of the pulleys and belt. Horizontal coupling can also be accomplished by building the motor and generator into a single frame or by coupling two separate frames on a base. Maximum isolation is attained by separate frames, electrically isolated, and connected by an insulating coupling (figure 5-32). Motor-generator sets with a common motor and generator in one rotor offer the smallest horizontal size but the least isolation of transients from input to output (figure 5-33).

5.6.3 AC motor-generator with flywheel

The addition of a flywheel adds mass and therefore increases the ride-through time of a motor-generator set. This increased ride-through time is achieved at the expense of weight, size, efficiency, bearing life, and higher initial system cost. Air friction (or *windage*) increases

**Figure 5-31—Horizontal coupling of stacked motor
and generator using pulleys and belts**

rapidly as the radius of the flywheel and its speed increase. Bearing friction causes further losses, decreasing the overall system efficiency. The flywheel takes more input power to start up, so inrush current-limiting circuits are usually necessary. The addition of a flywheel also requires a larger motor for the extra horsepower necessary to restore the r/min to the flywheel that are lost during input power sags or loss. Provision for the higher current input must be made.

Flywheel motor-generator sets are available with up to several seconds of ride-through time. Larger flywheels have proven to be impractical. It takes a mass of steel approximately 6 inches thick and 4 ft in diameter to maintain a 30 kVA load with less than 1 Hz frequency change for 0.5 s.

Maintenance of motor-generator sets consists of periodic checks for bearing noise. Motor-generator sets have a proven track record of very long *mean time between failure* (MTBF). The bearings are the most likely failure point. Their failure is predictable, so replacement prior to failure (typically once every 7–10 years) is the largest maintenance cost.

**Figure 5-32—Horizontal coupling of motor and generator using
two separate frames on a base**

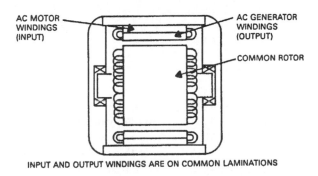

INPUT AND OUTPUT WINDINGS ARE ON COMMON LAMINATIONS

Figure 5-33—Motor and generator with common rotor

The construction of a motor-generator set can make bearing replacement easy or difficult. For example, some vertical motor-generators have the load support bearing on top to allow easy access. This allows the main bearing to be changed without pulling the rotor out of the case.

5.6.4 Battery/dc motor/ac motor-generator set

This UPS uses a standard motor-generator set for continuous power conditioning (see figure 5-34). When the normal power source is available, the dc motor is controlled by a field voltage control circuit to operate as a generator, maintaining the battery voltage. When the normal power source is disturbed or fails, the dc motor is changed by a field voltage control circuit from a generator to a motor. The dc motor draws battery power to continue driving the ac motor-generator without interruption.

Advantages include the following:

— Excellent power conditioning and load isolation
— Excellent overload and short-circuit capacity
— Maintenance and repairs do not require specially qualified personnel.
— Failure of dc circuits or motor does not affect power conditioning.

The disadvantage is as follows:

— Dc motor brushes require maintenance and replacement.

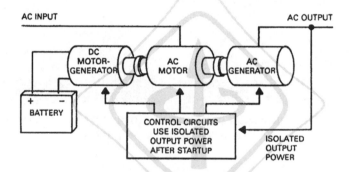

Figure 5-34—Battery/dc motor/ac motor-generator set

5.6.5 Battery/dc motor/ac generator

This UPS (figure 5-35) uses a dc motor to continuously drive the ac generator. A rectifier/charger converts the ac input to dc for the motor and battery. This system is less expensive than the system described in 5.6.4, but it cannot continue to condition and isolate the power line if any failure occurs. Some manufacturers of this type of system have separate circuits for the dc motor and the battery charger, and add a flywheel to ride through switchover time during the failure of the normal power source. Other manufacturers have simplified the system by reducing circuits and eliminating the flywheel.

Advantages include the following:

— Output frequency can be regulated very closely at all times.
— It conditions power and isolates the load from the utility.
— Maintenance and repairs do not require specially trained personnel.
— Cost is lower than systems with both an ac and dc motor.
— The output frequency remains stable over varying input frequencies.
— It may be used as a frequency changer.

Disadvantages include the following:

— Failure of the dc circuits prevents power conditioning.
— Efficiency is reduced by rectifier circuits.
— Dc motor brushes require maintenance and replacement.

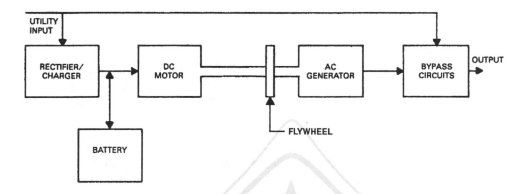

Figure 5-35—Battery/dc motor/ac generator

5.6.6 Off-line inverter/motor-generator system

This UPS system (figure 5-36) substitutes a solid-state ac inverter for the dc motor in previous examples. The ac motor-generator set provides continuous power-line conditioning even if the dc and inverter circuits fail. Normally the inverter is off. Upon loss of the normal power, the inverter is turned on and converts stored battery energy to ac to drive the motor-generator set.

Advantages include the following:

— Power-line conditioning and isolation is provided even if dc circuits fail.
— Efficiency is high because the inverter is normally off.
— No brush maintenance or replacement is required.

Disadvantages include the following:

— An inverter may not be as reliable as a dc motor.
— Inverter failure may not be detected until it is turned on.

5.6.7 On-line inverter/motor-generator system

This UPS system, called a hybrid UPS and shown in figure 5-37, differs from the off-line system only in that the rectifier and inverter are always operating. The inverter and rectifier are bypassed in case of failure of either component.

167

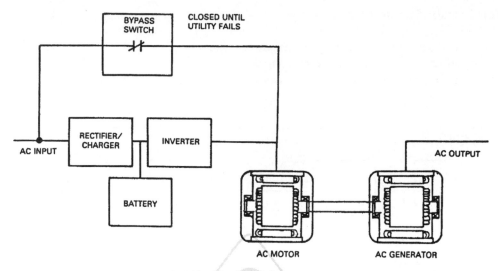

Figure 5-36—Off-line inverter/motor-generator system

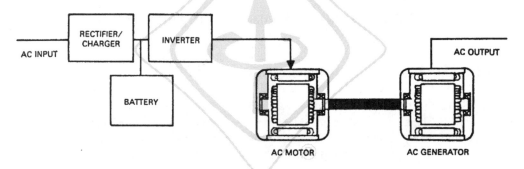

Figure 5-37—On-line inverter/motor-generator system

The advantage is as follows:

— A failure in rectifier or inverter does not affect power conditioning.

The disadvantage is as follows:

— An inverter is not as reliable as a dc motor.

5.6.8 Engine motor-generator system

This system (shown in figure 5-38) consists of an internal combustion engine, an electro-mechanical clutch or a magnetic clutch, a horizontal axis flywheel, an ac generator, and an ac motor (plus control and transfer equipment). In normal operation, the normal power source to the ac motor drives the flywheel and ac generator, which in turn supplies power to the load. The flywheel stores kinetic energy.

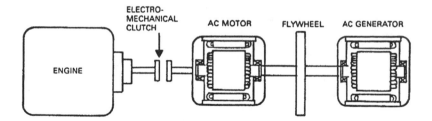

Figure 5-38—Engine/motor-generator system

When the normal power source is interrupted, the flywheel drives the ac generator and starts the engine through the clutch. The engine then drives the ac generator, which continues to supply power to the load without interruption. With proper selection of components to minimize the start-up and run-up times of the engine, the frequency dip can be kept to approximately 1.5–2 Hz without paying a premium. Thus, with a steady-state frequency of 60.0 Hz, the transient frequency would be from 58–58.5 Hz. The time for the engine to start, come up to speed, and take the load, is normally less than 2–3 s.

Advantages include the following:

— Operating time after a normal power loss is limited only by fuel supply.
— It offers excellent overload and short-circuit capacity.
— Maintenance and repairs do not require specially qualified personnel.
— The system has predictable failure modes.
— There is no battery to maintain.

Disadvantages include the following:

— The mechanical clutch suffers wear and tear during each start and requires costly and frequent maintenance.
— The engine crankshaft experiences high axial loads that require a special design; its maintenance and replacement parts are costly.
— An additional engine generator must be provided to supply the air conditioning, lighting, and other similar loads if long-term operation is desired.

5.6.9 Engine generator/motor-generator system

This system consists of an ac motor-generator set with a flywheel and an engine-generator set (figure 5-39). In normal operation the normal power source supplies the ac motor-generator set, which in turn supplies power to the load. The flywheel stores kinetic energy.

When the normal power source is interrupted, the flywheel energy supports the speed of the ac motor-generator set. A transfer switch disconnects the normal power from the motor-generator and connects the engine-generator output to the motor-generator. Simultaneously, the engine is started. As its speed increases, the output voltage rises, exciting the motor-generator

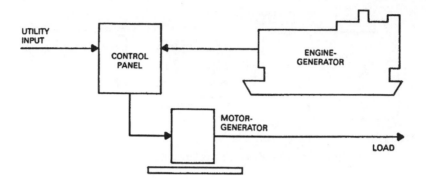

Figure 5-39—Engine-generator/motor-generator system

set motor to act momentarily as a generator, assisting the engine in achieving full operating speed.

Engine-generator sets, under 100 kW in rating, have been found to accelerate to full speed within 2 s. The backup generator has sufficient extra power to feed loads such as lights and air conditioning.

Advantages include the following:

— Cost is less than that of both battery backup UPS and engine-generators.
— Operating time during an interruption of normal power is limited only by fuel supply.
— It offers excellent overload and short-circuit capacity.
— The transfer of driving power to start the internal combustion engine is effected smoothly with electromagnetic action, thereby avoiding clutching and destructive forces in the engine crankshaft.
— Installation, service, repairs, and maintenance do not require specially qualified personnel.

The disadvantage is as follows:

— Frequency is always below 60 Hz, since an induction motor is used.

5.6.10 Parallel systems

Most rotating UPS systems described here can be connected in parallel for additional output power. In most cases some added control circuits are necessary to sense and adjust the phase angle of each ac generator output voltage to ensure they are synchronized when switching. An exception is the case of synchronous ac motors and generators operating on the normal power source. These motor-generator sets are always at synchronous speed. However, if two synchronous motor-generator sets are backed up by a dc battery and motor, control circuits are required to maintain synchronism during dc operation. Once connected together, synchronous ac generators will remain in synchronism.

5.6.11 Redundant systems

Most rotating systems described here may be connected to create redundant outputs. This may be accomplished by parallel operation at less than half power per system, or by connection through a sensing and switching circuit.

Induction motor-generator sets are more difficult to parallel than synchronous sets due to the continuous slip of the induction motor. With one unit loaded, the other unit being brought on-line must be loaded with an external load bank until the two generator outputs are in phase. Only then may the outputs be connected to each other to supply the load in parallel.

5.6.12 Bypass circuits

UPS systems that have the same frequency and voltage input and output are usually supplied with a bypass circuit. This circuit consists of a static transfer switch or an electromechanical transfer switch, or both. The purpose of the bypass circuit is threefold: First, to connect the bypass source to the load in case of failure of the UPS; second, to enable bypass of the UPS for maintenance; third, to assist the UPS output in supplying fault current if a fault occurs. However, most motor-generators and motor-generator-based UPS systems do not require ac bypass to the utility to clear faults, since they have enough overload capacity to clear the faults without assistance. Care should be taken to ensure that the output of the UPS or system is in phase with the normal power supply (i.e., input). The initiation of an out-of-phase closure (e.g., during maintenance) of the bypass represents both a safety and equipment hazard.

5.7 References

This chapter shall be used in conjunction with the following publications:

IEEE Std 100-1992, The New IEEE Standard Dictionary of Electrical and Electronics Terms (ANSI).[3]

IEEE Std 450-1995, IEEE Recommended Practice for Maintenance, Testing, and Replacement of Vented Lead-Acid Batteries for Stationary Applications.

IEEE Std 484-1996, IEEE Recommended Practice for Installation Design and Installation of Vented Lead-Acid Batteries for Stationary Applications.

IEEE Std 485-1983, IEEE Recommended Practice for Sizing Large Lead Storage Batteries for Generating Stations and Substations.

IEEE Std 946-1992, IEEE Recommended Practice for the Design of DC Auxiliary Power Systems for Generating Stations (ANSI).

---

[3]IEEE publications are available from the Institute of Electrical and Electronics Engineers, 445 Hoes Lane, P.O. Box 1331, Piscataway, NJ 08855-1331, USA.

IEEE Std 1106-1995, IEEE Recommended Practice for Installation, Maintenance, Testing, and Replacement of Vented Nickel-Cadmium Batteries for Stationary Applications (ANSI).

IEEE Std 1115-1992, IEEE Recommended Practice for Sizing Nickel-Cadmium Batteries for Stationary Applications (ANSI).

IEEE Std 1184-1994, IEEE Guide for the Selection and Sizing of Batteries for Uninterruptible Power Systems.

IEEE Std 1187-1996, IEEE Recommended Practice for Installation Design and Installation of Valve-Regulated Lead-Acid Storage Batteries for Stationary Applications.

IEEE P1188, Draft Recommended Practice for Maintenance, Testing, and Replacement of Valve-Regulated Lead-Acid Batteries for Stationary Applications, Oct. 1995.[4]

IEEE P1189, Draft Guide for Selecting and Sizing Valve-Regulated Lead-Acid Batteries for Stationary Applications, Oct. 1995.[5]

5.8 Bibliography

Additional information may be found in the following sources:

[B1] ANSI C84.1-1989, American National Standard Voltage Ratings for Electric Power Systems and Equipment (60 Hz).[6]

[B2] ANSI/NFPA 101-1994, Code for Safety to Life from Fire in Buildings and Structures.[7]

[B3] ANSI/NFPA 111-1993, Stored Electrical Energy Emergency and Standby Power Systems.

[B4] ANSI/UL 924-1990, Safety Standard for Emergency Lighting and Power Equipment.[8]

[B5] ANSI/UL 1778-1991, Uninterruptible Power Supply Equipment.

[B6] Bell Laboratories, "Lead-acid Battery," *The Bell System Technical Journal,* vol. 49, no. 7, pp. 1249–1470.

---

[4]This IEEE standards project was not approved by the IEEE Standards Board at the time this publication went to press. For information about obtaining a draft, contact the IEEE.

[5]See footnote 4.

[6]ANSI publications are available from the Sales Department, American National Standards Institute, 11 West 42nd Street, 13th Floor, New York, NY 10036, USA.

[7]NFPA publications are available from Publications Sales, National Fire Protection Association, 1 Batterymarch Park, P.O. Box 9101, Quincy, MA 02269-9101, USA.

[8]UL publications are available from Underwriters Laboratories, Inc., 333 Pfingsten Road, Northbrook, IL 60062-2096, USA.

[B7] Griffith, D. C., *Uninterruptible Power Supplies,* New York: Marcel Dekker, Inc., 1989.

[B8] Harrison, A. I., "Thermal Management of High Energy Density Battery Equipments," *Conference Paper 92CH3195-5,* Presented at 1992 IEEE INTELEC Conference, pp. 28–34.

[B9] IEEE Committee Report, "Reliability of Electrical Equipment, Part 1," *IEEE Transactions on Industry Applications,* vol. IA-10, pp. 213–235, Mar./Apr. 1974.

[B10] IEEE Std 241-1990, IEEE Recommended Practice for Electric Power Systems in Commercial Buildings (The Gray Book) (ANSI).

[B11] IEEE Std 493-1990, IEEE Recommended Practice for the Design of Reliable Industrial and Commercial Power Systems (The Gold Book) (ANSI).

[B12] IEEE Std 602-1986, IEEE Recommended Practice for Electric Systems in Health Care Facilities (The White Book) (ANSI).[9]

[B13] IEEE Std 1100-1992, IEEE Recommended Practice for Powering and Grounding Sensitive Electronic Equipment (The Emerald Book) (ANSI).

[B14] Kiehne, H. A., *Battery Technology Handbook,* New York: Marcel Dekker, Inc., 1989.

[B15] Linden, D., *Handbook of Batteries and Fuel Cells,* New York: McGraw-Hill, 1984.

[B16] Migliaro, M. W., "Considerations for Selecting and Sizing Batteries," *IEEE Transactions on Industry Applications,* vol. IA-23, no. 1, pp. 134–143, Jan./Feb. 1987.

[B17] Migliaro, M. W., "Stationary Batteries-Selected Topics," *Proceedings of the American Power Conference,* vol. 55-I, pp. 23–33, 1993.

[B18] Migliaro, M. W., and Albér, G., "Sizing UPS Batteries," *Proceedings of the Fourth International Power Quality Conference,* vol. 4, pp. 285–290, 1991.

[B19] Migliaro, M. W., and Mazzoni, O. S., "Battery Problems That Can Spell Disaster," Disaster Avoidance & Recovery '93 Conference, May 1993.

[B20] Misra, S. S., Noveske, T. M., and Williamson, A. W., "Thermal Effects in VRLA Cells and Comparison with Wet Lead-Acid Cells Under Different Operating Conditions," Conference Paper 92CH3195-5, Presented at 1992 IEEE INTELEC Conference, pp. 35–40.

[B21] NEMA PE 1-1993, Uninterruptible Power Systems.[10]

---

[9]As this standard goes to press, IEEE Std 602-1996 is approved but not yet published. The draft standard is, however, available from the IEEE. Anticipated publication date is December 1996. Contact the IEEE Standards Department at 1 (908) 562-3800 for status information.

[10]NEMA publications are available from the National Electrical Manufacturers Association, 2101 L Street NW, Washington, DC 20037, USA.

[B22] NFPA 70-1996, National Electrical Code®.[11]

[B23] NFPA 99-1996, Health Care Facilities Code.

[B24] Platts, J., and St. Aubyn, J., *IEE Power Series 14: Uninterruptible Power Supplies.* London: Peter Peregrinus, 1992.

[B25] Vinal, G. W., *Storage Batteries,* Fourth Edition. New York: John Wiley & Sons, 1955.

[11]NFPA publications are available from Publications Sales, National Fire Protection Association, 1 Batterymarch Park, P.O. Box 9101, Quincy, MA 02269-9101, USA.

Chapter 6
Protection

6.1 Introduction

This chapter is presented to discuss recommended practices and guidelines for protection of emergency and standby power systems. Even though standard practice for protection of equipment should always be given full consideration when applying the equipment in emergency and standby use, reliability often warrants special consideration when a power supply for critical loads is designed. Although compliance with all national, state, and local codes and standards applicable to protection of the components that make up the emergency or standby power system are necessary, it may be desirable to exceed these codes and standards in the design process. It is not the intent of this chapter to list all applicable codes and standards, but some pertinent ones are referenced where necessary to aid these recommended practice and guidelines.

Protection for individual components that make up the most common emergency and standby power systems is discussed, with emphasis on maintaining the required integrity and reliability of the system. Proper application and maintenance of systems are discussed in other chapters and should be considered an important aspect of protection.

6.2 Short-circuit current considerations

Of the many areas of concern for protection of components that make up an emergency or standby power system, one needing special consideration is that of magnitude and duration of short-circuit current available from the emergency or standby power source. Fault conditions obviously have a direct effect on the availability of the power supply to serve its intended purpose. Studies should be made to determine available short-circuit current throughout the system supplied by an emergency or standby power supply, especially at switching and current-interrupting devices.

In evaluating the performance of an emergency or standby generator under fault conditions, a critical. concern is whether sufficient fault current is available for sufficient duration to selectively trip overcurrent devices in a properly coordinated system. In most cases, emergency or standby power sources do not produce as much fault current as the normal source. When both sources are designed to supply a distribution system, through automatic or manual switching devices, the magnitude of the fault current available from the normal supply usually determines the required interrupting or withstand rating of the system components. Careful planning is necessary to design a system that assures optimum selectivity and coordination with both power sources. An emergency or standby generator's available short-circuit current should be compared to the ratings of system overcurrent devices to determine how this coordination is to be achieved. Normally the emergency or standby power source should be connected into the power system so as to be physically and electrically as close to the loads as practical. This will minimize the number and size of distribution system circuit breakers involved and the number of coordination levels required.

Selective coordination of overcurrent devices is the process of applying these devices so that one will operate before another under given levels of fault currents, thereby allowing effective isolation of the faulted circuit from unfaulted circuits. For a detailed analysis of the principals of selective coordination, see IEEE Std 242-1986.[1]

Evaluating the available fault current from an emergency or standby generator includes determining the magnitude of the fault current and how long the fault current will exist and how it may change. Test information on generator short-circuit characteristics may be necessary from the manufacturer. One should not assume that the speed of the generator will remain unchanged for a fault fed only by the generator; the effects of frequency changes and prime mover load should also be accounted for. The coordination of the mechanical and electrical stored energy in a generator set and the type of excitation system will determine how long the engine and generator will sustain fault current and how rapidly this fault current will decay. In some cases, the initial power to a fault is higher (sometimes several times higher) than the prime mover power rating. The result can be a rapid reduction in speed. This overloading of the prime mover is more likely in small generator set applications than in larger power systems since the X/R ratios of both the generator windings and distribution circuits in small systems are lower.

An excitation system usually will not respond fast enough to significantly affect the first one or two cycles of fault current, so at this point the type of excitation system does not matter. If the fault is not cleared in the first 2–4 cycles, a serious concern is whether or not the generator set can recover, after the fault is finally cleared, to maintain acceptable service to unfaulted branch circuits. For systems where the fault current decays rapidly to levels below instantaneous and delayed overcurrent trip settings, tripping will only be possible in the first few cycles. This diminishes the ability to selectively trip the overcurrent devices, leaving only the instantaneous settings to work with.

Figure 6-1 illustrates the rate of decay of three-phase fault current from tests on three typical generators; the first two are separately excited (with fixed excitation) and tested at no load. The curves are approximations of actual test results. In figure 6-1(a), about 40 cycles elapse before the fault current decays to the full-load rating of the generator. In figure 6-1(b), the fault current decayed to the full-load rating in about 25 cycles. The quicker decline of fault current from the smaller generator is a common occurrence. The current (I) shown is in per unit (pu) based on generator full-load current rating. Figure 6-1(c) illustrates an approximation of short-circuit current of a shunt-excited generator without short-circuit sustaining capability. In this case, the current has decayed to full-load rating in 10 cycles and to nearly zero in 20 cycles.

When two circuit breakers equipped with instantaneous trips are applied in series, even though the upstream breaker is substantially larger, selective instantaneous tripping is not assured on faults below the downstream breaker unless the momentary fault current is less

---

[1]Information on references can be found in 6.11.

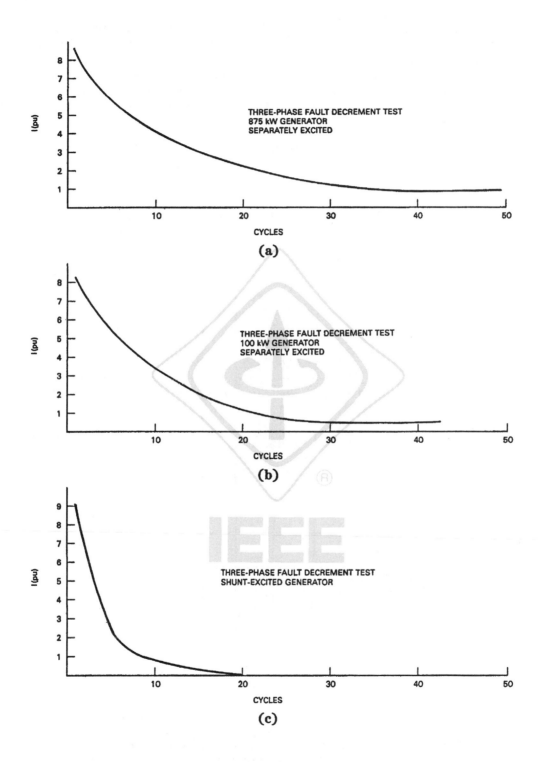

Figure 6-1—Three-phase decrement curves for engine-generators

than the minimum instantaneous trip level of the larger upstream breaker. This concept is illustrated in figure 6-2. The figure shows a case where the fault current, taken from figure 6-1(b), is above the maximum instantaneous pickup current of the larger breaker. This may unlatch and trip this larger breaker, so that both breakers trip and power is lost to unfaulted branch circuits. The decay of the current during the unlatching time of the breaker, which may be less than .01 s, is insignificant compared to the pickup tolerance of the trip unit or the variation in the asymmetrical component of the current. Once the breaker is unlatched, it is committed to trip.

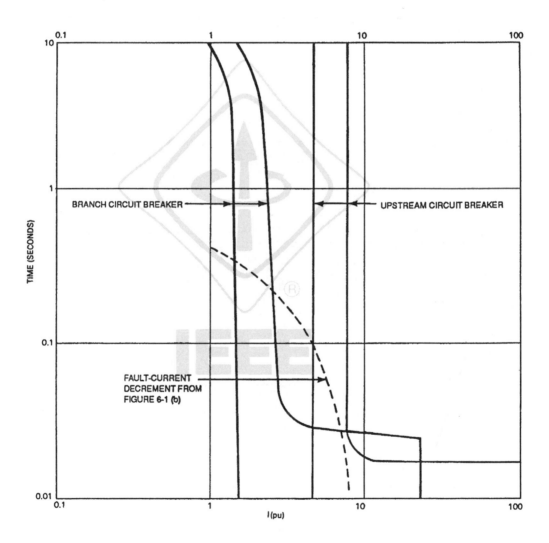

Figure 6-2—Three-phase short-circuit current versus molded-case circuit breakers in series

For the cases illustrated in figure 6-1, only three-phase fault conditions are shown. In actual practice, unbalanced faults are much more common, especially line-to-ground in grounded systems. For this reason, evaluating only three-phase fault conditions in the application of an engine-generator is insufficient. Shunt exciter systems may derive their power from line-to-line, line-to-neutral, or from all three phases. Depending on the particular design, it is possible that faults occurring line-to-line or line-to-neutral may not decay to a self-protecting level as shown in figure 6-1. The degree to which this can be a problem should be determined on a case-by-case basis. It is possible for a generator and excitation system to be designed to assure collapse of the generator terminal voltage and fault current on any kind of fault at the generator terminals. Generator and excitation systems are also available to assure a predicted level of fault current. A user should specify the type of system that best fits his needs.

Figure 6-3 is an approximation of an actual test on a turbine-driven generator with and without excitation support under three-phase fault conditions. The curves show how little influence the excitation system has in the first few cycles, but the sustained fault current is substantially different from that without excitation support.

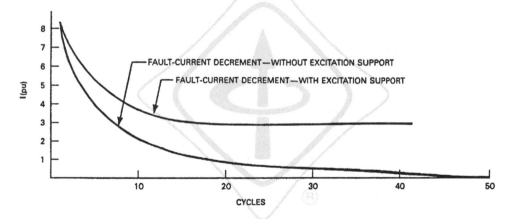

Figure 6-3—Three-phase decrements for 900 kW turbine generator

This type of fault-sustaining support will produce even higher than 3 pu fault current for line-to-line and line-to-ground faults. These values are typically 5 pu and 8 pu, respectively.

6.3 Transfer devices

6.3.1 Codes and standards

Several codes and standards that relate to transfer devices are cited throughout this subclause. These are as follows:

— ANSI C37.16-1988
— IEEE Std C37.13-1990
— IEEE Std C37.26-1972

— IEEE Std C37.90-1989
— IEEE Std 141-1993
— NEMA ICS 1-1993
— The National Electrical Code (NEC) (NFPA 70-1996)
— ANSI/NFPA 110-1993
— ANSI/UL 1008-1989
— CSA C22.2/No. 178-1987

Other standards not cited in this subclause that may serve as useful bibliographic references are as follows:

— ANSI/NEMA ICS 2-1993 [B2][2]
— NFPA 99-1996 [B17]
— IEEE Std 241-1990 [B12]

Codes and standards applicable to protection of transfer devices vary somewhat between different usages of the equipment. The NEC, for instance, is limited in its requirements for transfer equipment in emergency and standby power applications. ANSI/UL 1008-1989 contains considerable information on construction and testing of automatic transfer switches. Most users today place considerable emphasis on adequacy of equipment as determined by nationally recognized testing laboratories. For this reason, testing has been given special attention in this subclause. The primary concern of these testing labs, however, is safety, and the user should recognize reliability considerations in the proper selection and application of a transfer switch. It should be noted that CSA C22.2/No. 178-1987, the Canadian standard on automatic transfer switches, is similar to ANSI/UL 1008-1989. Also, because of worldwide need, the International Electrotechnical Commission (IEC) has prepared a standard on automatic transfer switches: IEC 947-6-1: 1989 [B11].

6.3.2 Current withstand ratings

Proper operation of transfer switches are a vital part of the proper operation of the system making careful application of the switches extremely important, maybe more so than other branch-circuit devices. The design, normal duty, and fault-current ratings of the switch play an important part in its application and protection scheme. It must be capable of closing into high inrush currents, of withstanding fault currents, and of severe duty cycle in switching normal-rated load. All are important capability characteristics and thus important to protection, but emphasis in this chapter will be mainly on fault withstandability. The coordination of overcurrent protection devices with transfer switch ratings, under fault conditions, is one of the most important aspects of maintaining the integrity and reliability necessary in the operation of a standby or emergency power system.

The destructive effects of high fault currents consist mainly of two components: (1) magnetic stresses that attempt to pry open the switch contacts and bend bus bars, and (2) heat energy developed that can melt, deform, or otherwise damage the switch. Either or both of these components can cause switch failure.

---

[2]The numbers in brackets preceded by the letter B correspond to those of the bibliography in 6.12.

A fault involving high short-circuit currents usually causes a substantial voltage drop that will be sensed by the voltage sensing relays in the automatic transfer switch. It is imperative for protection that the switch contacts remain closed until protective devices can clear the fault. Separation of contacts, prior to protective device operation, can develop enough arcing and heat to damage the switch. Normally employed time delay to prevent immediate transfer of mechanically held mechanisms and contact structures specifically designed with high contact pressure, in some cases utilizing electromagnetic forces to increase contact pressure, combine to provide the reliability and protection necessary in automatic transfer switch operation. It follows that proper application of the switch within its withstand rating is important to prevent contacts from welding together and to prevent any other circuit path joints and connections from overheating or deforming, thus prolonging the life and increasing reliability of the switch.

ANSI/UL 1008-1989 presents specific test requirements to ensure the withstand capabilities of switches. Included are methods and types of overcurrent device application, available short-circuit currents required, and allowable damage criteria while still remaining operable. Also, power factor requirements of the test circuit are given. Manufacturers should be consulted to determine the method of testing applied to transfer switches. Determining whether a fuse or circuit breaker (and what size and type) was used, and determining the X/R ratio of the test circuit are both important aids in judging whether or not the switch is suitable for its intended application. Current-limiting fuses or current-limiting circuit breakers, for example, would considerably limit the duration of short-circuit current compared to the application of ordinary circuit breakers. This is discussed further in 6.3.4. Specifications of switches should be carefully examined to recognize when asymmetrical and instantaneous peak fault currents are used to avoid being misled by specifications giving seemingly high numbers that may actually be asymmetrical or peak current ratings. Normally, symmetrical rms amperes should be used when coordinating time-current characteristics of switches and protective devices.

Additionally, ANSI/UL 1008-1989 establishes withstand ratings for transfer switches using either integrally designed overcurrent protection or external overcurrent protective devices. In the case where circuit breakers are integrally incorporated into the design, it should be noted that the transfer switch contacts will not remain closed for the duration of a short circuit, but instead will interrupt the current. Thus the withstand rating can be considered the same as the interrupt rating. This interchange of the terms *interrupting* and *withstand* can lead to confusion, especially when transfer switches of the integral circuit breaker type with the trip units removed are used with external overcurrent protective devices. Caution is advised when evaluating the withstand rating for this case, since eliminating the trip unit can reduce the interrupting rating and therefore the withstand rating by as much as 2 or 3 times.

Table 6-1 shows an example of a manufacturer's switch withstand current ratings when protected by current-limiting fuses or ordinary circuit breakers. This table illustrates the difference in withstand current ratings for switches, owing to the inherent differences between ordinary breakers and fuses. The normal and emergency contacts have the same withstand ratings even though the emergency contacts do not usually have to withstand currents as high as those of the normal source. The table is not intended as a guide for all switches as the data will vary among manufacturers and types of switches.

Table 6-1—Example of automatic transfer switches suitable for available fault current

Switch rating (amperes)	Available symmetrical amperes rms at 480 Vac and X/R ratio of 6.6 or less			
	When used with class J and L current-limiting fuses		When used with molded-case circuit breakers	
	Withstand current rating	Maximum fuse size (amperes)	Withstand current rating	Maximum circuit breaker trip rating (amperes)
30	100 000	60	10 000	50
100	100 000	300	22 000	150
260	200 000	400	22 000	600
400	200 000	800	35 000	600
600	200 000	1200	42 000	2500
800	200 000	1200	42 000	2500
1000	200 000	2000	65 000	2500
1200	200 000	2000	65 000	2500
1600	200 000	3000	85 000	2500
2000	200 000	3000	85 000	2500
4000	200 000	6000	100 000	5000

NOTE—X/R ratio, size of overcurrent protective devices, and withstand current ratings vary depending upon the manufacturer.

6.3.3 Significance of X/R ratio

It is the X/R ratio of a circuit that determines the maximum available peak current and thus the maximum magnetic stresses that can occur. As the X/R ratio increases, both the fault with-standability of the switch and the capability of an overcurrent protective device must also increase. Power factors, X/R ratios, and their relationships to peak current can be found in Table 2 of IEEE Std C37.26-1972. In many instances a circuit breaker symmetrical current interrupting rating or a transfer switch withstand rating must be reduced if applied at an X/R ratio greater than what the device safely withstood at test.

When current-limiting fuses are employed as protective devices for switches, the peak instan-taneous let-through current passed by the fuse should be no more than the instantaneous peak current for which the switch has been tested. Also, the fuse interrupting rating and test X/R ratio should be greater than the circuit available fault current and rated X/R ratio, respectively.

Tables 6-2 through 6-4 show how circuit breaker interrupting ratings, fuse interrupting ratings, and transfer switch withstand ratings vary with X/R ratios.

Table 6-2—Molded-case and low-voltage circuit-breaker-interrupting requirements

Interrupting rating (symmetrical amperes)		Test power factor (%)	X/R ratio
Molded-case circuit breakers	Power circuit breakers		
10 000 or less	—	45–50	1.73–1.98
10 001–20 000	—	25–30	3.18–3.87
20 001 and more	—	15–20	4.9–6.6
—	All ratings	15 maximum	6.6 minimum

Sources: IEEE Std C37.13-1990 and ANSI/UL 489-1991 [B8].

Table 6-3—Automatic transfer switch withstand requirements

Withstand test available current (symmetrical amperes)	Test power factor (%)	X/R ratio
10 000 or less	45–50	1.73–2.29
10 001–20 000	25–30	3.18–3.87
20 001 and more	20 maximum	4 minimum

Source: ANSI/UL 1008-1989.

6.3.4 Withstand ratings with respect to time

Fault-current magnitude and time of duration determine the heat energy and thermal stress developed during a fault, and this energy is normally designated as I^2t. In addition to current magnitude withstand ratings, automatic transfer switches have I^2t ratings that, if exceeded, can damage or possibly even destroy a switch.

Available I^2t at a switch will vary with the magnitude of fault current and the clearing time of the overcurrent device protecting the switch. Thus, to know the available I^2t, the type of overcurrent protective device must be known since different protective devices allow different

Table 6-4—Fuse-interrupting test requirements

Fuse class	Interrupting test current (symmetrical amperes)	Test power factor (%)	X/R ratio
H	10 000	45–50	1.73–1.98
K	50 000	20 maximum	4.9 minimum
	100 000		
	200 000		
J	200 000	20 maximum	4.9 minimum
L	200 000	20 maximum	4.9 minimum
R	200 000	20 maximum	4.9 minimum
T	200 000	20 maximum	4.9 minimum

Sources: ANSI C97.1-1972 [B1] and ANSI/UL 198B-1995 [B3], ANSI/UL 198C-1986 [B4], ANSI/UL 198D-1995 [B5], ANSI/UL 198E-1995 [B6], and ANSI/UL 198H-1988 [B7].

magnitudes of fault-current let-through and have different clearing times. Clearing time of a fuse will differ from that of a circuit breaker, and each will differ among different specific types. Current-limiting fuses introduce an additional parameter to be considered, called peak let-through current. When applying current-limiting fuses, the time factor reduces to a fraction of a cycle.

ANSI/UL 1008-1989 permits an automatic transfer switch to be tested without an overcurrent protective device so long as the time of the test is at least as long as the opening time of a specified protective device at a specified level of fault current. Although the switch under these conditions may be capable of withstanding several cycles of the specified fault current, it might not be labeled as rated for this number of cycles. In actual applications, it is not uncommon for switches to be required to carry fault current for several cycles. If this if the case, the user is bound to assure that the available fault current does not cause the I^2t rating of the switch to be exceeded.

Table 6-5 shows typical transfer switch ratings in I^2t as related to different peak let-through currents of fuses. These values will vary among different switch manufacturers. The manufacturer provides a list of the breakers or fuses that will protect the transfer switch.

Table 6-5—Typical transfer switch characteristics when used with fuses

Switch rating (amperes)	Available rms symmetrical fault current (amperes)	Peal let-through current (amperes)	I^2t (amperes^2-seconds)
125	200 000	26 000	600×10^3
225	200 000	45 000	2500×10^3
400	200 000	80 000	$12\,000 \times 10^3$
600	200 000	100 000	$12\,000 \times 10^3$
1000	200 000	150 000	$35\,000 \times 10^3$

6.3.5 Automatic transfer switch dielectric strength

In addition to current-carrying capabilities, automatic transfer switches must be able to withstand voltage surges to satisfy their reliability requirements. Control devices in an automatic transfer switch initiate the operation of transfer or retransfer and thus heavily affect the reliability of the switch. However, these control devices do not have the physical size and dielectric space inherent in the main load current-carrying parts of the switch. For this reason, it is important that high-quality products suitable for emergency equipment use are employed in the switch.

ANSI/UL 1008-1989 requires dielectric voltage withstand tests of 1000 V plus twice-rated voltage. But the requirements are unclear as to what specific devices are to be tested and whether or not control devices are to be included. ANSI/UL 1008-1989 requirements are intended mainly for safety, but to satisfy the reliability requirements of an emergency or standby power system, consideration should be given to additional surge protection depending on the exposure of the switch to voltage surges. Some considerations helpful in protecting the dielectric strength of an automatic switch are

— Arc-breaking capability to minimize flashover between sources and deterioration of dielectric.
— Contact construction to minimize heat generated at high currents.
— Readily accessible contacts and components for easy visual inspection and replacement.

Some common causes of voltage transients in ac systems that might affect automatic transfer switches are switching inductive loads, energizing and de-energizing transformers, and lightning and commutation transients. In most cases, it is impossible to eliminate all the causes of transients, and thus the transients themselves, so the next step is to assume they will occur and then take measures to protect sensitive equipment. It is recommended that transfer switches meet impulse withstand voltage test requirements as designated in ANSI/NEMA

ICS 1-1993 and voltage surge withstand capability as designated in IEEE Std C37.90-1989. This is particularly important if solid-state voltage and frequency sensing is used.

IEEE Std 141-1993 provides an in-depth analysis of causes and effects of various kinds of overvoltages.

6.3.6 Protection with circuit breakers

Principals of coordination and selectivity between the breakers and devices to be protected in the distribution system follow those of most typical systems (assuming adequate fault-current availability). Reliability of power to critical loads will depend on selective breaker tripping. Two areas of concern regarding breakers and automatic transfer switches are evident: protecting the switch according to its withstand rating and, at the same time, achieving proper selectivity for service reliability. Selectivity becomes more of a problem when transfer switching and overcurrent protection are combined as an integral unit. The integral protective device fault clearing characteristics must be known to allow coordination with external overcurrent devices.

Figures 6-4 and 6-5 show a simple illustration of a typical small system protected with circuit breakers. Complete coordination is achieved by employing time delay in the short time region on breakers A and B. The transfer switch is protected for any fault downstream of the switch by breakers B and C. In this case, the capability of the cable associated with the trans-

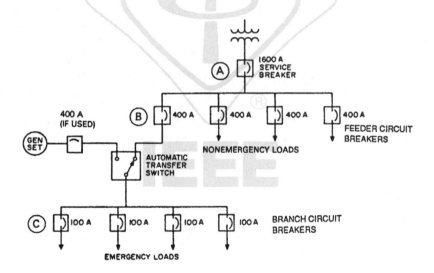

Figure 6-4—Emergency power system with circuit breakers

fer switch is the limiting factor and reduces the apparatus withstand rating. The switch by itself would have a higher rating. Also, in achieving coordination, the switch and associated wiring are required to withstand as much as 6 cycles of fault current for a fault between the switch and the branch breakers before the fault current is cleared in the short time region. The rating of this switch will accommodate this requirement if the fault current does not exceed

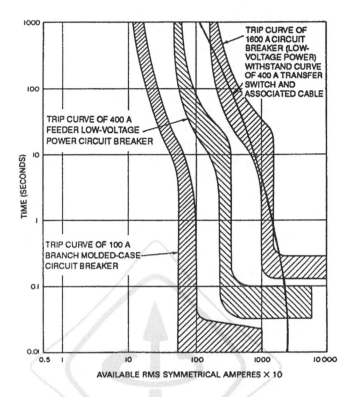

**Figure 6-5—Coordination chart of emergency power system
with circuit breakers**

20 000 A. An assumption in this illustration is that the generator will provide sufficient fault current to trip a branch breaker for a fault below one of these breakers. In most instances, available fault current from an emergency or standby generator will be substantially less than that of the normal source. When this is the case, the emergency or standby source should be located as close as possible to the critical load from a distribution standpoint to minimize the number of coordination levels and breaker sizes. As previously stated, proper selectivity in breaker operation is no different from that in most distribution systems. However, by investing in a time-delay trip feature for an upstream breaker, an additional advantage is gained in the selectivity in preventing nuisance starting of and transfer to the emergency or standby source.

When applying circuit breakers for protection, the transfer switch I^2t rating must correlate with the maximum clearing time of the breaker protecting it even with instantaneous tripping. For instance, it is possible for a transfer switch to have a withstand rating of 100 000 symmetrical amperes when used with a specific current-limiting fuse, but may only have a withstand rating of 30 000 symmetrical amperes when used with a specific circuit breaker with an instantaneous trip. The same reasoning applies for breakers with different fault-clearing times, especially considering time-delayed trips versus instantaneous trips. ANSI C37.16-1988 recognizes this by requiring reduced short-circuit interrupting ratings of circuit breakers for short-time delay applications. For example, a 225 A frame low-voltage power circuit breaker, with an instantaneous trip unit, has a 22 000 symmetrical amperes interrupting rating at 480 V. The same breaker without an instantaneous trip has a reduced rating of 14 000 symmetrical amperes at 480 V.

It is often difficult to predict future expansion with the present emphasis on cost-effective systems. It is especially difficult to justify added capital expenditures for speculated load growth. A situation not so unusual is for available short-circuit current to eventually exceed breaker and transfer switch interrupting and withstand ratings when the normal supply transformer bank is increased in rating to accommodate unexpected load growth. A solution is to add current-limiting fuses in line with the existing breakers in accord with UL series ratings to protect the equipment whose rating has been exceeded. The fuses should be applied in accordance with recommendations from the circuit breaker manufacturers. This offers an economical compromise of limiting short-circuit current and I^2t let-through and still maintaining some operating flexibility. However, coordination can be compromised. An alternative solution is to apply current-limiting reactors whereby overcurrent device coordination can be maintained, providing X/R ratios do not become excessive.

6.3.7 Protection with fuses

First cost often favors fuse application over circuit breakers. Another advantage is that fuses can safely interrupt higher short-circuit currents than breakers and with faster clearing times. A disadvantage is the requirement to replace fuses after fault clearing. Breakers offer an advantage where loads include three-phase motors, since their operation will not create a single-phase condition.

When fuses are used, peak let-through current and I^2t energy let-through should be coordinated with the same characteristics of the transfer switch to be protected. These characteristics vary among fuse manufacturers and types of fuses and, therefore, the manufacturer should be consulted for each particular fuse considered. Additionally, transfer switches may be rated for operation in series with a specific fuse for which they were tested. If another class of fuse with the same ampere rating and interrupting rating is substituted, the transfer switch could possibly fail under fault conditions if the substitute fuse permits a higher peak current and I^2t energy let-through. The same reasoning applies when comparing a current-limiting fuse to a circuit breaker equipped with an instantaneous trip with a clearing time as fast as 1-1/2 cycles. The circuit breaker will permit a higher peak current and I^2t energy let-through than the current-limiting fuse, which can clear in a fraction of a cycle.

Table 6-1 shows an example of necessary application data for certain types of transfer switches suitable for use with fuses by specifying the circuit test data and fuse classes. Table 6-5 illustrates an example of application data by specifying the peak current and I^2t let-through limits of certain kinds of switches. Again, these characteristics will vary among different manufacturers. In one case, the specific overcurrent protective devices are given along with the short-circuit test data, and in the other case the maximum limits of the switch ratings are given. The user can compare the switch capabilities with any type of fuse to be employed.

Figures 6-6 and 6-7 show the example system previously discussed with figures 6-4 and 6-5 except that current-limiting fuses are used instead of circuit breakers. The transfer switch has a specific maximum allowable peak let-through current rating. Peak let-through curves based on available fault current and the clearing time of the fuses in the current-limiting range are available from fuse manufacturers.

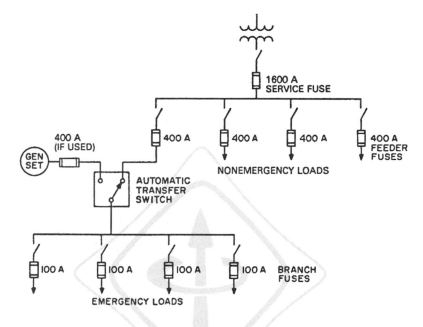

Figure 6-6—Emergency power system with fuses

6.3.8 Ground-fault protection

Although ground-fault protection of equipment is not normally required on the alternate source for emergency systems, ground-faults can occur on such systems and they can result in equipment burn-down. Because of the emergency nature of such systems, automatic disconnect in the event of a ground-fault is not required by code. However, detection of such a fault is desirable. It is good practice to provide an audible and visual signal device to indicate a ground-fault condition. Instructions should also be provided to advise what course of action should be taken in the event of a ground-fault indication. Additional consideration should be given to the possibility of a ground-fault on the load side of the transfer switch when energized from either source. For further discussion, see Chapter 7.

6.4 Generator protection

When an emergency generator is running, it supplies the power for critical loads. In this role it is the most critical and vital element in the power supply. Manufacturers may not always provide all the basic protection needs for generators and also leave options to choice by the

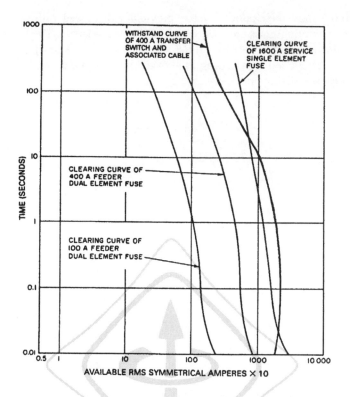

Figure 6-7—Coordination chart of emergency power system fuses

user. In any application, the user should evaluate his needs and the critical nature of the load before deciding on the best protection scheme. The protection scheme chosen should ensure reliability of this power source. Unlike applying standard practice in generator protection, a user should also rely on operating experience and sound-judgment in determining whether standard protection schemes allow the required reliability of emergency power. For instance, whether an installation is remotely or locally operated may determine if an audible or visual alarm will suffice in a condition where normally an automatic shutdown is used. Where power is extremely critical, it is wise to evaluate the consequences of loss of power to critical loads versus damage to the emergency power source. Caution should be exercised, however, when emphasizing reliability, to ensure that applicable codes and standards are not over-looked.

6.4.1 Codes and standards

Some codes and standards that address emergency or standby generator protection are listed in 6.11 as IEEE Std 141-1993, IEEE Std 242-1986, ANSI/NEMA MG 1-1993, NFPA 70-1996 (the NEC), EGSA 101P-1995.

6.4.2 Armature winding protection

Of most concern in winding protection is overcurrent, primarily from short circuits and over-loads. The basic protective devices employed are circuit breakers or fuses. But the size of the generator set can drastically influence the method of use and trip levels for such devices. Also, overvoltage protection needs will differ between large and small machines (that is, high-voltage and low-voltage ratings).

6.4.2.1 Overcurrent protection

The need for overcurrent protection for large machines is commonly taken for granted. For purposes of this chapter, these are machines that have enough mechanical and electrical stored energy, and thus available short-circuit current, to allow easy coordination between the generator and other load-side overcurrent protective devices. Overcurrent protection of the generator windings becomes important due to the cost of investment and also because protection will not seriously compromise reliability of the power supply to critical loads since over-current device selectivity is reasonably easy. Design of the protection scheme should follow standard practice, as a rule. Standard practice can vary from a single, simple, molded-case circuit breaker to a larger power circuit breaker with zone-selective interlocking. IEEE Std 242-1986 provides a useful guideline for recommended generator protection.

Smaller generator sets pose a more perplexing problem regarding available short-circuit cur-rent. These are machines with relatively little mechanical and electrical stored energy and typically low system X/R ratios, and under bolted fault conditions can slow down very rap-idly and have difficulty in supplying sustained fault current. This has been discussed, to some extent, in 6.2. Many users and specifiers of engine-generators often assume the need for a generator breaker for protection of the windings under short-circuit conditions. There are conditions where unregulated short-circuit current is capable of damaging a small generator. However, it is probable that the output of the generator, with a specified excitation system, will reduce to practically zero before any serious damage occurs. Even for separate excita-tion, the output can be specified to reduce to the full-load rating or less. This was illustrated in figure 6-1. In this sense, it is inherently protected and an overcurrent device serves little pur-pose in protecting the windings against short-circuit current. The dangers of assuming inher-ent protection are the uncertain conditions of unbalanced faults. For instance, excitation could be supplied from an unfaulted phase and unwanted sustained fault current could occur. If inherent protection is necessary, the user should specify this feature.

The initial per-unit fault current of a generator is $1/x''d$, where $x''d$ is the subtransient reac-tance of the generator and is determined from a short-circuit test of the generator. The initial short-circuit current induces very high currents in the field and damper windings of the rotor (8–10 times the no-load value is common). The generator losses under a fault condition, therefore, involve not just stator winding losses, but also field and damper losses, as well as extra stray load losses in both rotor and stator steel. It is possible for these losses to break couplings and tear loose generator mounts if the generator is not securely mounted. At the present time there are no reliable parameters available in the industry to determine the exact losses, but calculations based on the positive, negative, and zero sequence reactances and resistances will give approximate values. For a close analysis, these losses can be compared to the stored kinetic energy and the mechanical shaft energy input to determine the effect of a fault on generator speed.

In the discussions above for large and small generator sets, obvious consequences and effects of generator damage are assumed. In reality, the damaging effects of short-circuit current on a generator are difficult to determine. Even for a manufacturer, the actual limits of short-circuit current and duration are difficult to determine, since the tolerable damage can vary from slight reduction in insulation life to actual physical winding damage rendering the machine inoperative. For the mechanical strength of a generator ANSI/NEMA MG 1-1993 specifies that a generator be capable of withstanding without injury a three-phase fault at its terminals for 30 s when operating at rated kVA and power factor with fixed excitation for 5% overvoltage. The sustained current in this case is typically less than rated current, as evidenced in figures 6-1(a) and (b), and hence does not test the windings for heating damage. Requirements are also given for unbalanced fault conditions.

Assuming that any generator has an accurate damage curve readily available for use in coordination of overcurrent devices is erroneous. Of additional concern, is the allowance of an extra 25 °C rise in winding temperature for emergency or standby application of a generator, as designated in ANSI/NEMA MG 1-1993. Sometimes the regulator/exciter system is the limiting factor in a damage curve. For instance, a common specification for a generator set is that it sustains 3 pu fault current for 10 s ($I^2t = 90$). This may actually be a limit for the regulator and exciter whereby the stator winding is capable of more. Further inquiry will reveal that rotor heating becomes a limiting feature during unbalanced faults. Rotor heating is caused by the negative sequence current. ANSI/NEMA MG 1-1993 requires that generators withstand negative sequence current only to an I_2^2t value of 40. During a line-to-line fault, which produces the highest negative sequence current content, this translates to a total I^2t of 120. However, if the protection is set at $I_2^2t = 120$, a separate device would be needed to protect the excitation system, if the excitation system is the limiting factor in the 90 I_2^2t calculation. Therefore, little is to be gained in coordinating capabilities by raising the overcurrent setting above the total system limit. Through consultation with a manufacturer, assuring that all conditions are understood, a reasonably accurate time-current limit can be estimated.

To avoid confusion and misconception about damage limit curves, a better descriptive might be *capability* limit. This is reasonable considering cases where it is difficult to determine limits other than from standards such as ANSI/NEMA MG 1-1993. The manufacturer should be consulted in determining the capability of a generator since it should account for all components in identifying the weakest part. These components would include the stator, rotor, damper, and exciter windings. Semiconductors, as well as components of the regulator, should be included.

Thus, with fault-sustaining capability, the possibility exists for damage to the generator windings (and possibly to the prime mover) if the fault condition is allowed to exist too long. Figure 6-8 helps to illustrate this point. The figure shows an assumed generator capability curve based on 90 I^2t thermal limit and its relation to the fault-current decrement curves for a generator with and without an excitation system designed to maintain fault current. The figure does not represent an actual case, but simply illustrates the maximum level at which the generator protective device must operate to provide minimum protection for the generator. The

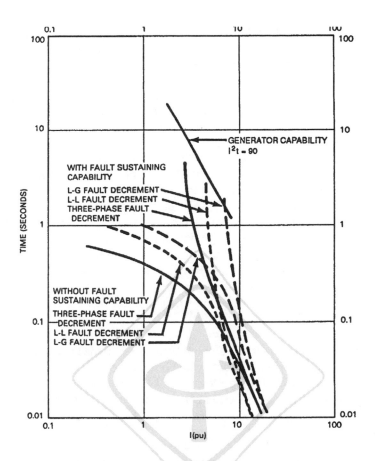

Figure 6-8—Generator balanced and unbalanced fault decrement curves relative to generator-capability curve

fault current available elsewhere in the system would have to be calculated since the engine-generator manufacturer can only provide information on available fault current at the generator terminals. Another observation, not normally evident without the use of fault-current decrement curves, is that the sustained fault currents for line-to-line and line-to-ground faults are typically higher than the three-phase value. When only the three-phase fault-current decrement curve is available, the user should be aware that the overcurrent devices must trip faster for line-to-line and line-to-ground faults.

When a main circuit breaker is to be used, an insulated case breaker or power breaker offers easy coordination with its adjustable tripping characteristics in long time delay, short time delay, and instantaneous ranges. However, molded-case breakers are smaller in size for a given rating. But without adjustable tripping characteristics, they are more difficult to coordinate with other overcurrent devices or with the generator-capability limits. Some electronic tripping devices offer constant I^2t characteristics that are suitable for generator protection. Relays offer either constant I^2t curves or extremely inverse curves which are a close approximation. Standard winding temperature detectors do not respond rapidly enough to provide this short-time thermal protection. Most fuses do not have a constant I^2t characteristic in the regions of the generator current, and so do not offer equal coordination with downstream breakers with variable generator fault currents as produced by different types of faults.

Proper selection and application of the overcurrent protective device will depend on the accuracy of the generator capability limit, available fault current, and the selected setting of the overcurrent device. Figure 6-9 shows an easy mistake to make in the application of a protective device. The generator in the example is rated 100 kW and 151 A at full load. A typical molded-case circuit breaker is applied at 125% of the generator rating, which assumes the load rating is equal to that of the generator. In this example, a 200 A breaker is selected. The dotted portion of the decrement curve shows that it would take at least 80 s for the breaker to initiate a trip for 3 pu sustained current, if the breaker does not trip in the instantaneous region. Thus the generator would have to have a pu I^2t rating of well over 720 to be adequately protected. And, of course, the long-time trip region of the breaker is well beyond an I^2t rating of 90, which in this case is the assumed protection limit of the generator. The fault decrement curve without short-circuit support (solid line) shows that the breaker's only chance of tripping is in the instantaneous region. Beyond 0.08 s the breaker will not pick up. However, since the current is well below the I^2t curve, the generator is inherently protected for this condition.

In the case illustrated by figure 6-9, if 3 pu fault current is provided by the generator, a better application of the same type circuit breaker could only be achieved if less than full-load rating of the generator is applied allowing a lower breaker trip setting in both the long-time and instantaneous regions. This requires a generator sized for more than the allowable load. Otherwise, a breaker with better and more extensive trip adjustments, or a properly rated fuse, should be applied.

As pointed out earlier, damage to a generator because of lack of an overcurrent protective device in the generator output can seriously affect its availability to serve its intended purpose. The problem often facing designers is whether or not a protective device adds reliability or decreases reliability. This is not always an easy analysis. However, when an overcurrent protective device is required for generator protection and is properly applied, it will not operate unless damage to the generator is imminent.

Differential relaying should be considered to identify internal faults when two generators are operated in parallel. This allows identifying the faulted machine with the relaying to operate the proper breaker. Overcurrent devices in the generator output alone would sense equal fault currents and both generators could be disconnected on the occurrence of a fault in only one generator. When more than two generators are applied in parallel operation, overcurrent devices on the generators' output can function selectively for internal faults since each would sense more fault current than the others. Automatic synchronizers will usually be employed for legally required systems or other systems where start-up time is critical. There should be an independent device to check the synchronizer's selected point of closure. The checking device should be of a quality that will not materially reduce system reliability. In addition, manual synchronizing should be available as a back-up, with a separate synchro-check device.

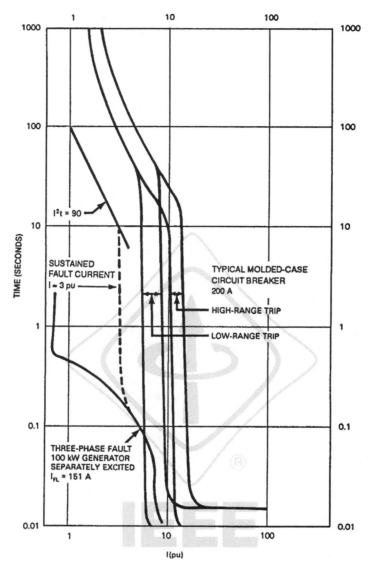

Figure 6-9—Misapplication of typical molded-case circuit breaker with limited short-circuit current

When the power system is grounded, the scheme employed warrants special attention. Multiple neutral ground connections can cause problems if ground current paths are not carefully designed. On large systems using special ground fault sensors for the generator protection, incomplete sensing or erroneous tripping can occur if the ground-fault current does not follow a predictable path. This problem is not so serious, as far as generator protection is concerned, on small systems that depend on a phase overcurrent device to operate on a ground fault. Likewise, with an ungrounded system ground currents are not a critical concern to generator overcurrent protection so long as proper detection is employed and single line-to-ground conditions are eliminated as soon as possible. Chapter 7 explores in detail various aspects of grounding and handling of the system neutral.

6.4.2.2 Overvoltage protection

Overvoltage protection of the main generator windings is a necessity sometimes taken lightly or even overlooked. Emergency and standby power systems and their associated distribution systems are relatively small in overall power rating and number of components compared to base-loaded systems (*normal* power supplies and distribution systems) and also often located well within the overall distribution system. Consequently, they are not usually subject to the same number and severity of overvoltage problems. But, because emergency and standby power must be reliable, if effectively applied, overvoltage protection should always be included in the design and application process. Certainly it would be an unusual case if an emergency generator were physically connected to an electric utility system such that it was subject to the same dangers of lightning transients. But other types of transient voltages from switching and restriking faults, for example, can be damaging and should be of concern.

Overvoltage protection is more critical for large generators with higher voltage ratings than for smaller ones with low voltage ratings (600 V). Protection of the investment is one reason, but another is the decreased margin of safety in the insulation as voltage ratings increase. That is, the ratio of insulating capacity to system voltage is normally higher for smaller units than for larger, higher voltage-rated units. ANSI/NEMA MG 1-1993, for instance, stipulates a suitable high potential test for armature windings of 1 000 V plus twice the rated voltage for most common types of ac generators. The test voltage for a 4160 V generator at this condition would be 12% higher than twice the rating. The test voltage for a 480 V generator would be about 100% higher than twice the rating.

Overvoltage conditions can be either of a transient nature or steady-state nature. The former is considered higher in magnitude and frequency, but of considerably less duration than the latter. Protection from each type of overvoltage condition is handled differently, but for the same reason: to preserve the integrity of the insulation. Although difficult to measure or calculate, any overvoltage condition, no matter how short the duration, will stress the insulation and shorten its life. So this is always a concern.

Protection against transient voltages is most commonly provided by surge arresters in combination with capacitors. But unless the transient is high, as it would be from a lightning strike, surge arresters are not always effective, although capacitors will attenuate a surge at any level. Switching surges would rarely reach the sparkover value of a lightning surge arrester. When an emergency or standby generator is situated to be subject to lightning-induced transients, surge arresters should be applied preferably at the generator terminals and, if necessary, at the boundaries of the exposed part of the system, such as at the ends of the exposed portion of an overhead line. The margin of safety is greatly influenced by the expected frequency and magnitude of the surges, something a designer would determine largely by judgment. Each occurrence of an overvoltage will shorten the insulation life of the windings with an inverse relation between the magnitude and allowable duration. The generator manufacturer can provide the necessary information on the withstand capability of the winding insulation.

This will aid in determining the upper limits of allowable overvoltage and duration. However, some additional margin of safety should be considered. IEEE Std 141-1993 suggests limiting the magnitude to approximately four fifths of the certified test voltage. The permissible rate of rise of the transient is suggested as no more than the 60 Hz high-potential test peak value at a uniform rise time of 10 µs. This rate of rise is controlled by the application of appropriate surge capacitors at the generator terminals.

Other types of transients, common to industrial and commercial systems, result from switching actions that force current to zero, which in turn generate a transient voltage from the rapid collapse of the magnetic field. This type of overvoltage can result from the operation of devices ranging from circuit breakers to SCRS. Even the opening of a circuit by a conductor burning itself free from a fault can produce a transient overvoltage. In ungrounded systems, the neutral is free to change its electrical reference to ground under certain conditions, which can. compound the transient effects of switching.

The most effective method of protecting an emergency generator from switching transients is careful design of the installation. Switching transients, as mentioned above, are rarely as severe as those from lightning and are not normally given the same consideration. Even though their occurrence can be more frequent than those from lightning, there is also more inherent protection within a distribution system, such as the number of cable circuits and connected equipment that act to greatly reduce the magnitude and slope of surge voltages. Grounding of a system neutral minimizes additional voltage-to-ground stress caused by switching surges and ground faults (especially restriking ground faults). Additionally, regardless of whether a system neutral is grounded or not, switching can cause overvoltage stress between windings from the oscillatory effect of voltage when a switch clears a fault. See IEEE Std 142-1991, Chapter 1.

IEEE Std 141-1993 provides a detailed analysis of the causes and effects of surge voltages along with recommended application practices that afford protection.

Steady-state overvoltage conditions are not as serious as transient overvoltages because of their lesser magnitude and because they are easier to control. They are of concern, however, because of their duration, and again it is emphasized, insulation life is shortened by these overvoltages. Some common causes are over-excitation, accidental contact with a higher voltage source (this can sometimes be of a transient nature), and shifting of the system neutral in ungrounded systems.

Overexcitation can result from unlimited control of an exciter and voltage regulator or excessive leading reactive power from external devices like capacitors that are designed only for use with the normal power supply. Accidental contact with a higher voltage source happens in rare cases. Perhaps as the result of insulation breakdown between a high and low winding in a transformer. In an ungrounded system, the neutral would be raised above ground reference by an amount equal to the high voltage and thus raise each phase above ground accordingly. The occurrence of this condition is so rare that deliberate measures to guard against it are rarely taken. Proper enclosures and shielding of the conductor systems provide a reasonable safeguard. In a grounded system, the ground of the secondary and primary (presuming the high-voltage side is physically referenced to ground) will complete a short-circuit path when the two voltage sources come in contact, allowing overcurrent devices to operate. An initial voltage transient is not prevented but the duration is minimized.

Shifting of a system neutral and corresponding phase overvoltage to ground under steady-state conditions in an ungrounded or resistance grounded system is caused from single line-to-ground faults. Ground detection serves to protect a generator from the deteriorating effects of overvoltage or a second internal or external ground fault, but only if prompt action is taken to correct the unbalance when it occurs. ANSI/NEMA MG 1-1993 and ANSI C50.10-1990 assure line-to-line voltage rating of the line-to-neutral winding in a wye-connected generator. Adherence with one of these standards should be specified.

6.4.2.3 Harmonics

The increased use of static power converters, fluorescent and high-intensity discharge lighting, adjustable frequency drives, and switching mode power supplies have brought with it an increased concern of the effects on emergency and standby power generators. Some of the most serious effects pertain to proper operation and quality of power. But, there is also cause for concern for generator protection. Some obvious concerns are as follows:

— High-frequency harmonies cause additional losses and heating in a generator. A significant portion of the losses occur in the rotor where heating is not measured.
— Overcurrent relays can become more sensitive because of the skin effect in the current-sensing elements. Electromechanical and static relays may have altered performances, with both the duration and amount of change following no predictable criteria. The overall result is that a relay may not operate as accurately as specifications show. NEMA AB 3-1991 provides information on the application of circuit-breakers with harmonic loads.
— Although little quantitative information exists on the effect of harmonics on circuit breakers and fuses, it is expected that their current-carrying capacity would be reduced, as heating of thermal elements is increased due to skin effect.

6.4.3 Rotor and excitation system

A field circuit breaker is a positive means of protecting the rotor and excitation system from damaging over currents due to external faults, underspeed, certain load conditions, or component failure within the excitation system. A field breaker, however, is not considered adequate protection by itself for the stator windings and should not replace an overcurrent device in the generator output, if one is required.

Solid-state exciter/regulator systems are commonly available. Common protection features include over- and under-excitation limiting, automatic voltage sensing between manual and automatic regulation circuits to allow smooth transfer from automatic to manual operation and vice versa, and failed rectifier detection.

In the brush-type machines (including those with static exciters) a field breaker may be located in the leads to the slip rings, in the field leads of an exciter, or in the regulator supply. On brushless generators only the last two locations are available, since the main rotor leads are not accessible. Location in the regulator power input is usually preferred since it provides short-circuit protection to the regulator and the regulator performs the field discharge function. In this position, the breaker may contain additional contacts that provide short-circuit protection for the voltage-sensing circuitry. Thus, excitation would be removed to prevent over-excitation when sensing is lost due to a fault or protective-device operation.

6.5 Prime mover protection

6.5.1 General requirements

The most direct form of overload protection, still maintaining some degree of reliability, would be load shedding. Depending on the severity of stability problems, circuit breaker status or frequency sensing might be used to initiate action. Instantaneous automatic load shedding where multiple generator sets are used, when one or more generators are lost, would assure available power for the remaining, more critical loads. On smaller systems, especially where only one generator is used, frequency sensing to shed load might provide a more reliable power supply if conditions do not always require load shedding. A combination of the two methods would allow a system to instantaneously shed selected loads, with frequency sensing employed as backup to shed additional load as necessary. It is common practice in some cases to employ underfrequency relays as secondary sensing devices to trip selected load breakers in multiple steps, with a time delay between each step. A stability study would determine frequency settings at each successive step. The study would also determine how fast load shedding should occur and thus determine the type and speed of equipment to be used. The scheme would normally be designed to maintain enough generation to prevent total blackout regardless of the load conditions.

Overload protection for a prime mover can also be aided by assuring that frequency sensitive voltage regulation is used. Maintaining a constant voltage-to-frequency ratio minimizes effects of overload and allows a unit to more easily regain normal voltage and frequency after an overload. The output voltage of the generating set would decrease in proportion to the frequency (prime mover speed). The use of a non-frequency-sensitive voltage reference could require, in some cases, a load reduction of from 50–60% to allow return to rated speed. Although some manufacturers can provide either type of voltage reference, it may be up to the user to specify his preference. Application of frequency sensitive voltage regulation, however, should not overshadow the importance of proper matching of generator or prime mover torque characteristics.

Reverse power relaying is an important form of protection for prime movers. It will prevent motoring when generator sets are operating in parallel and in another application prevents overload of a generator set by fast relaying when power flow is into an electric utility system. In prevention of generator motoring, the user should be aware that some prime movers are less susceptible to damage than others. Sensitivity is more critical, for instance, on turbines than reciprocating engines, and nuisance tripping can occur if this is not accounted for.

Protection against motoring of a prime mover guards against overheating or cavitation of blades on a turbine and possible fire or explosion from unburned fuel in a reciprocating engine. A relay to detect reverse power flow would normally be applied as backup protection to mechanical devices designed to detect these conditions. A time delay can be applied to prevent nuisance tripping on momentary reverse power surges such as may occur during synchronizing. Some typical values are listed below showing reverse power required to motor a generator when a prime mover is being spun at synchronous speed without input power:

— Condensing turbine: 3% of nameplate, in kilowatts
— Noncondensing turbine: 3% of nameplate, in kilowatts
— Diesel engine: 25% of nameplate, in kilowatts
— Hydraulic turbine: 0.2–2.0% of nameplate, in kilowatts

6.5.2 Equipment malfunction protection

Standard protective devices and numerous options are provided with prime movers by manufacturers. The equipment investment and nature of critical loads determine how to apply this protection. Some shutdown devices might be considered for alarm only, such as where installations are attended, and a malfunction can be quickly investigated. When it is determined that a shutdown is necessary for a malfunction condition, protection integrity can be maintained and power supply reliability enhanced if the malfunction is such that an alarm and subsequent shutdown can be employed.

High water temperature, high oil temperature, low oil pressure, overspeed, high exhaust temperature, and high vibration are typical examples of malfunctions that lend themselves to two-level protection as suggested above. On large machines, this is usually an insignificant investment to make. It is common practice in many installations and often required by machine manufacturers to also provide meters or displays for continuous monitoring of the above parameters by personnel on site or at remote locations. When remote controlled machines are located in areas not easily accessible, readouts of individual machine parameters become more significant. Cases have occurred where engines and turbines have been damaged because operating personnel with remote control capability restarted the units or continued operation of the units under malfunction conditions without knowing specifically which malfunctions existed.

Large generator sets requiring sophisticated and complex control systems often utilize uninterruptible power supply (UPS) systems for control power. Protection of power supplies of this nature is vital to the total machine protection.

Reciprocating engines and turbines require different philosophies for protection by nature of their design and operation. Smaller reciprocating engines typically have protection furnished for high water temperature, low oil pressure, overspeed, and failure to start. Larger units might also include high oil temperature, high vibration, antimotoring, and protection for complex control and excitation systems.

Protection for combustion turbines would add such protective devices as failure to light, failure to reach self-sustaining speed, and exhaust temperature limits and control. Overspeed and vibration are obviously more critical on turbines due to high-speed operation.

Electric motor-driven auxiliary equipment on large generator sets, such as lube oil pumps and cooling water pumps, are vital to the protection and reliability of the generator set. Reliability might be increased and protection maintained in locally operated critical installations by removing thermal overload trips from motor-control circuits and alarming only on an auxiliary motor overload. In this instance, lube oil temperature and levels, cooling water temperature, and auxiliary motor loading should be closely monitored to protect equipment investment.

6.5.3 Fuel system protection

The importance of protection for fuel systems needs very little explanation regarding the reliability of the power supply. For instance, it is obvious that low pressure and level alarms can prevent needless shutdown or failures of emergency generator sets requiring a high degree of reliability. Building codes and fire insurance regulations aid in determining optimum locations of self-contained fuel systems. Refer to Chapter 4 for storage recommendations and ANSI/NFPA 30-1993 for requirements on protection for fuel piping.

It should be noted that gasoline and diesel fuels can deteriorate if left standing unused for long periods of time. Some provision should be made for periodically burning or replacing the fuel at regular intervals and for treatment with appropriate additives.

6.6 Electric utility power supply

A second electric utility supply serving in a *standby* (*emergency*) role is typically protected no differently than if it were the *normal* (*preferred*) supply, except for the problems associated with connecting the two sources simultaneously. Usually this is intentionally prohibited by the equipment, but if not, the two sources must be in synchronism before being closed simultaneously (paralleled). However, if allowed, two sources may be operated continually in parallel to share the duty of providing power, with either one standing by to assume the entire load if the other source is lost. These may also be referred to as redundant sources.

Unlike the standby generator the standby utility source voltage is immediately available. If the load contains large motors these motors must be protected from the closing of the standby source when the residual voltage on the motors is out of phase with the standby source. If the transfer is initiated by loss of the normal source, the motors will have slowed and will become out of phase. Transfer will need to be delayed by timer or voltage relay until voltage has decayed to the acceptable level of 35%, as specified in ANSI/NEMA MG 1-1993. There is often some delay introduced to prevent transfer initiation by momentary dips in the utility voltage. If the transfer is to be between two sources both of which are at normal voltage, a "fast transfer" can be made if the two sources are first determined to be in phase. Alternately, a closed transition (momentary paralleling) transfer may be made. Refer to 4.3.8 for further discussion.

Switching from a standby power supply back to the normal supply would demand the same synchronizing requirements whether the standby source is an electric utility or an in-plant generator. In either case, closed or open transition can be employed depending on load requirements, and the issue of synchronizing would be the same.

Because of the exposure of an electric utility line to uncontrollable disturbances, this source is rarely employed as an *emergency* source, as defined in this standard. Therefore, special techniques and protective equipment to preserve reliability, such as those recommended for other in-plant emergency or standby sources, are not considered necessary or practical. Standard guidelines for protective equipment for electric utility ties are covered quite well in IEEE Std 242-1986. It will suffice to say that close cooperation between engineering representatives of the electric utility and user is necessary to assure the needs of each are clearly defined and understood. An accurate description of the load and its effects on the utility supply is essential in establishing proper protection of the supply while maximizing reliability. One additional important concern is that of ownership of the service equipment. If the user requires protection and control equipment not normally employed by the utility, he may choose to furnish and own the substation equipment to maintain this control. An electric utility may allow the customer to specify equipment not normally supplied by the electric utility, but require reimbursement for additional cost.

Protective schemes vary in complexity depending on the size, economic investment of the system, and consequences of power loss, but the objectives are the same. The utility supply must be protected from the effects of faults and abnormalities in the user's system and, conversely, the user's system must be protected against the possible adverse conditions in the electric utility system.

Protection against ground faults raises special issues. Ground-fault sensing can be a problem if not carefully planned; see Chapter 7 for methods and considerations in handling ground faults.

6.7 Uninterruptible power supply (UPS) system

The basic components of a static UPS system are the battery, rectifier or battery charger, inverter, and often a static transfer switch. Technically, a motor-generator set is also a UPS system, but is often referred to as a mechanical stored energy or rotary system. The discussion here is limited to the static UPS system.

6.7.1 Battery protection

Batteries provide the source of emergency or standby power in the application of a UPS system. The reliability of the system will heavily depend on the protection provided for the battery. Much of the protection provided is inherent in good maintenance practice as discussed in Chapter 8, but the importance of this subject warrants further discussion in this subclause.

Lead-acid batteries are especially susceptible to adverse effects from both being undercharged and overcharged. Continual undercharging promotes lead sulfate buildup, which reduces battery capacity. Overcharging causes gassing of vented cells and heating of valve-regulated cells. A lead-antimony battery experiences objectionable water consumption if a float voltage is too high and thus reduced battery life. Lead-calcium batteries are less susceptible to high water consumption.

Most battery specifications and recommendations are based on an ambient temperature of 77 °F (25 °C). Float charging or equalize charging a lead-acid battery in an ambient temperature higher than this *optimum* value can reduce battery life below its designed life if the voltage is not reduced accordingly. Typical recommended float voltages for fully charged lead-acid batteries are shown in the following table. However, in any specific installation a manufacturer's recommended values are the preferred choice.

Battery	Volts per cell
Lead-antimony	2.15–2.17
Planté	2.17–2.19
Lead-calcium 1.215 sp gr 1.250 sp gr 1.300 sp gr	2.17–2.25 2.23–2.33 2.28–2.37

When equalize charging by constant voltage is necessary to bring all cells to an acceptable charge state, a voltage level higher than a normal float voltage is used (provided the voltage level does not exceed the maximum tolerable level for connected loads). Equalize charging has a protection benefit for lead-antimony batteries because it counteracts the degradation of natural transfer of antimony from the positive to negative plate in an undercharged battery. An equalize charge maintains the integrity of a battery, but should not be applied longer than necessary. The worst condition for hydrogen evolution is forcing maximum current into a fully charged battery. Some recommended voltages and time periods for equalizing lead-acid batteries are shown in the following tables. These values are based on cell temperatures in the range of 70 °F (21 °C) to 90 °F (32 °C). As with the recommended values of float voltages in the table above, manufacturers should be consulted for specific or unusual installations and especially for charging requirements for other temperatures. Additionally, charging equipment should be evaluated as to whether it is ambient temperature compensated, thus accounting for different cell temperatures.

Lead-antimony and Planté	
Volts per cell	Time (hours)
2.24	80
2.27	60
2.30	48
2.33	36
2.36	30
2.39	24

Lead-calcium			
Volts per cell	Time (hours)		
	1.215 sp gr	1.250 sp gr	1.300 sp gr
2.24	222	—	—
2.27	166	—	—
2.30	105	—	—
2.33	74	166	—
2.36	50	118	200
2.39	34	80	134
2.42	—	54	91
2.45	—	36	62
2.48	—	—	42

The initial charging of a lead-acid battery after shipment or installation is very much like equalize charging after a discharge. The difference is that the time period is longer—typically twice as long.

An important protection feature for a lead-calcium battery is correct sizing of the ampere-hour capacity. A lead-calcium battery cannot take deep discharges, so control of the discharge end voltage is more critical than for other battery types.

Nickel-cadmium (NICAD) batteries, because of their construction and chemical composition, are more tolerable to high charge rates and high ambient temperatures than lead-acid batteries. However, overcharging (continued charge current after full charge reached) still causes oxygen and hydrogen evolution. A sealed cell would experience pressure buildup and temperature rise.

A vented cell would experience gassing and loss of water from the electrolyte. Approximate charge voltages per cell related to battery temperature are shown in figure 6-10 for vented-cell NICAD batteries.

The detrimental effects of overcharging batteries are compounded with high ambient temperatures that add to the increased temperature resulting from charging. High temperature increases water consumption by evaporation, and the resulting increased charging current from high temperature causes more water consumption through oxygen and hydrogen evolution. Acid fumes from lead-acid batteries corrode terminals (and other equipment in close proximity). Hydrogen evolution can create an explosive atmosphere if the area is not adequately ventilated. Sealed cells can build up dangerous pressures if temperature is too high. For these reasons, controlling ambient temperature may be the single best protection for preserving battery integrity and maximizing life.

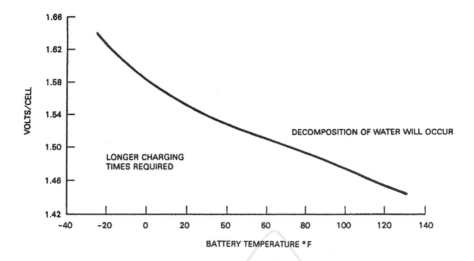

**Figure 6-10—Charge voltage versus temperature
for vented-cell NICAD batteries**

When the environmental conditions, such as ambient temperature, cannot be controlled adequately, chargers should be equipped with the ability to automatically compensate for temperature changes by reducing charge potential with increasing temperature. Some battery manufacturers incorporate devices within the cells of the battery to protect against the effects of overcharging and over-discharging. For instance, semiconductor devices can be used to shunt part of the charging current if voltage and temperature become uncoordinated or they can prevent cell polarity reversal on excessive discharge.

Good practice would be to maintain the battery environment between 60 °F (16 °C) and 90 °F (32 °C) with the optimum temperature at or near 77 °F (25 °C). The battery area should be adequately ventilated to prevent hydrogen buildup with exhaust to the outside atmosphere. Under normal conditions, the lower explosive limit of hydrogen mixed with air is 4%, so ventilation should be adequate to ensure a mixture well below this level. Internal gases in the cell can also ignite from an external ignition source. If this can be a problem, consideration should be given to installing *explosion-resistant vents* to prevent this ignition. Cells should be located so that an even distribution of temperature between cells is possible. Outside devices that might cause concentrated sources of heat to some cells should be avoided in the location of the battery.

An area of battery protection often omitted is overcurrent protection. Because of the usual critical nature of a battery, overcurrent protection for the battery and its cables may be considered as adversely affecting reliability. However, a designer should be aware that without fast overcurrent protection a battery can be damaged and, in some cases, the battery cable may inadvertently be the only fuse protection available. A battery sized for 50 A for 2 h might be capable of 2000 A of short-circuit current. The short-circuit current available from a battery is the voltage rating of the battery divided by the resistance between the battery terminals; more simply, it is the cell voltage divided by the internal resistance of the cell as expressed by the formula

$$I_{sc} = \frac{\text{voltage per cell}}{\text{internal resistance per cell}}$$

The internal resistance of a cell is not normally published in most literature available from manufacturers. If this is the case, consult manufacturers for this information. A useful guide in estimating the internal resistance of a battery or cell is by the use of the two rated end voltages along with the rated current at each of these voltages. For best results the time period chosen to obtain these voltage and current values should be short, typically 1 min or less. With this information, the internal resistance R between the points of voltage measurement (such as individual cell or the whole battery) is simply

$$R = \frac{\Delta E\,(1\ \text{min})}{\Delta I\,(1\ \text{min})}$$

or

$$R = \frac{E_1 - E_2}{I_2 - I_1}$$

As an example, assume a 200 Ah lead-acid battery is being considered. Specifications show 382 A for 1 min to an end voltage of 1.75 V/cell and 748 A for 1 min to an end voltage of 1.50 V/cell. The cell internal resistance R is estimated by

$$R = \frac{1.75 - 1.50}{748 - 382} = 0.000683\ \Omega$$

The battery nominal voltage should be used when calculating the maximum short-circuit current. Tests have shown that an increase in electrolyte temperature (above 25 °C) or elevated battery terminal voltage (above nominal voltage) will have no appreciable effect on the magnitude of short-circuit current delivered by a battery.

Elevated battery terminal voltage during float and equalize charge does not increase the chemical energy available from the battery during a short circuit. The effective voltage driving the short-circuit current is dependent of the acid concentration in direction contact with the active material in the plates of the cell. Therefore, the battery nominal voltage should be used in calculating the maximum short-circuit current.

In this example, the short circuit, I_{sc}, available at a nominal 2.00 V/cell is

$$I_{sc} = \frac{2.00}{0.000683} = 2928\ \text{A}$$

When the discharge characteristics are presented as "per positive plate" values, the above calculation for R will result in ohms per positive plate. This value must be divided by the number of positive plates (plates connected in parallel) to obtain the cell resistance.

For the purpose of determining the maximum available dc short-circuit current (e.g., the required withstand and interrupting capability of the distribution buses and disconnecting devices), the total short-circuit current at its source is the sum of that delivered by the battery, charger, and motors (as applicable).

In current-limited chargers, the current-limiting circuits will typically act to reduce the current after the first zero crossing (i.e., 1/2 cycle, 8 ms or less) if internal protective devices, such as rectifier fuses, have not already acted to clear the fault. It is therefore conservative to assume that the maximum sustained fault current after 8 ms is the current-limiting value, a current not greater than the charger current-limit rating.

Tests on some current-limited SCR-type battery chargers have shown that the initial short-circuit current can exceed the current-limit value. A large transient current spike may occur due to the stored energy in filter circuits (capacitors). This peak short-circuit current may approach a value 200 times the charger rated value. However, the time of duration of the initial transient is so short (in the order of 5 μs) that it need not be considered in determining the required interrupting capability of external protective devices or the withstand rating of buses. After the stored energy in the filter circuits is dissipated, the magnitude of the transient short-circuit current is dependent on the X/R ratio of the ac supply as well as the inductance and resistance of the transformer-rectifier-fault circuit.

The fault current from a large lead storage battery resulting from a bolted short at the battery terminals will typically exhibit a rate-of-rise that delivers the peak current within 17 ms. The fault current for a short at the dc distribution switchgear or panelboard will peak later (typically within 34–50 ms), due to the inductance of the dc system in series with the fault. The magnitude of the fault current for a short at the distribution bus will also be lower than the value at the battery due to the resistance of the cables between the battery terminals and the bus.

For a typical dc system, the short-circuit current from the charger will already peak and decay before the short-circuit current from the battery reaches its peak. Due to this battery time constant, the maximum coincident short-circuit current can be conservatively calculated as the sum of that from the battery and that from the charger.

Dc motors, if operating, will contribute to the total fault current. The maximum current that a dc motor will deliver at its terminals is limited by the effective transient armature resistance r_d of the range of 0.1–0.15 per unit. Thus, the maximum fault current for a fault at the motor terminals will typically range from 7–10 times the motors rated armature current. Therefore, it is conservative to estimate the maximum current that a motor will contribute is 10 times the motor's rated full-load current. When a more accurate value is required, the short-circuit current should be calculated using specific rd data or from test data obtained from the motor manufacturer. (The reference for this information is IEEE Std 946-1992. For additional information, see IEEE Std 666-1991 [B13].)

Loads supplied by UPS systems are critical and low-voltage alarms are necessary to alert personnel when the power supply integrity is in danger, so this protection feature is recommended with any type of battery system. However, a lead-acid battery is especially susceptible to damage if excessively discharged, so a low-voltage alarm serves to protect the battery as well as the load.

6.7.2 Battery charger protection

Overcurrent protection for a battery charger, like most devices, should account for both overload and short-circuit conditions. In the case of a charger, the current required in charging a severely discharged battery can easily cause overload conditions aside from the inverter load. Simple overload protection should allow for the charging requirements of a battery.

To charge a battery that has been discharged to any large extent requires that the charger output current be regulated to stay within acceptable limits. This protects both the charger and the battery. Of particular concern in a charger is the rectifier circuit, especially if it is connected directly to the output. Current ratings should be known in order to assure good protection.

Most chargers are provided with a current-limiting feature for protection. Not all chargers have the same current-limiting characteristics. A user should evaluate the particular charger under consideration and the short-circuit characteristics of its output to assure proper overcurrent protection. Some chargers have current limiting features designed primarily for protection in charging a discharged battery. Other simple overload conditions would also be protected against. However, the charger may not be able to withstand a bolted fault on its output. The fault current at zero voltage could easily be higher than the charger's current-limit value. In this case, additional output protection is needed, such as breakers or fuses, unless the charger is equipped to automatically shut down when a dead short occurs. Some charger specifications include current limiting designed to allow withstand of a dead short on the output, even continually. In this case, an output breaker or fuse adds flexibility but is only redundant for short-circuit protection.

Regardless of the reason for a condition of current limiting, if it is expected to occur frequently or for long durations, consideration should be given to adding thermal protection in addition to the current limiting feature. Some chargers are equipped with a thermal circuit that automatically reduces output current if a predetermined temperature is exceeded.

If heavy inrush currents are possible (loads other than battery-charging current), a problem with the charger going into current limiting or tripping of the output protective device can occur. This can affect the applied load by dropping all or part of it off-line. Some chargers can be equipped to allow gradual load application to prevent nuisance tripping or current limiting.

A protective device on the ac input to the charger is also necessary to protect the charger from extensive damage from internal faults. Manufacturers provide charger input ratings making protective device ratings easy to determine.

Optional protective devices that would usually be supplied with a battery charger, although not necessarily part of the protection scheme for the charger alone, should also be mentioned here. Ground detection with light indication or voltmeter readout can be supplied for ungrounded dc systems. High and low dc voltage relays serve to protect the load and charger. High-voltage detection serves to protect semiconductors, since high-voltage increases leakage current which increases temperature. On some chargers an ac power failure disconnect relay can be furnished to open the input circuit of the charger and thus protect the battery from unnecessary discharge back through the charger.

6.7.3 Inverter protection

Protecting an inverter from overcurrent conditions and still maintaining a reliable power supply to critical loads takes careful planning and evaluation of the load and power supply requirements. An inverter is considered a soft source in that it normally does not have abundant short-circuit current capability. Protecting the output allows very little tolerance between the inverter rating and protective-device rating, but at the same time normal inrush currents must be tolerated.

Like battery chargers, inverters also are commonly supplied with current-limiting capability for protection. This adds to the difficulty in sizing branch circuit overcurrent devices because they must operate fast enough on branch circuit faults to prevent current-limiting action by the inverter and still allow enough flexibility for inrush currents. Typical ratings of an inverter might be 125% of full load for 10 min and 150% of full load for 10 s. Often this is sufficient for selective coordination of branch circuit devices if the load is distributed among a sufficient number of branch circuits. Still, high-speed fault clearing is likely necessary to prevent inverter current limiting. For example, the inverter would start current-limiting action at 150% of its rating (some inverters would start limiting current before this value is reached), so branch circuit overcurrent devices must be set well below this value. This could pose a problem even for fuses if they are designed for the inrush requirements of some inductive loads.

Manufacturer's overload ratings for inverters state the output magnitude and duration possible without damage. It is possible for an overload to exist without reaching the current-limit action but still exceed the magnitude and time overload rating of the inverter. These ratings can easily be plotted on a time-current graph allowing proper device tripping characteristics to be compared and applied. A branch circuit overcurrent device should be given careful consideration to assure a low-level fault or overload will not go undetected before exceeding the inverter rating. Figure 6-11 shows a problem commonly encountered. The branch circuit overcurrent device in figure 6-11 is assumed to be a standard molded-case circuit-breaker with a 15 A trip rating. This trip rating is in the range of settings often selected for a distribution system of the size suggested by the inverter ratings. It would be desirable for the tripping characteristic of the breaker to fall under the limits for an inverter to assure protection. A problem occurs with inadequate protection of the 10 kVA inverter, in this example, in the short-time region. However, the 15 kVA inverter is protected by the 15 A circuit-breaker. Smaller trip ratings for the branch breakers (or possibly a different overcurrent device with better suited tripping characteristic) used with the 10 kVA inverter would help the protection problem. An alternate course would be to employ the larger inverter. This might be the best solution when loads cannot be distributed between enough branches to reduce overcurrent device ratings.

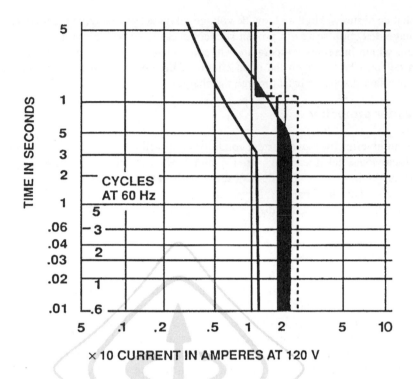

Source: Potts, Charles D., "A User's Guide to UPS Protection," IEEE Technical Paper No. 89-37, presented at the IEEE IAS Annual Meeting, 1989.

Figure 6-11—Inverter protection—15 A branch breaker

One solution to this problem of preserving the integrity of the power supply to the load is a design allowing the static transfer switch to switch to the alternate ac supply on fault or heavy inrush current conditions. The alternate supply would have the short-circuit capability to easily allow clearing of the fault or the inrush current requirements and then automatic retransfer to the inverter would take place. This alleviates the problem of precise coordination of the branch circuit overcurrent device with the current-limiting action of the inverter. It should be understood, however, that if the alternate ac source is not available at the time of necessary transfer, the inverter will go into current limiting, if it has this feature, and all loads will be affected if the faulted branch circuit does not clear. If the UPS system is designed for total dependency on transfer to the alternate source for branch circuit overcurrent conditions (that is, current-limiting feature not provided), the inverter will shut down, trip off, or be damaged and, again, all of the load will be affected.

The reliability required of the power supply for the load will determine how the distribution system is designed and the type of protection provided for the UPS system. There are various ways to protect the inverter from overcurrent, but for each, reliability is affected to some extent. High-speed semiconductor fuses can be applied at the inverter output, but this makes coordination with branch circuit overcurrent devices difficult, if not impossible. These fuses could be applied to the branch circuits to make fast clearing of branch circuit faults possible.

The main disadvantage here is the high cost of these fuses. As mentioned above, available short-circuit capacity can sometimes be a problem. An oversized inverter would help to alleviate this problem but, again, investment cost would be high. Applying a transfer scheme to automatically transfer high inrush currents and short-circuit currents to an alternate power supply offers a relatively simple approach to overcurrent protection. This makes selective coordination of overcurrent devices much easier. This protects the inverter and, in short-circuit conditions, allows isolation of the faulted circuit, thus minimizing the disturbance.

Even though inverters are provided with current-limiting action, they are not always rated to tolerate short-circuit conditions. To protect against the event of an alternate ac source not being available to handle short-circuit current conditions, an overcurrent device should be provided in the inverter output. Since fuses are generally faster than breakers, they should be given first consideration. However, since semiconductor devices are involved, even a fuse cannot guarantee preventing all damage, but it can assure minimizing the damage. Another overcurrent condition that should be protected against on the output is out-of-phase switching.

Another common problem in the application of UPS systems is inadequate ventilation for the inverter. Inverters generate a considerable amount of heat and some means of removing this heat should be provided. Good ventilation is the best method of preventing overheating. The installation design should assure that this ventilation is not blocked, and personnel should be made aware of the danger to the inverter if ventilation is blocked. Each inverter has a maximum operating temperature rating, and exceeding this temperature should be prevented. Inverters can also overheat under prolonged short-circuit conditions even though they may be rated to withstand a continuous short circuit on their output. Thermal cutouts can be provided to protect against this heating effect. Rare cases have even been reported where overheating occurred at no-load conditions.

Input overcurrent devices for inverters will minimize damage caused by internal faults. Again, fuses should be given first consideration for high-speed clearing. Another source of high current in the input protected against by fuses or breakers is an accidental reverse polarity connection. An important option offered for most inverters is a low-input voltage alarm. Since the input is connected to batteries in a UPS and to the output of a battery charger, the possibility always exists for low-input voltage. The inverter can only maintain a specified voltage at its output if the input is within specified limits. Strictly speaking, this feature provides protection for the battery against excessive discharge, but it also provides protection for the load against the adverse effects of low voltage, especially if transfer to an alternate ac source is initiated when the output low-voltage limit is reached.

6.7.4 Static transfer switch protection

Protecting a static transfer switch from excessive overcurrent requires coordination of the switch rating with the available fault current from the ac supply with the highest available fault current. Static transfer switches commonly have a short-circuit rating at least 1000% of the continuous rating for 1–5 cycles. This is more than adequate for the fault-current availability of an inverter, but careful overcurrent device setting will be required when the fault current is from a larger alternate source. Again, since semiconductor devices are involved, fast fuse operation is necessary for adequate protection. Another feature that adds protection to the switch is fast removal of gating voltage, which effectively opens the switch. Most commonly, switches are protected by applying the overcurrent device on the input side. The manufacturer or UPS supplier should be consulted for static transfer switch withstand ratings for proper application of overcurrent protection.

Even though the inverter source is not likely to supply a lot of short-circuit current, especially if it goes into current limiting on a short circuit, an inverter output protective device serves also to protect the static switch. This can be the case when a fault occurs on the load side of the switch (or an overload) and the alternate source is unavailable for transfer.

A rating of 1000% for 1 cycle, along with semiconductor fuse ratings (when fuses are applied to project SCRs, for example) can be coordinated with the overcurrent device in the branch circuit. See figure 6-12.

6.7.5 Overvoltage protection

As previously stated, the basic components of a UPS system are the battery, a rectifier or battery charger, inverter, and often a static transfer switch. These devices contain semiconductors making protection uniquely different from that of more tolerant equipment, such as motors, generators, transformers, electromechanical transfer switches, etc. In dealing with semiconductors, surge protection becomes a critical application criteria. Simply increasing insulation thickness and dielectric strength is not feasible because of the necessary properties of the devices, so effective protection must be applied externally. Sources of surges and transients are many, and without proper protection semiconductors can be easily damaged. Even if the damage is not visible, they can be stressed such that their life is drastically shortened. Even a relay coil can produce a surge in the order of thousands of volts under fast-contact current-interrupting action if it is not itself equipped with surge suppression such as a diode or varistor to handle the steep wavefront and high-frequency surge associated with the interruption.

Equipment manufacturers are usually best suited to determine proper surge protection for the semiconductors in their equipment. However, they cannot always be accurate in their assessment of the application of the equipment. Even though surge protection may be standard with some manufacturers, the source and magnitude of possible voltage transients and application conditions are often underestimated. It is not uncommon for a surge suppressor to be damaged if operating conditions allow the suppressor to be subjected to steady-state voltages exceeding its rating. If the user supplies this type of protection, he must know the dielectric strength of the semiconductors to be protected to determine the rating of the surge suppressor.

There are many types of surge suppressors available with different operating characteristics. Some are fast acting but may allow a higher let-through voltage than another that is slower acting but capable of lower threshold settings. Some of the more expensive surge suppressor packages employ a combination of both characteristics for improve.d protection.

Isolating transformers provide some measure of surge protection because of the physical isolation effect on circuits. But because of their magnetic coupling and distributed capacitance

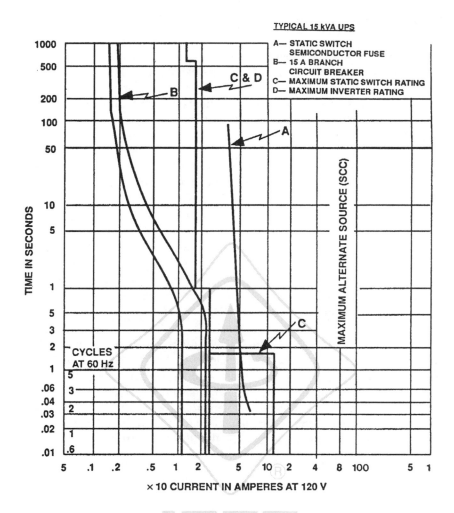

Source: Potts, Charles D., "A User's Guide to UPS Protection," IEEE Technical Paper No. 89-37, presented at the IEEE IAS Annual Meeting, 1989.

Figure 6-12—Static transfer switch fuse and branch breaker coordination

between windings, they are not perfect isolators and often additional surge protection is required. So-called *line conditioners* offer the best protection in that they provide line isolation, surge protection, high-speed voltage regulation, and, in some cases, a degree of waveshape filtering for protection against harmonic distortion, all in an integrated package.

Methods used in grounding equipment cabinets affect the magnitude of insulation stress to ground especially when equipment is exposed to high transients typical of lightning strikes. The inductive voltages (due to inductance of grounding conductors) can stress equipment insulation. Shortening ground conductor lengths or paralleling ground conductors, or both, are effective methods in reducing the inductance of ground circuits. Each installation will be unique in proper procedures for adequate protection and personnel safety.

6.8 Equipment physical protection

Engine-generator sets and fuel supplies and their associated equipment require careful planning in application to prevent damage from physical abuse and environmental conditions. Radiator cooling on engines should be given special consideration, when possible, since a self-contained cooling system does not require external piping connections that could be subject to damage. Some climates, such as where dust is prevalent, require that air inlet filters be of special design.

Most other devices and equipment discussed previously, when applied in emergency and standby use, are usually located where only qualified personnel have access. When this is not possible, enclosures should be designed to prevent easy access. Provisions for locking enclosures with hinged panels and doors can easily be supplied by most manufacturers. Manufacturers should also be thoroughly knowledgeable of the location and environmental conditions for application of proper enclosures, materials, and seismic protection. For example, corrosive or humid atmospheres may require heaters or special coating or materials to protect exposed metal parts or circuits. Locations in proximity to large reciprocating machinery might require special seismic protection. Fuel systems require special consideration in protection from leaks, contaminants, etc.

Manufacturers can usually provide suitable racks for batteries that provide protection and easy maintenance. It is important to have properly sized racks that space cells to minimize overheating and corrosion problems, allow easy maintenance, and still utilize available space in an optimum manner. Connections between cells should minimize strain on battery posts. Manufacturers can also assist in designing installations for extreme seismic conditions, such as where earthquakes are a problem. Additional information on installation and environmental conditions can be found in Chapter 5 of ANSI/NFPA 110-1993.

6.9 Grounding

Reliable ground fault protection schemes require a careful analysis of the system- and equipment-grounding arrangements. Chapter 7 covers the basic functions and requirements for system and equipment grounding. Several grounding arrangements that are applicable to emergency and standby power systems are illustrated in Chapter 7.

6.10 Conclusions

Protection of emergency and standby power systems determines to a great degree the reliability of the systems. Although the total system should be considered in the protection scheme, overall system protection and reliability is only as good as that of the individual components. With emphasis on protecting power supply investment, a designer must assure that the desired reliability of the system is achieved. The designer should carefully evaluate standard and optional protection supplied with equipment and apply the design best suited for equipment protection and power supply reliability.

6.11 References

This chapter shall be used in conjunction with the following publications:

ANSI C37.16-1988, American National Standard Preferred Ratings, Related Requirements, and Application Recommendations for Low-Voltage Power Circuit Breakers and AC Power Circuit Protectors.[3]

ANSI C50.10-1990, American National Standard for Rotating Electrical Machinery—Synchronous Machines.

ANSI/NEMA ICS 1-1993, Industrial Control and Systems General Requirements.[4]

ANSI/NEMA MG 1-1993, Motors and Generators.

ANSI/NFPA 30-1993, Flammable and Combustible Liquids Code.[5]

ANSI/NFPA 110-1993, Emergency and Standby Power Systems.

ANSI/UL 1008-1989, Safety Standard for Automatic Transfer Switches.[6]

CSA C22.2/No. 178-1987 (Reaff 1992), Automatic Transfer Switches.[7]

EGSA 101P-1995, Performance Standards: For Engine Driven Generator Sets.[8]

IEEE Std C37.13-1990, IEEE Standard for Low-Voltage AC Power Circuit Breakers Used in Enclosures (ANSI).[9]

IEEE Std C37.26-1972 (Reaff 1990), IEEE Guide for Methods of Power-Factor Measurement for Low-Voltage Inductive Test Circuits (ANSI).

IEEE Std C37.90-1989, IEEE Standard for Relays and Relay Systems Associated with Electric Power Apparatus (ANSI).

---

[3]ANSI publications are available from the Sales Department, American National Standards Institute, 11 West 42nd Street, 13th Floor, New York, NY 10036, USA.

[4]NEMA publications are available from the National Electrical Manufacturers Association, 2101 L Street NW, Washington, DC 20037, USA.

[5]NFPA publications are available from Publications Sales, National Fire Protection Association, 1 Batterymarch Park, P.O. Box 9101, Quincy, MA 02269-9101, USA.

[6]UL publications are available from Underwriters Laboratories, Inc., 333 Pfingsten Road, Northbrook, IL 60062-2096, USA.

[7]CSA publications are available from the Canadian Standards Association (Standards Sales), 178 Rexdale Blvd., Rexdale, Ontario, Canada M9W 193.

[8]EGSA publications are available from the Electrical Generating Systems Association, 10251 W. Sample Rd., Suite B, Coral Springs, FL 33065.

[9]IEEE publications are available from the Institute of Electrical and Electronics Engineers, 445 Hoes Lane, P.O. Box 1331, Piscataway, NJ 08855-1331, USA.

IEEE Std C37.95-1989, IEEE Guide for Protective Relaying of Utility-Consumer Interconnections (ANSI).

IEEE Std 141-1993, IEEE Recommended Practice for Electric Power Distribution for Industrial Plants (IEEE Red Book) (ANSI).

IEEE Std 142-1991, IEEE Recommended Practice for Grounding of Industrial and Commercial Power Systems (IEEE Green Book) (ANSI).

IEEE Std 242-1986, IEEE Recommended Practice for Protection and Coordination of Industrial and Commercial Power Systems (IEEE Buff Book) (ANSI).

IEEE Std 946-1992, IEEE Recommended Practice for the Design of DC Auxiliary Power Systems for Generating Stations (ANSI).

NFPA 70-1996, National Electrical Code®.

6.12 Bibliography

Additional information may be found in the following sources:

[B1] ANSI C97.1-1972 (Reaff 1978), American National Standard Low-Voltage Cartridge Fuses 600 Volts or Less.[10]

[B2] ANSI/NEMA ICS 2-1993, Industrial Control and Systems, Controllers, Contractors, and Overload Relays Rated Not More Than 2000 Volts AC or 750 Volts DC.

[B3] ANSI/UL 198B-1995, Safety Standard for Class H Fuses.

[B4] ANSI/UL 198C-1986, Safety Standard for High-Interrupting Capacity Fuses, Current-Limiting Types.

[B5] ANSI/UL 198D-1995, Safety Standard for Class K Fuses.

[B6] ANSI/UL 198E-1995, Safety Standard for Class R Fuses.

[B7] ANSI/UL 198H-1988, Safety Standard for Class T Fuses.

[B8] ANSI/UL 489-1991, Molded-Case Circuit Breakers and Circuit-Breaker Enclosures.

[B9] Castenschiold, R., Goldberg, D.L., Johnston, F.C., and O'Donnell, P., "New Rating Requirements for Automatic Transfer Switches," *IEEE Conference Record*, Paper no. 78CH1302-91A, June 1978.

---

[10]ANSI C97.1-1972 has been withdrawn; however, copies can be obtained from the American National Standards Institute, 11 West 42nd Street, 13th Floor, New York, NY 10036, USA.

[B10] Castenschiold, R., "Plant Engineer's Guide to Understanding Automatic Transfer Switches," *Plant Engineering*, Mar. 3, 1983.

[B11] IEC 947-6-1: 1989, Low-voltage switchgear and controlgear—Part 6: Multiple function equipment. Section One—Automatic transfer switching equipment.[11]

[B12] IEEE Std 241-1990, IEEE Recommended Practice for Electric Power Systems in Commercial Buildings (IEEE Gray Book) (ANSI).

[B13] IEEE Std 666-1991, IEEE Design Guide for Electric Power Service Systems for Generating Stations (ANSI).

[B14] IEEE Tutorial Course Text, "Surge Protection in Power Systems," IEEE Paper no. 79EH0144-6-PWR.

[B15] Johnson, G. S., "Overcurrent Protection for Emergency and Standby Generating Systems," *Electrical Construction and Maintenance*, Apr. 1983. *See also:* Stromme, G., Discussion, Aug. 1983; Johnson, G. S., Discussion, Aug. 1983; Phelps, E. J., Jr., Discussion, Nov. 1983; Editor's Note, Nov. 1983; Griffith, M. S., Discussion, Nov. 1983; Johnson, G. S., Discussion, Feb. 1984.

[B16] NEMA AB 3-1991, Molded-Case Circuit Breakers and Their Applications.

[B17] NFPA 99-1996, Health Care Facilities Code.

[B18] Reichenstein, H. W., and Castenschiold, R., "Coordinating Overcurrent Protective Devices with Automatic Transfer Switches in Commercial and Institutional Power Systems," *IEEE Transactions on Industry Applications*, vol. IA-11, no. 6, Nov./Dec. 1975.

---

[11]IEC publications are available from IEC Sales Department, Case Postale 131, 3 rue de Varembé, CH-1211, Genève 20, Switzerland/Suisse. IEC publications are also available in the United States from the Sales Department, American National Standards Institute, 11 West 42nd Street, 13th Floor, New York, NY 10036, USA.

Chapter 7
Grounding

7.1 Introduction

7.1.1 General

This chapter discusses recommended practices and guidelines for system and equipment grounding of emergency and standby power systems rated 600 V or less.

Fundamental design principles for system and equipment grounding and basic factors that influence the selection of the type of system grounding are covered in detail in other IEEE Color Books, including IEEE Std 141-1993,[1] IEEE Std 142-1991, and IEEE Std 1100-1992. Ground-fault protection is an important consideration that is covered in detail in IEEE Std 242-1986. The purpose of this chapter is to further define these fundamental grounding requirements and to illustrate grounding arrangements for several types of system grounding and transfer schemes that are most often selected for emergency and standby power systems in industrial and commercial installations.

7.1.2 Grounding requirements

Grounding requirements for emergency and standby power systems are unique because of multiple power sources, ground-fault sensing conditions, and special code stipulations. The requirements for grounding vary depending upon the type of system (emergency, standby, or optional standby), whether or not the alternate power is a separately derived source, and whether ground-fault protection is provided. Furthermore, reliable operation and protection requires coordinated design, proper installation, and maintenance of the following:

— Circuit-protective equipment
— Systems grounding
— Equipment grounding
— Transfer switching equipment

7.1.3 Circuit-protective equipment

Various types of circuit protection are satisfactory for ground-fault protection. Some commonly used types are circuit breakers with series trips, circuit-interrupting equipment tripped by ground-fault current-sensing devices, and, to a lesser extent, fuses. Selection and application of circuit-protective equipment requires a detailed analysis of each system and circuit to be protected, including the system and equipment grounding arrangements.

---

[1]Information on references can be found in 7.14.

In addition to providing proper ground-fault protection, it is essential to coordinate over-current protective devices and transfer switches with maximum available short-circuit currents. See Chapter 6 for further information on overcurrent protection.

7.1.4 Transfer switching equipment

Transfer switches transfer load conductor connections from one power source to another. These load conductors may or may not include the grounded conductor connection (neutral), thus determining whether the system is separately derived. This determines the design of the grounding system, selection of transfer switching equipment, and feasibility of ground-fault protection. See Chapter 4 for basic information on transfer switches.

7.2 System and equipment grounding functions

7.2.1 General

System grounding pertains to the manner in which a circuit conductor of a system is intentionally connected to earth, or to some conducting body that is effectively connected to earth or serves in place of earth. The following types of system grounding are discussed in this chapter:

— *Solidly grounded.* A grounding electrode conductor connects a terminal of the system to the grounding electrode (s) and no impedance is intentionally inserted into the connection.
— *Resistance grounded.* A grounding resistor is inserted into the connection between a terminal of the system and the grounding electrode(s).
— *Ungrounded.* None of the circuit conductors of the system is intentionally grounded.

Equipment grounding is the process of bonding together, with equipment-grounding conductors, all conductive enclosures for conductors and equipment within each circuit. These equipment-grounding conductors are required to run with or enclose the circuit conductors, and they provide a permanent, low-impedance conductive path for ground-fault current. In solidly grounded systems, the equipment-grounding conductors are bonded to the grounded circuit conductor and to the system-grounding conductor(s) per the National Electrical Code (NEC) (NFPA 70-1996), Section 250-50(a), at specific points, as shown in figures 7-1 and 7-2.

7.2.2 System grounding functions

Systems and circuit conductors are grounded to overvoltages due to lightning, line surges, or unintentional contact with higher voltage lines, and to stabilize the voltage-to-ground during normal operation. Systems and circuit conductors are solidly grounded to facilitate overcurrent device operation in case of ground faults, and to stabilize voltage-to-ground during fault conditions.

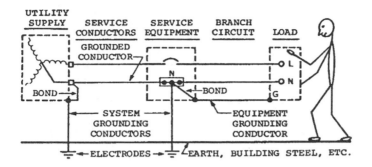

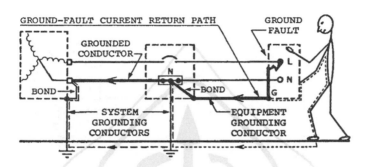

Figure 7-1—System and equipment grounding for solidly grounded, service-supplied system

Grounding electrodes and the grounding electrode conductors that connect the electrodes to the system-grounding conductor are not intended to conduct ground-fault currents that are due to ground faults in equipment, raceways, or other conductor enclosures. In solidly grounded systems, the ground-fault current flows through the equipment-grounding conductors from a ground fault anywhere in the system to the bonding jumper between the equipment-grounding conductors and the system-grounding conductor, as shown in figures 7-2 and 7-3.

In solidly grounded service-supplied systems, the ground-fault current return path is completed through the bonding jumper in the service equipment and the grounded service conductor to the supply transformer.

Although the term "system grounding" is used in figures 7-2 and 7-3 for neutral grounding of utility transformers as well as for neutral grounding of service equipment, there is no intention to imply that these two forms of grounding are functionally equivalent.

7.2.3 Equipment grounding functions

Equipment grounding systems, consisting of interconnected networks of equipment-grounding conductors, perform the following basic functions:

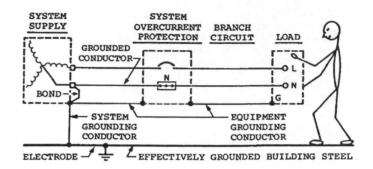

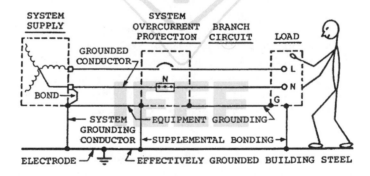

Figure 7-2—System and equipment grounding for solidly grounded, separately derived system

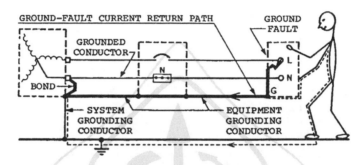

Figure 7-3—Supplemental equipment bonding for separately derived system

— They limit the voltage to ground (shock voltage) on the exposed noncurrent-carrying metal parts of equipment, raceways, and other conductor enclosures in case of ground faults.

— They safely conduct ground-fault currents of sufficient magnitude for fast operation of the circuit-protective devices.

— They reduce electromagnetic interference (EMI), common-mode noise, and other electronic interference.

In order to ensure the performance of the above basic functions, equipment-grounding conductors should

— Be permanent and continuous;
— Have ample capacity to safely conduct any ground-fault current likely to be imposed on them;
— Have impedance sufficiently low to limit the voltage to ground to a safe magnitude and to facilitate the operation of the circuit-protective devices.

As illustrated in figures 7-1 and 7-2, a person contacting a conductive enclosure in which there is a ground fault will be protected from shock injury if the equipment-grounding conductors provide a shunt path of sufficiently low impedance to limit the current through the person's body to a safe magnitude. In solidly grounded systems, the ground-fault current actuates the circuit-protective devices to automatically de-energize a faulted circuit and remove any destructive heating, arcing, and shock hazard.

The same network of equipment-grounding conductors should be provided for solidly grounded systems, high-resistance grounded systems, and ungrounded systems. Equipment-grounding conductors are required in resistance grounded and ungrounded systems to provide shock protection and to present a low-impedance path for phase-to-phase fault currents in case the first ground fault is not located and cleared before another ground fault occurs on a different phase in the system.

7.3 Supplemental equipment bonding

Exposure to electrical shock can be reduced by additional supplemental equipment bonding between the conductive enclosures for conductors and equipment and adjacent conductive materials.

The supplemental equipment bonding shown in figure 7-3 contributes to equalizing the potential between exposed noncurrent-carrying metal parts of the electric system and adjacent grounded building steel when ground faults occur. The inductive reactance of the ground-fault circuit will normally prevent a significant amount of ground-fault current from flowing through the supplemental bonding connections.

Ground-fault current will flow through the path that provides the lowest ground-fault circuit impedance. The ground-fault current path that minimizes the inductive reactance of the ground-fault circuit is through the equipment-grounding conductors that are required to run with or enclose the circuit conductors. Therefore, practically all of the ground-fault current will flow through the equipment-grounding conductors, and the ground-fault current through the supplemental bonding connections will be no more than required to equalize the potential at the bonding locations.

7.4 Objectionable current through grounding conductors

System and equipment-grounding conductors should be installed and connected in a manner that will prevent an objectionable flow of current through the grounding conductors or grounding paths. If a grounded (neutral) circuit conductor is connected to the equipment-grounding conductors at more than one point, or if it is grounded at more than one point, stray neutral current paths will be established. Stray neutral currents that flow through paths other than the intended grounded (neutral) circuit conductors during normal operation of a system will be objectionable if they contribute to any of the following:

— Interference with the proper operation of equipment, devices, or systems that are sensitive to electromagnetic interference, such as electronic equipment, communications systems, computer systems, etc.;
— Interference with the proper sensing and operation of ground-fault protection equipment;
— Arcing of sufficient energy to ignite flammable materials;
— Detonation of explosives during production, storage, or testing;
— Overheating due to heat generated in raceways, etc., as a result of stray current;
— Electrochemical action, particularly in soil, that may damage nearby metallic elements.

If the supply transformer is utility-owned and is located outside the building, the grounded service conductor should be grounded on the secondary side of the supply transformer by the utility. The grounded service conductor of service-supplied systems must be grounded at the service equipment to meet NEC requirements. A grounding connection should not be made to any grounded (neutral) circuit conductor on the load side of the service disconnecting means.

When the transformer is owned by the user, the secondary power supply is referred to as a "separately derived" source. Such a separately derived source has to have its neutral grounded at the transformer location per NEC, Section 250-26.

The stray neutral current illustrated in figure 7-4 is due to multiple grounding of the grounded service conductor. Such multiple grounding of the neutral circuit conductor may cause stray currents that are likely to be objectionable and will cause ground-fault current to flow in paths that may adversely affect the operation of ground-fault protection equipment.

Objectionable stray neutral currents are frequently caused by unintentional neutral-to-ground faults as shown in figure 7-5. Neutral-to-ground faults are difficult to locate, but should be suspected if there are objectionable stray neutral currents (Zipse 1972 [B11]).[2]

The NEC requires a disconnecting point for the grounded circuit conductor for test purposes when a system is commissioned or updated. This connection can be temporarily opened in order to test and assure that no downstream ground connection to the neutral exist. While this connection is open, safety precautions should be taken because of possible backfeed from the emergency or standby power source (Castenschiold and Hogrebe 1993 [B5]).

---

[2]The numbers in brackets preceded by the letter B correspond to those of the bibliography in 7.15.

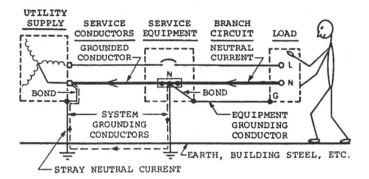

Figure 7-4—Stray neutral current due to multiple grounding of grounded service conductor

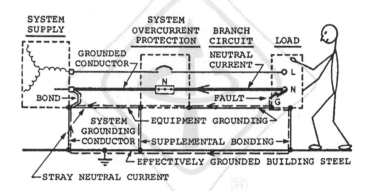

Figure 7-5—Stray neutral current due to unintentional grounding of a grounded circuit conductor

7.5 System grounding requirements

Alternating-current systems of 50–1000 V should be solidly grounded where the maximum voltage to ground on the ungrounded conductors will not exceed 150 V. Systems that supply phase-to-neutral loads should also be solidly grounded. The following commonly used systems are required to be solidly grounded:

— 120/240 V single-phase, three-wire

— 208Y/120 V three-phase, four-wire

— 480Y/277 V three-phase, four-wire

— 240/120 V three-phase, four-wire delta (midpoint of one phase used as a grounded circuit conductor)

The following commonly used systems are not required to be solidly grounded:

— 240 V delta, three-phase, three-wire
— 480 V three-phase, three-wire
— 600 V three-phase, three-wire

Although most emergency and standby power systems are solidly grounded, there is a growing trend towards resistance grounding where phase-to-neutral loads need not be served. This is particularly so for 480 V and 600 V three-phase systems in industrial facilities. High resistance system grounding combines some of the advantages of solidly grounded systems and ungrounded systems. System overvoltages are held to acceptable levels during ground faults, and the potentially destructive effects of high-magnitude ground-fault currents that occur in high-capacity, solidly grounded systems are eliminated. Ground-fault current is limited by the system grounding resistor to a magnitude that permits continued operating of a system while a ground fault is located and cleared. However, if a ground fault is not located and cleared before another ground fault occurs on another phase in the system, the high magnitude phase-to-phase fault current will flow through the equipment-grounding conductors and operate the circuit-protective equipment. Factors that influence selecting the type of system grounding are covered in the standards referenced in 7.1.1. With high-resistance grounding, ground fault currents are usually limited to 10 A or less.

Low-resistance grounding may be used for systems where no neutral connected loads are involved as described above, and where limiting the ground-fault current is important. Such grounding may be used to limit damage to large motors or generators. There is also somewhat of a protective aspect to the limitation of ground fault current for personnel who may be working on or near the system. The size of the resistor can be set to limit the ground fault current to at least 100 A; however, the 200–1000 A range is more typical. This provides sufficient current to operate the system-protective devices with a one line-ground fault.

7.6 Types of equipment-grounding conductors

Equipment grounding conductors represented in the diagrams in this chapter may be any of the types permitted in the NEC, Section 250-91(b), if this section is adopted by the authority having jurisdiction. Where raceway, cable tray, cable armor, etc., are used as equipment grounding conductors, all joints and fittings must be made tight to provide an adequate conducting path for ground-fault currents.

Earth and the structural metal frame of a building may be sued for supplemental equipment bonding, but they should not be used as the sole equipment-grounding conductor for ac systems. Equipment grounding conductors for ac systems should run with or enclose the conductors of each circuit. These requirements are mandatory per Article 25? of the NEC.

Where copper or aluminum wire is used as equipment-grounding conductors for circuits having paralleled conductors in multiple metal raceways, an equipment-grounding conductor should be run in each raceway. The size of each paralleled equipment-grounding conductor is a function of the rating of the circuit overcurrent protection.

Section 250-91(b) of the NEC permits the metallic enclosure or raceway containing the conductors to serve as the equipment-grounding conductor. The equipment-grounding conductors will either be the grounding conductor run with the current-carrying conductors or the enclosure (or both where applicable). Even through the code permits the enclosure to be used as the equipment-grounding conductor, a separate grounding conductor run in this enclosure is often elected or may be required by the specifying authority for purpose of avoiding contact resistances of enclosure joints, lower equipment-grounding conductor impedance, and greater reliability.

All equipment-grounding conductors in one premise must ultimately connect to the grounding electrode conductors. A separate grounding system for specific equipment such as computers, is not only a violation of the NEC, but risks the damage to or misoperation of sensitive systems and possibly danger to life.

— There are small differences in potential throughout the various components of an electrical system. These differences can cause faulty information transfer or erroneous control operations for sensitive equipment.

— With transients or surges that may be caused by switching, lightning (including induced currents or voltages), or faults, equipment may be damaged or misoperate. In the case of lightning, an improper grounding system may cause serious damage to equipment or injury to personnel.

Section 250-74, Exception 4, of the NEC does permit an "isolated" equipment-grounding conductor for purposes of electrical noise (EMI) control for sensitive equipment. However, this isolated conductor may run through one or more panelboards without connection to the grounding bar, but it must ultimately connect to one of the equipment-grounding conductors in a panelboard, and must run with the power conductors of the equipment to be grounded.

7.7 Grounding for separately derived and service-supplied systems

Basic grounding connections for solidly grounded separately derived and service-supplied systems are illustrated in figure 7-6 with reference to NEC Sections in which the grounding requirements are specified.

The grounding requirements for separately derived systems and service-supplied systems are similar, but there are three important differences:

a) The system-grounding conductor for a separately derived system should be grounded at only one point. The single system-grounding point is specified as the source of the separately derived system and ahead of any system disconnecting means or overcurrent devices. Where the main system disconnecting means is adjacent to the generator or transformer supplying a separately derived system, the grounding connection to the system-grounding conductor may be made at, or ahead of, the system-disconnecting means.

The system-grounding conductor for a service-supplied system should be grounded at the service equipment and elsewhere on the secondary of the transformer that sup-

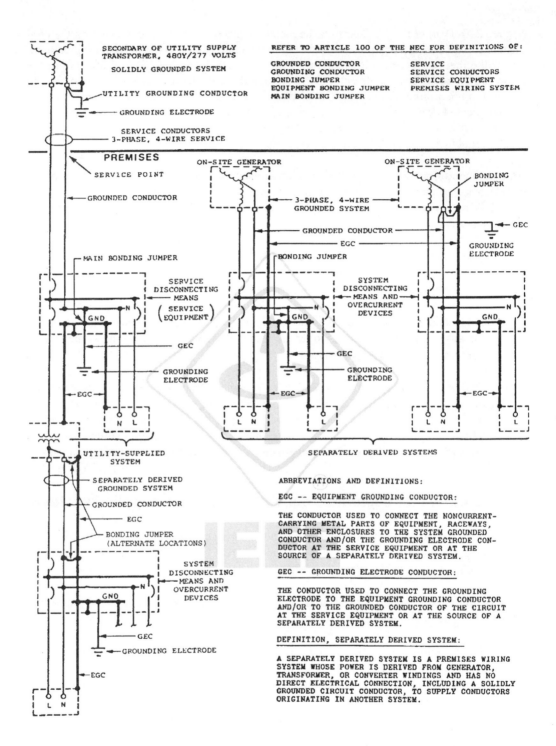

Figure 7-6—System and equipment grounding for separately derived and service-supplied systems

plies the service, if the supply transformer is not in the same building as the service equipment.

b) The preferred grounding electrode for a separately derived system is the nearest effectively grounded structural metal member of the structure or the nearest effectively grounded water pipe. The grounding electrode system for a service supplied system should be in accordance with established code requirements.

c) In solidly grounded separately derived systems, the equipment-grounding conductors should be bonded to the system-grounding conductor and to the grounding electrode conductor at or ahead of the main system disconnecting means or overcurrent device. The equipment-grounding conductor should always be connected to the enclosure of the supply transformer or generator, as shown in figure 7-6.

In solidly grounded utility-supplied systems, the equipment-grounding conductors should be bonded to the system-grounding conductor and to the grounding electrode conductor at the service equipment. The grounded service conductor may be used to ground the noncurrent-carrying metal parts of equipment on the supply side of the service disconnecting means, and the grounded service conductor may also serve as the ground-fault current return path from the service equipment to the transformer that supplies the service.

7.8 Grounding arrangements for emergency and standby power systems

A primary consideration in designing emergency and standby power systems is to satisfy the user's needs for continuity of electrical service. The type of system grounding that is employed, and the arrangement of system and equipment-grounding conductors, will affect the service continuity. Grounding conductors and connections must be arranged so that objectionable stray neutral currents will not exist and ground-fault currents will flow in low-impedance, predictable paths that will protect personnel from electrical shock and assure proper operation of the circuit-protective equipment.

Where phase-to-neutral loads must be served, systems are required to be solidly grounded. However, 600 V and 480 V systems may be high- or low-resistance grounded or ungrounded where a grounded circuit conductor is not used to supply phase-to-neutral loads. High-resistance grounded or ungrounded systems may provide a higher degree of service continuity than solidly grounded systems.

This chapter discusses grounding arrangements for emergency and standby power systems that are solidly grounded, high-resistance grounded, and ungrounded.

7.9 Systems with a grounded circuit conductor

Where grounded (neutral) conductors are used as circuit conductors in systems that have emergency or standby power supplies, the grounding arrangement should be carefully planned to avoid objectionable stray currents. For example, stray neutral currents and ground-fault currents in unplanned, undefined conducting paths may cause serious sensing errors by ground-fault protection equipment. A precautionary note is included in Section 230-95 of the NEC, which states, "Where ground-fault protection is provided for the service disconnecting means and interconnection is made with another supply system by a transfer device, means or devices may be needed to assure proper ground-fault sensing by the ground-fault protection equipment."

7.9.1 Solidly interconnected multiple-grounded neutral

A grounded (neutral) circuit conductor is permitted to be solidly connected in the transfer equipment. Therefore, a neutral conductor is permitted to be solidly interconnected between a service-supplied normal source and an on-site generator that serves as an emergency or standby source, as shown in figure 7-7. However, this is not always a recommended practice. Rather, for most emergency and standby power systems with ground-fault switches, switching of the grounded circuit conductor by the transfer switch is the recommended practice.

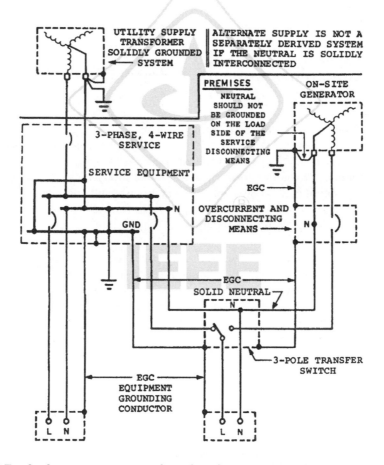

Figure 7-7—An incorrect connection showing a solidly interconnected neutral conductor grounded at service equpment and at source of alternate power supply

Grounding connections to the grounded (neutral) conductor on the load side of the service disconnecting means is not recommended, so the grounding connection to the generator neutral in figure 7-7 *should not be made*. Such multiple grounding of the neutral circuit conductor may cause stray currents that are likely to be objectionable and will cause ground-fault current to flow in paths that may adversely affect the operation of ground-fault protection equipment.

a) *Figure 7-7.* The grounding connection to the neutral conductor at the on-site generator in figure 7-7 is on the load side of the service disconnecting means, and is not recommended and may not satisfy code requirements. Where the grounded (neutral) conductor is solidly connected in the transfer equipment, the system supplied by the on-site generator is not considered as a separately derived system.

b) *Figure 7-8.* The grounding connection to the neutral conductor at the on-site generator in figure 7-8 completes a conducting path for stray neutral current. The magnitude of the stray current will be a function of the relative impedances of the neutral current paths. Where ground-fault protection is provided at the service disconnecting means,

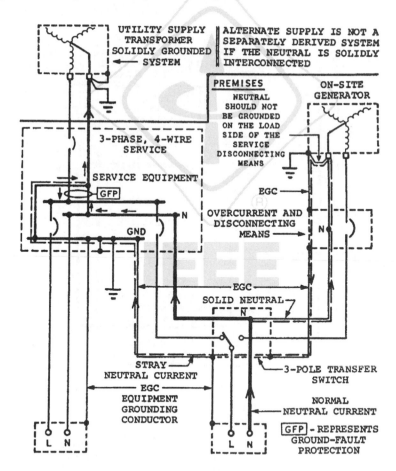

Figure 7-8—Stray neutral current due to grounding the neutral conductor at two locations

the stray neutral current may adversely affect the operation of the ground-fault protection equipment.

c)   *Figure 7-9.* The grounding connection to the neutral, which is on the opposite side of the ground-fault sensor from the service entrance grounding, can cause ground-fault current to return through the neutral, thus cancelling the sensing of this current by the ground-fault sensor. It may also allow zero-sequence current to flow in the neutral, even though no phase conductor is faulted, thus causing unwarranted tripping of the service entrance breaker.

If ground-fault protection is applied on the feeder to the transfer switch, it may be similarly affected. If neutral current continues to flow subsequent to tripping of the feeder breaker, it may damage the ground-fault relay. This flow of neutral current is not caused by the multiple grounds; they merely enable the flow. The current must be drive 'n by some source, such as the induction due to unequal bus spacing, or even voltages from a different system.

Where ground-fault protection is applied to a feeder from the service equipment to the transfer equipment, the ground-fault current illustrated in figure 7-9 could not be accurately detected by a zero-sequence ground-fault current sensor for the feeder.

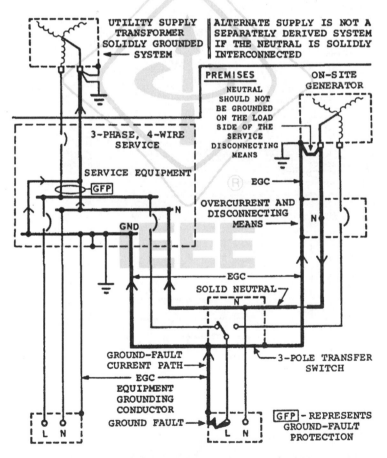

Figure 7-9—Ground-fault current return paths to normal supply, neutral grounded at two locations

d)   *Figure 7-10.* The multiple-grounding connections to the solidly interconnected neutral in figure 7-10 permit a portion of the ground-fault current returning to the on-site generator to pass through the sensor for the ground-fault protection at the service equipment. This arrangement could result in tripping the service disconnecting means by ground-fault current supplies from the on-site generator.

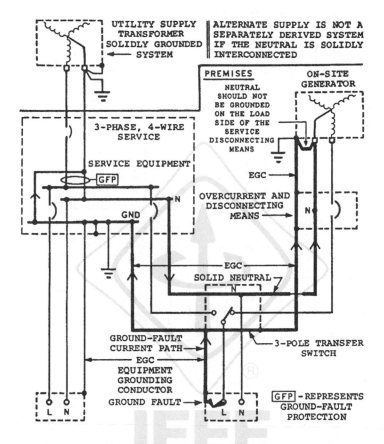

Figure 7-10—Ground-fault current return paths to alternate supply, neutral grounded at two locations

7.9.2 Neutral conductor transferred by transfer means

The transfer switch may have an additional pole for switching the neutral conductor, or the neutral may be transferred by make-before-break overlapping neutral contacts in the transfer switch. Where the neutral circuit conductor is transferred by the transfer equipment, an emergency or standby system supplied by an on-site generator is a separately derived system. A separately derived system with a neutral circuit conductor should be solidly grounded at or ahead of the system disconnecting means.

a)   *Figure 7-11.* The neutral conductor between the service equipment and the on-site generator in figure 7-11 is completely isolated by the transfer switch and is solidly

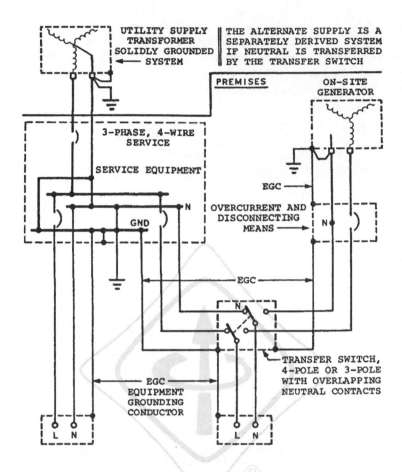

Figure 7-11—Transferred neutral conductor grounded at service equipment and at source of alternate power supply

grounded at the service equipment and at the on-site generator. Where the neutral circuit conductor is switched by the transfer equipment, the stray neutral current paths and the undesirable ground-fault current paths illustrated in figures 7-10, 7-11, and 7-12 are eliminated.

The normal supply and the alternate supply in figure 7-13 are equivalent to two separate radial systems because all of the circuit conductors from both supplies are switched by the transfer switch. Since both systems are completely isolated from each other and are solidly grounded, ground-fault sensing and protection can be applied to the circuits of the normal source and the emergency or standby source as it is applied in a single radial system.

b) *Figure 7-12.* This diagram shows that unintentional neutral grounds will cause stray neutral currents that may be objectionable. Therefore, in addition to carefully planning the intentional grounding connections, systems should be kept free of unintentional grounds on the neutral circuit conductors.

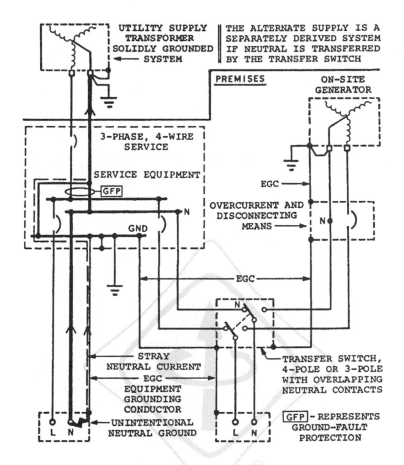

**Figure 7-12—Stray neutral current enabled by unintentionally
grounded neutral conductor**

c) *Figure 7-13.* This diagram is similar to figure 7-11 except there are two on-site generators connected for parallel operation and the neutral conductor is grounded at the
generator switchgear instead of at the generator. Where the generator switchgear is
adjacent to the generators, the grounding connections may be made in the generator
switchgear, as shown in figure 7-13.

Switching of the neutral conductor permits grounding of the neutral at the generator
location. This may be desirable for the following reasons:

1) An engine-generator set is often remotely located from the grounded utility service entrance, and in some cases the ground potentials of the two locations may
not be exactly the same.

2) Good engineering practice requires the automatic transfer switch to be located
as close to the load as possible to provide maximum protection against cable or
equipment failures within the facility. The distance of cable between incoming
service and the transfer switch and then to the engine-generator set may be substantial. Should cable failure occur with the neutral conductor not grounded at

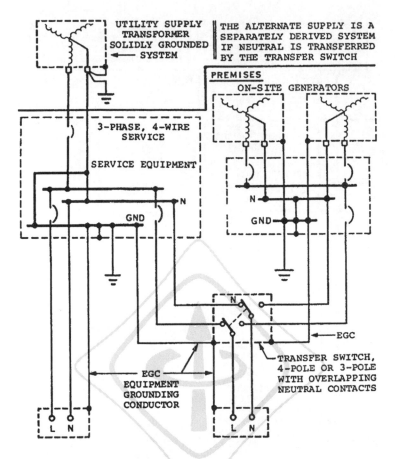

Figure 7-13—Transferred neutral conductor grounded at servide equipment and at switchgear for two on-site generators connected in parallel

the generator location, the load would be transferred to an ungrounded emergency power system. Concurrent failure of equipment (breakdown between line and equipment ground) after transfer to emergency may not be detected.

3) Some local codes require ground-fault protection while the engine-generator is operating. This may present a sensing problem if the neutral conductor of the generator is not connected to a grounding electrode at the generator site and proper isolation of neutrals is not provided. This may also present a problem in providing a ground-fault signal as required according to NEC, Section 700-7(e).

4) When the transfer switch is in the emergency position, other problems may occur if the neutral is not grounded at the engine-generator set. A ground-fault condition, as shown in figure 7-17(b), could cause nuisance tripping of the normal source circuit breaker, even though load current is not flowing through the breaker, and still not be cleared.

The normal neutral conductor and the emergency neutral conductor would then be simultaneously vulnerable to the same ground-fault current. The ground-fault relay can be damaged. Thus a single fault could jeopardize power to critical loads even though both utility and emergency power are available. Such a condition may be in violation of codes requiring independent wiring and separate emergency feeders.

7.9.3 Neutral conductor isolated by a transformer

Where a transferable load is supplied by a system that is derived from an on-site isolating transformer and the transfer equipment is ahead of the transformer, as illustrated in figure 7-14, a grounded (neutral) circuit conductor is not always required from either the normal or alternate supply to the transformer primary. The isolating transformer permits phase-to-neutral transferable loads to be supplied without a grounded (neutral) circuit conductor in the feeders to the transfer switch.

This type of connection is practical where a power-conditioning module incorporating an isolation transformer is used to improve "power quality" and be a source of neutral current for computer or other applications.

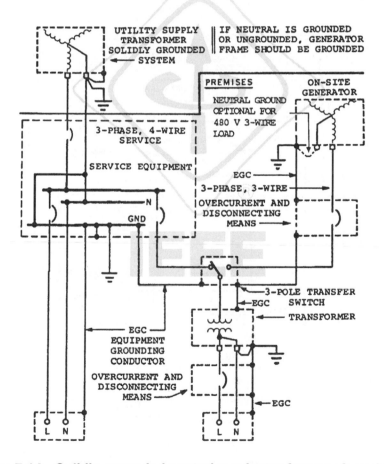

Figure 7-14—Solidly grounded neutral conductor for transferred load isolated by transformer

a) *Figure 7-14.* The system supplied by the isolating transformer in figure 7-14 is a separately derived system, and if it is required to be solidly grounded, it should be grounded in accordance with code requirements. The neutral circuit conductor for the transferable load in figure 7-14 is supplied from the secondary of the isolating transformer and should be grounded according to NEC, Section 250-26.

If the on-site generator in figure 7-14 is rated 480Y/277 V or 600Y/347 V, its neutral may not need to be solidly grounded because the neutral is not used as a circuit conductor. Therefore, the type of system grounding for such a generator is optional. For a three-wire system, it is generally recommended that the neutral of the on-site generator not be grounded so as to reduce circulating neutral currents within the ground system. In any case, the generator frame should be solidly grounded whether its neutral is ungrounded, high-resistance grounded, or solidly grounded.

b) *Figure 7-15.* This figure illustrates ground-fault current return paths where the grounded (neutral) circuit conductor of a transferable load is isolated by a transformer. Any stray neutral current or ground-fault current on the secondary of the isolating transformer will have no effect on ground-fault protection equipment at the service equipment or at the generator.

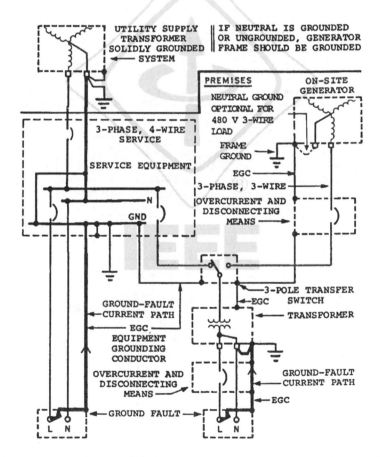

**Figure 7-15—Ground-fault current return paths transferred load
isolated by transformer**

7.9.4 Solidly interconnected neutral conductor grounded at service equipment only

Where the grounded (neutral) circuit conductor is solidly connected (not switched) in the transfer equipment, an emergency or standby system supplied by an on-site generator should not be considered a separately derived system. The solidly interconnected grounded (neutral) conductor needs only to be grounded at the service equipment.

a) *Figure 7-16.* The solidly interconnected neutral conductor in figure 7-16 is grounded at the service equipment only and there are no conducting paths for stray neutral currents. However, this arrangement does not readily lend itself to sensing ground-fault current on the emergency side of the transfer switch as required by the NEC, Section 700-7(d).

b) *Figures 7-17(a) and 7-17(b).* Where the solidly interconnected neutral conductor is grounded at the service equipment only, as shown in figure 7-17(b), the ground-fault current return path from the transferable load to the on-site generator is through the equipment-grounding conductor from the transfer switch to the service equipment,

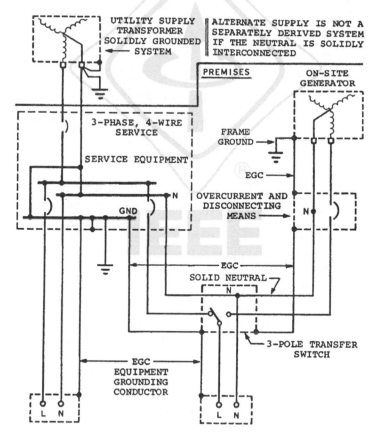

Figure 7-16—Solidly interconnected neutral conductor grounded at service equipment only

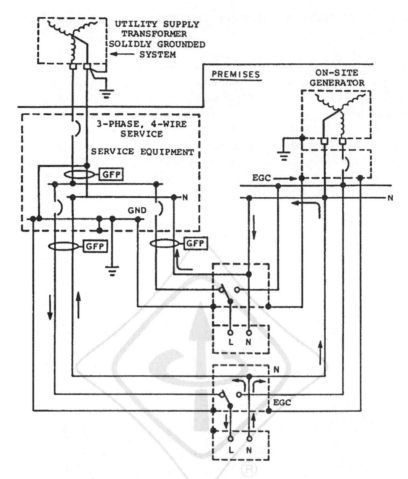

**Figure 7-17 (a)—Two transfer switches with multiple neutral return paths—
ground fault indicated though none exists**

then through the main bonding jumper in the service equipment and the neutral conductor from the service equipment to the generator.

The ground-fault current shown in figure 7-17(b) might trip the service disconnecting means, even though the ground fault is on a circuit supplied by the generator. A signal could be derived from the ground-fault sensor on the generator neutral conductor to block the ground-fault protection equipment at the service in case of ground faults while the system is transferred to the generator. Such blocking signals require careful analysis to ensure proper functioning of the ground-fault protection equipment.

If the neutral conductor between the service equipment and the transfer switch in figures 7-17(a) and 7-17(b) is intentionally or accidentally disconnected, the generator will be ungrounded. Therefore, the integrity of the neutral conductor should be maintained from the service equipment to the transfer switch while the load is transferred to the generator. The equipment-grounding conductor should also be maintained from the service equipment to the transfer equipment in order to provide a ground-fault current return path from the transferable load to the generator.

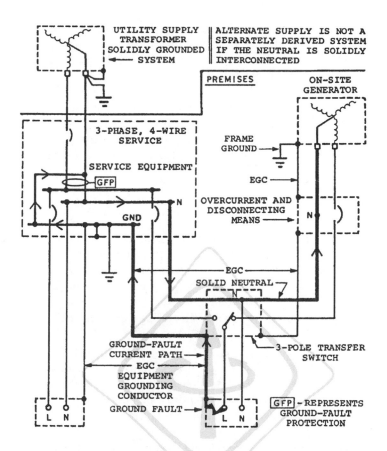

**Figure 7-17 (b)—Ground-fault current return path to alternate supply, neutral
conductor grounded at service equipment only**

7.9.5 Multiple transfer switches

For increased reliability, multiple transfer switches, located close to the loads, are often used
rather than one transfer switch for the entire load. In such cases, consideration should be
given to the possibility of cable or equipment failure between the service equipment and the
transfer switches, thus possibly causing an emergency or standby power system to become
ungrounded. This is particularly important if a solidly interconnected neutral conductor is
grounded at the service equipment only.

When multiple transfer switches are used with ground-fault detection on the distribution circuit level, there is a possibility of tripping the ground-fault circuits when no ground fault
exists. Figure 7-17(a) illustrates a typical system with multiple three-pole transfer switches.
Power is supplied from the normal source to the load through a transfer switch; the neutral
current returns to the transfer switch where multiple return paths are presented. The current
will divide between the paths depending on the relative impedance of the path. Some portion
of the current will return by the normal return path. The remainder of the current will flow
through the neutral conductor of the emergency supply to the transfer switch, through the

neutral conductor of the emergency distribution bus, through the neutral conductor of the emergency supply to the second transfer switch, then through the neutral conductor of the normal supply to the second transfer switch to the neutral conductor of the normal distribution bus, and finally back to the normal source.

This situation can occur independently of the grounding means chosen for the system, and can cause tripping of both normal and emergency service distribution breakers if they are protected by ground-fault devices even when no ground-fault exists. This problem can be corrected by the use of the three-pole transfer switches with overlapping neutral or four-pole transfer switches.

7.9.6 Multiple engine-generator sets

When several engine-generator sets are connected in parallel and serve as a common source of power, each generator neutral is usually connected to a common neutral bus within the paralleling switchgear which, in turn, is grounded. The associated switchgear containing the neutral bus should be located in the vicinity of the generator sets. A single system-grounding conductor between the neutral bus and ground simplifies the addition of ground-fault sensing equipment. This also permits the use of a single grounding resistor for multiple engine-generator sets.

It may be argued when individual grounding resistors are used, circulation of harmonic currents between paralleled generators is not a problem, since the resistance limits the circulating current to negligible values. However, if third harmonics are suppressed in the engine-generator sets, circulating currents are usually not a problem.

Multiple engine-generator sets that are physically separated and used for isolated loads may necessitate additional neutral-to-ground connections. However, by using multiple four-pole transfer switches or three-pole switches with overlapping neutral contacts, proper isolation and ground-fault sensing can be obtained.

7.9.7 Transferring neutral conductor

The foregoing discussion and circuit diagrams indicate that four-pole transfer switches are synonymous with three-pole transfer switches having overlapping neutral contacts. This is true from the standpoint of providing isolation as needed for ground-fault protection. However, there are other considerations.

Four-pole transfer switches can be satisfactorily applied where the loads are passive and relatively balanced. However, unbalanced loads may cause abnormal voltages for as long as 10–15 ms when the neutral conductor is momentarily opened during transfer of the load. Transfer switches may be called upon to operate during total load unbalance caused by a single-phasing condition. Inductive loads may cause additional high transient voltages in the microsecond range. Contacts of the fourth switch pole do interrupt current and are, therefore, subject to arcing and contact erosion. A good maintenance program is recommended to reaffirm at intervals the integrity of the fourth pole as a current-carrying member with sufficiently low impedance.

With overlapping neutral contacts, the only time the neutrals of the normal and emergency power sources are connected is during transfer and retransfer. The operating time of the ground-fault relay should be set higher than the overlap time of the particular transfer switch used.

With overlapping neutral transfer contacts, the load neutral is always connected to one source of power. When the transfer switch operates, abnormal and transient voltages, which can produce common-mode noise, are kept to a minimum because there is no momentary opening of the neutral conductor. Also, there is no erosion of the overlapping contacts due to arcing.

7.10 Ground-fault alarm

Most of the discussion on ground faults in this chapter has pertained to protection on the normal side of the transfer switch. However, ground faults can also occur between the transfer switch and the on-site generator. It is usually not desirable that emergency loads be automatically disconnected from the on-site generator should such a ground-fault occur.

However, for the purpose of safety and to minimize the possibility of fire and equipment damage, a visual and audible alarm to indicate a ground fault in larger emergency power systems is often recommended. This could alert personnel that corrective action should be taken. Instructions should be provided at or near the sensor location stating what course of action is to be taken in the event of a ground-fault indication.

Usually a ground-fault condition will show up during routine testing of the on-site generator. This then provides time to take corrective steps prior to an actual emergency condition.

7.11 Systems without a grounded circuit conductor

Three-phase, three-wire, 480 V and 600 V systems, which are extensively used in industrial establishments, do not require the use of grounded conductors as circuit conductors. There are more system-grounding options where emergency and standby power systems do not require a grounded circuit conductor to supply phase-to-neutral loads.

7.11.1 Solidly grounded service

In many installations, the utility service to the premises will be solidly grounded, three-phase, four-wire, where a grounded (neutral) circuit conductor is not required for loads that are provided with an on-site emergency or standby supply. An on-site emergency or standby supply is not always required to have the same type of system grounding as the normal supply to the premises.

a) *Figure 7-18.* The generator in figure 7-18 supplies a three-phase, three-wire system. If the generator is rated 480Y/277 V or 600Y/347 V, the neutral need not be used as a circuit conductor.

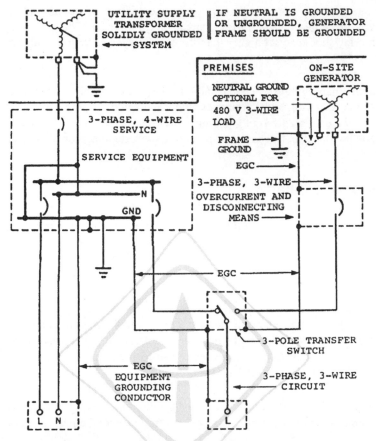

Figure 7-18—Three-pole transfer switch for transfer to an alternate power supply without a grounded circuit conductor

An on-site generator that is not required to be solidly grounded may be high-resistance grounded or ungrounded. A high-resistance grounded or ungrounded emergency or standby power supply provides a high degree of service continuity because the circuit-protective equipment will not be tripped by the first ground fault on the system.

If the generator in figure 7-18 is solidly grounded, it should be grounded at or ahead of the generator-disconnecting means.

b) *Figure 7-19.* Interlocked circuit breakers are used as the transfer means in figure 7-19. The grounding arrangements in figures 7-18 and 7-19 are the same. Where a grounded (neutral) circuit conductor is not required, the type of transfer equipment that is employed is not a consideration in selecting the type of system grounding for the emergency or standby supply.

Interlocked circuit breakers that provide overcurrent protection should not be selected as a transfer means without considering additional means to isolate the normal and alternate circuit conductors and equipment for maintenance work. If an on-site transformer is provided for emergency lighting, it should be supplied from the normal service and the emergency or standby supply through automatic transfer

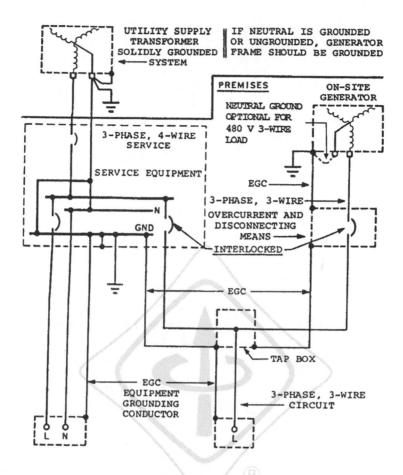

Figure 7-19—Interlocked circuit breakers for transfer to an alternate power supply without a grounded circuit conductor

switching equipment. Ground-detection equipment should be installed to help prevent a prolonged single-fault condition.

While it might not be a code violation to operate a generator as a three-wire ungrounded system, as shown in figures 7-18 and 7-19, a situation of lesser reliability and increased safety problems may develop.

c) *Figure 7-20.* A 480 V or 600 V, three-phase, three-wire, on-site generator that is high-resistance grounded may serve as an emergency or standby power supply for a three-phase, three-wire system that is normally supplied by a solidly grounded service, as shown in figure 7-20.

7.11.2 High-resistance grounded service

Where the three-phase, three-wire, critical load is relatively large compared with loads that require a grounded (neutral) circuit conductor, a high-resistance grounded service with a high-resistance grounded emergency or standby power supply is sometimes considered. This

245

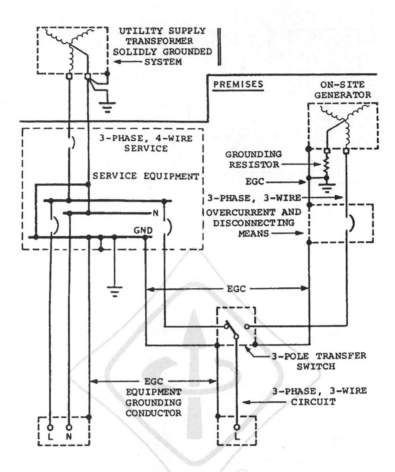

**Figure 7-20—High-resistance grounded alternate power supply without a
grounded circuit conductor**

arrangement requires an on-site transformer for loads that require a neutral circuit conductor.
If an on-site transformer is provided for emergency lighting, it should be supplied from the
normal service and the emergency supply through automatic transfer equipment.

a) *Figure 7-21.* The supply transformer for normal service and the on-site generator in
    figure are both high-resistance grounded. There are no provisions in this diagram to
    supply phase-to-neutral loads.
b) *Figure 7-22.* The ground-fault current return path to the on-site generator in figure
    7-22 is completed through the grounding resistor. The grounding resistor limits the
    line-to-ground fault current to a magnitude that can be tolerated for a time, allowing
    the ground fault to be located and removed from the system.

High-resistance grounded systems should not be used unless they are equipped with ground-
fault indicators or alarms, or both, and qualified persons are available to quickly locate and
remove ground faults. If ground faults are not promptly removed, the service reliability will

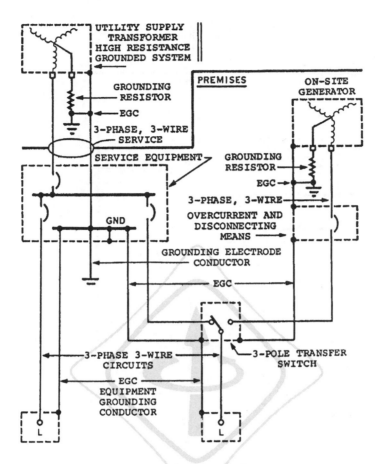

Figure 7-21—High-resistance grounded systems for normal service and alternate supply

be reduced. A possible aid in locating ground faults is applying a pulsed current that can be traced to the fault. Ground-detection equipment is essential for both systems. If the fault is in the load and not detected, undesirable transfer into a system with one fault may occur (IEEE Std 141-1993; Bridger 1983 [B2]).

7.12 Mobile engine-generator sets

The basic requirements for system grounding and equipment grounding that are discussed and illustrated in this chapter also apply to mobile engine-generator sets when they are used to supply emergency or standby power for systems rated 600 V or less. Grounding arrangements that are acceptable for emergency or standby power supplied by fixed generators are also acceptable where such systems are supplied from mobile engine-generators. If ground-fault-protection equipment is used for the normal service or for a mobile generator that supplies emergency or standby power, the system and equipment grounding connections should

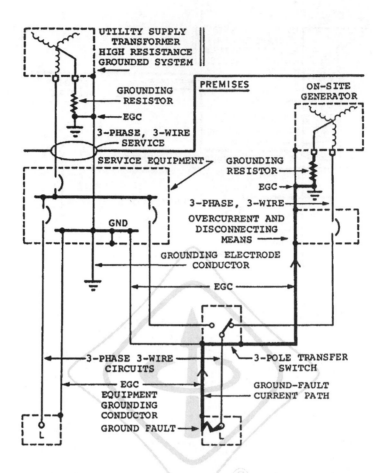

**Figure 7-22—Ground-fault current return path to high-resistance grounded
alternate supply**

be arranged to prevent stray neutral currents and ground-fault currents in paths that cause
improper operation of the ground-fault protection devices.

Where mobile generators are used to supply emergency or standby power for systems similar
to figure 7-11 in which the neutral is grounded at the generator, it may be desirable to install
permanent, pretested, system-grounding electrodes at locations designated for operating the
mobile equipment. If small mobile generators are operated at locations where permanent
grounding electrodes are not available, and the generator neutral is required to be grounded,
plate electrodes should be considered because they can be installed quickly. Plate electrodes
for equipment grounding should be located close to the generator and should be placed on the
surface (ground) with sufficient hold-down weight to ensure electrical bypass between the
operator's feet and the generator frame. However, this approach is a second choice to connecting the generator neutral to an existing permanent grounding electrode.

Equipment grounding conductors should be provided with the mobile generator circuit conductors as illustrated in the figures in this chapter. If flexible cords or cables are used to connect mobile generators to emergency or standby power systems, each cord or cable should have an equipment-grounding conductor.

Supplemental equipment bonding, which is discussed in 7.3, will reduce the risk of electrical shock for persons who contact the exposed noncurrent-carrying metal parts of the mobile equipment. Supplemental equipment bonding should be installed between the mobile generator frame and adjacent conductive surfaces such as structural steel, metal piping systems, and metal equipment enclosures. If the neutral of a mobile generator is not grounded, the generator frame should be connected to a grounding electrode, as shown in figure 7-17(a), in addition to its connection to the equipment-grounding conductor network.

7.13 Uninterruptible power supply (UPS) systems

As with any electrical system, correct grounding procedures are essential to overall safety and operation of a UPS system. In particular, personnel safety, equipment safety, equipment protection, and sensitive electronic system performance can all be jeopardized by incorrect or ineffective grounding systems. The grounding of the UPS system is very important when such systems supply power to critical computer loads.

The NEC does not require the installation of UPS systems, and much of Articles 517, 700, and 701 is not applicable. However, Articles 250 and 645 are applicable to the grounding of UPS systems.

Many UPS system modules have a wye-connected inverter output, and require the bypass input to be fed from a wye-connected source. The inverter portion of the UPS system module is a separately derived source, in that the input to the rectifier/charger is electrically isolated from the inverter output. However, because the bypass input neutral is directly connected to the inverter output neutral, the UPS system may or may not be considered a separately derived system, depending on the particular arrangement for the bypass input neutral.

The design of UPS systems vary considerably, thus affecting the grounding schemes. For further discussion, see IEEE Std 142-1991.

7.14 References

This chapter shall be used in conjunction with the following publications:

IEEE Std 141-1993, IEEE Recommended Practice for Electric Power Distribution for Industrial Plants (The Red Book) (ANSI).[3]

---

[3]IEEE publications are available from the Institute of Electrical and Electronics Engineers, 445 Hoes Lane, P.O. Box 1331, Piscataway, NJ 08855-1331, USA.

IEEE Std 142-1991, IEEE Recommended Practice for Grounding of Industrial and Commercial Power Systems (The Green Book) (ANSI).

IEEE Std 242-1986 (Reaff 1991), IEEE Recommended Practice for Protection and Coordination of Industrial and Commercial Power Systems (The Buff Book) (ANSI).

IEEE Std 1100-1992, IEEE Recommended Practice for Powering and Grounding Sensitive Electronic Equipment (The Emerald Book) (ANSI).

NEMA PB 2.2-1988 (Reaff 1994), Application Guide for Ground Fault Protective Devices for Equipment.[4]

NFPA 70-1996, National Electrical Code®.[5]

ANSI/NFPA 110-1993, Emergency and Standby Power Systems.

7.15 Bibliography

Additional information may be found in the following sources:

[B1] Bloomquist, W. C., Owen, K. J., and Gooch, R. L., "High-Resistance Grounded Power Systems—Why Not?" *IEEE Transactions on Industry Applications*, vol. IA-12, pp. 574–579, Nov./Dec. 1976.

[B2] Bridger, B., Jr., "High-Resistance Grounding," *IEEE Transactions on Industry Applications*," vol. 1A-19, pp. 15–21, Jan./Feb. 1983.

[B3] Brinks, J. W., and Wolfinger, J. P., Jr.,"Systems Grounding, Protection, and Detection for Cement Plants," *IEEE Transactions on Industry Applications*, vol. IA-17, pp. 587–596, Nov./Dec. 1981.

[B4] Castenschiold, R., "Grounding of Alternate Power Sources," *Conference Record of the 1977 IEEE Industry Applications Society*, Technical Conference, paper 77CH 1 1246-8-IA, pp. 67–72.

[B5] Castenschiold, R., and Hogrebe, L. F., "Factors to Consider When Upgrading Transfer Switching Equipment to Present Codes and Standards," *IEEE Transactions on Industry Applications*, vol. IA-29, no. 3, pp. 510–514, May/June 1993.

---

[4]NEMA publications are available from the National Electrical Manufacturers Association, 2101 L Street NW, Washington, DC 20037, USA.

[5]NFPA publications are available from Publications Sales, National Fire Protection Association, 1 Batterymarch Park, P.O. Box 9101, Quincy, MA 02269-9101, USA.

[B6] Castenschiold, R., "Ground-Fault Protection of Electrical Systems With Emergency or Standby Power," *IEEE Transactions on Industry Applications*, vol. IA-13, pp. 517–523, Nov./Dec. 1977.

[B7] Kaufmann, R. H., "Some Fundamentals of Equipment-Grounding Circuit Design," *AIEE Transactions (Applications and Industry)*, pt. 11, vol. 73, pp. 227–232, Nov. 1954.

[B8] Richards, J. H., "Generator Neutral Grounding," *Electrical Construction, and Maintenance*, p. 122, May 1984.

[B9] West, R. B., "Equipment Grounding for Reliable Ground Fault Protection in Electrical Systems Below 600 V," *IEEE Transactions on Industry Applications*, vol. IA-10, pp. 175–189, Mar./Apr. 1974.

[B10] West, R. B., "Grounding for Emergency and Standby Power Systems," *IEEE Transactions on Industry Applications*, vol. IA-15, pp. 124–136, Mar./Apr. 1979.

[B11] Zipse, D. W., "Multiple Neutral to Ground Connections," *Conference Record of the 1972 IEEE Industrial and Commercial Power Systems*, Technical Conference, paper 72CH0600-7-IA, pp. 60–64.

Chapter 8
Maintenance

8.1 Introduction

Once it has been determined by building codes, ANSI/NFPA 101-1994,[1] or a reliability study that an emergency or standby power system is justified or required, available systems must be evaluated to select one that satisfies the economic requirements. While economic considerations are primary, installation practices and maintenance procedures should be significant factors in selecting the proper system. After the system has been selected and the responsibility for maintenance established, plans for preventive maintenance must be made. The goal of preventive maintenance is to ensure that the system is in optimum operating condition. Without proper emphasis on maintenance from design stage through operation, the system can rapidly become unreliable and fail to perform its intended function.

Preventive maintenance can be thought of as a science of anticipation and prediction of failures. The system's important emergency and standby function makes preventive maintenance a great challenge.

8.1.1 General description of preventive maintenance practices

Preventive maintenance for electrical equipment consists of planned inspections, testing, cleaning, drying, monitoring, adjusting, corrective modification, and minor repair in order to maintain equipment in optimum operating condition and maximum reliability. In addition to routine preventive maintenance, it is important to maintain written records that document maintenance performance and test measurements. Also, drawings, such as connection wiring diagrams, one line diagrams, and block diagrams, are necessary in assistance with maintenance work.

8.1.2 Precautionary measures

Vital precautionary measures that should be considered a part of preventive maintenance are as follows:

— It should be made certain that the installation and ventilation of the emergency or standby power systems will not be adversely affected by unauthorized storage or accumulations of dirt.
— Regular test responsibilities should be placed on trained personnel, and tests should be scheduled frequently to assure reliable operation.

   NOTE—Use manufacturer's recommended procedure frequencies to establish program and adjust from experience.

— Gasoline and, to a lesser extent, diesel fuels deteriorate when stored for extended periods of time. Inhibitors can be used to reduce the rate of deterioration, but it is

---

[1]Information on references can be found in 8.9.

sound practice to operate a system utilizing these fuels such that total operating time will result in a complete fuel change cycle every few months.

— In case of life-limited components, a sufficient quantity of spares should be maintained, and they should be replaced according to the manufacturer's directions.

8.1.3 Personnel requirements

Personnel who maintain standby or emergency power systems should be required to have specific training and qualifications, as well as certain tools, manuals, and access to equipment, in order to ensure that preventive maintenance can be carried out effectively.

A list of these personnel requirements are as follows:

— An understanding of ANSI/NFPA 101-1994 and manufacturer's test procedures and frequency.
— Special training at manufacturer's location for equipment start and routine maintenance.
— A complete set of specialized and normal tools for required maintenance procedures on site.

    NOTE—Manufacturer can assist in developing this tool set.

— A complete set of shop manuals and list of required spare parts (with location notes).
— A manual of test procedures with step-by-step details.
— Physical access to system equipment to perform tests within required frequencies.
— Management/supervisory support to perform the tests within required frequencies.

8.1.4 How to use this chapter

Many different types of emergency and standby power systems are on the market today. This chapter presents a consolidation of general preventive maintenance recommendations that are organized into subclauses (8.2–8.12) according to system components. These general recommendations can then be applied to emergency and standby power systems that are formed from the various components.

8.2 Internal combustion engines

8.2.1 General

Internal combustion engines that are commonly available include those that use natural and bottled gas, gasoline, and diesel fuel. Since there are more similarities than differences in their maintenance requirements, these engines are grouped together.

Long life and high reliability are characteristics to be expected from these types of prime movers, but only if properly maintained. Preventive maintenance programs will greatly contribute to the service life and reliability.

In establishing a preventive maintenance program for these engines, the best starting point is the manufacturer's service manual. This will provide a guide for specific points to be checked and for frequency of inspection. These reference points can then be modified to fit particular installation and operating conditions.

8.2.2 Operating factors affecting maintenance

More than any other factor, lubrication determines an engine's useful life. Various parts of the engine may require different lubricants and different frequencies of lubricant application. It is important to follow the manufacturer's recommendations as to type and frequency of lubrication.

Because dirt and corrosion are major causes of equipment failure, no engine should be considered properly maintained if it is not cleaned to a "like new" condition. Dirt increases the difficulty of inspecting engine parts and interferes with heat conduction. Before performing any inspection on service, carefully clean all fittings, caps, fillers, level plugs, and their adjacent surfaces to prevent contamination of lubricants and coolants. Keep all dirt, dust, water, and sediment out of the fuel to prevent engine damage and clogging of fuel filters and injectors. In addition, bacteria in the presence of water can form sludge over an extended period of time, which will exacerbate the clogging of fuel filters and injectors. Frequently draining the water from the bottom of the fuel tank is the best method to prevent sludge. Visual and laboratory tests of sample is also of great value.

8.2.3 Typical maintenance schedule

NOTE—The following maintenance items or schedule are significant but not necessarily complete. Each system should have its own schedule developed from experience and early test results. In addition, table A-6-3.1 (a) from ANSI/NFPA 110-1993 can be helpful.

a) *Weekly inspections.* The following checks should be made weekly. Corrective action shall be taken for any item found to be deficient.
   1) Check cooling system and lubrication oil levels.
   2) Check air intake cleaner.
   3) Check engine for oil, fuel leaks, and cooling system operation.
   4) Check for oil heater and/or jacket heater operation.
b) *Monthly inspections.* The following checks should be made monthly. Corrective action shall be taken for any item found to be deficient.
   1) Check radiator for restrictions.
   2) Check belt tension.
   3) Check fuel system level.
c) *Semiannual inspections.* The following action shall be made semiannually:
   1) Change lubrication oil and replace filters.
   2) Change coolant filter.
   3) Drain sediment and check fuel-line connections.
d) *Annual inspections.* The following action shall be made annually:
   1) Clean fan hub, pulley, and water pump.
   2) Replace fuel float tank breather.
   3) Tighten exhaust manifold bolts.

8.3 Gas turbine

8.3.1 General

The combustion gas turbine, as with any rotating power equipment, requires a program of scheduled inspection and maintenance to achieve optimum availability and reliability. The combustion gas turbine is a complete, self-contained prime mover. This combustion process requires operation at high temperatures. When inspection marking on stainless steel parts is necessary, a grease pencil should be used. Graphite particles from lead pencils will carburize stainless steel at the high temperature of gas turbine operation.

Starting reliability is of prime concern since a delay in starting usually means the need for the unit has passed.

8.3.2 Operating factors affecting maintenance

The factors having the greatest influence on scheduling of preventive maintenance are type of fuel, starting frequency, environment, and reliability required.

a) *Fuel.* The effect of the type of fuel on parts is associated with the radiant energy in the combustion process and the ability to atomize the fuel. Natural gas, which does not require atomization, has the lowest level of radiant energy and will produce the longest life, and the crude oils and residual oils, with higher radiant energy and more difficult atomization, will provide shorter life of parts.

    Contaminants in the fuel will also affect the maintenance interval. In liquid fuels, dirt results in accelerated wear of pumps, metering elements, and fuel nozzles. Contamination in gas fuel systems can erode or corrode control valves and fuel nozzles. Filters must be inspected and replaced to prevent carrying contaminants through the fuel system. Clean fuels will result in reduced maintenance and extended lives of parts.

b) *Starting frequency.* Each stop and start subjects a gas turbine to thermal cycling. This thermal cycling will cause a shortened parts life. Applications requiring frequent starts and stops dictate a shorter maintenance interval.

c) *Environment.* The condition of inlet air to a combustion gas turbine can have a significant effect on maintenance. Abrasives in the inlet air, such as ash particles, require that careful attention be paid to inlet filtering to minimize the effect of the abrasives. In the case of corrosive atmosphere, careful attention should be paid to inlet air arrangement and the application of correct materials and protective coatings.

d) *Reliability required.* The degree of reliability required will affect the scheduling of maintenance. The higher the reliability desired, the more frequent the maintenance required.

8.3.3 Typical maintenance schedule

NOTE—The following maintenance items or schedule are significant but not necessarily complete. Each system should have its own schedule developed from experience and early test results. In addition, table A-6-3.1 (a) from ANSI/NFPA 110-1993 can be helpful.

a) *Weekly inspections.* The following checks should be made weekly. Corrective action shall be taken for any item found to be deficient.
   1) Check oil level.
   2) Check fuel oil pressure.
   3) Check all nuts and other fasteners.
   4) Check for lubrication oil and fuel leakage.
   5) Check lines and hoses for wear.
   6) Check inlet air and exhaust for obstructions.
b) Every 250 hours of operation. The following checks or action shall be made:
   1) Replace oil filter.
   2) Replace fuel filters.
   3) Blow out air lines and filters with dry low-pressure air.
   4) Lubricate auxiliary motors.
c) Every 1000 hours of operation. The following checks or action shall be made:
   1) Inspect spark plug.
   2) Inspect fuel injectors and combustion parts.
   3) Blow dry low-pressure air through exhaust and combustion drain lines.
   4) Inspect entire engine for discoloration, cracks, wear, or chafing of hoses, lines, and other unusual operating conditions.

8.4 Generators

8.4.1 General

The generator requires consideration for ambient temperature control, since the unit is in a de-energized state most of the time. Also, a program of scheduled inspections and maintenance is required to achieve optimum availability and reliability.

8.4.2 Operating factors affecting maintenance

Keeping equipment clean is of primary importance in generator preventive maintenance. Dust, oil, moisture, or other substances should not be allowed to accumulate on the equipment. Ventilation ducts should be kept clean to allow maximum cooling air in the generator. The importance of keeping windings clean cannot be overemphasized; dust, dirt, and other foreign matter can restrict heat dissipation and deteriorate winding insulation. A layer of dust as thin as 30 mil can raise the operating temperature of generator windings 10 °C.

The best method for cleaning a generator of loose and dry particles is to use a vacuum cleaner with proper fittings. Blowing with 30 lb/in^2 compressed air can also be employed, but this method has a tendency to redeposit the particles. Wiping with a soft, clean rag has the disadvantage of not being able to remove dust from grooves and inaccessible places. Buildup of grease and oil can be removed by conservative use of non-flammable solvents such as trichloroethylene. Megohmmeter readings should be taken after cleaning and drying. If the resistance is too low, dry out the machine with heat for several days. If low resistance persists, the cleaning should be repeated and followed by drying.

Regularly scheduled inspections should include checking for tightness, checking of all wires for chafed, brittle, or otherwise damaged insulation; checking bearings brushes, and commutator for proper operating condition. Inspect for leakage of bearing grease inside generator. If moisture has accumulated in the generator, the unit must be dried and strip heaters or other methods must be utilized to prevent the condition from recurring. To dry the unit, external heat should be applied to reduce the moisture content. Internal heat may then be applied by introducing a low-voltage current through the windings. The winding temperature must be monitored to prevent insulation damage during the drying operation.

Brushes and connecting shunts should be inspected for wear and deterioration. Remove the brushes one at a time and check for length. Be sure the brushes move freely in their holders. Brush holders should be checked for proper tension. Most brushes will operate satisfactorily with 2.5–3.0 lb/in^2 of brush cross section, but manufacturer's recommendation should be checked. Replace or repair brush holders that cannot provide adequate tension. Brushes should be replaced when worn to the point that tension cannot be adjusted properly, usually a brush length of about 1/2 in. In most cases, replace complete sets rather than single brushes. Be sure the shunt leads are properly connected. After placing new brushes in their holders, carefully fit the contact surface of the brushes to the commutator by using first #1, then #00, abrasive paper (aluminum oxide is recommended). Cut the abrasive paper into strips slightly wider than one brush. Insert the strip under the brush with the smooth side toward the commutator. Draw the strip in direction of rotation only until 90% contact has been made with arc of commutator. After the brushes have been seated, clean the carbon dust from the commutator and brush assemblies.

Examine brushes for sparking under load. Commutator brushes may have slight sparking; slip ring brushes should have none at all. Examine brushes for chattering, or for frayed shunts or chipped brushes indicative of chattering. If correction of spring tension does not alleviate the chattering, consult an expert for advice on brush grades, brush current density, brush pressure, etc.

Commutators should be smooth and have a light-to-medium-brown color. A rough or blackened generator commutator may be lightly polished with a commutator dressing stone fitted to the curvature of the commutator, but the underlying cause should be determined. If not available, use #00 abrasive paper with a block of wood shaped to fit the curvature of the commutator. *Do not use emery cloth.* All brushes should be lifted and the generator driven while slowly moving the polishing block back and forth. The mica insulation between commutator bars should be undercut 1/16–1/32 in. As the commutator wears down, the mica will cause ridges resulting in bouncing of the brushes. If this condition exists the mica must be undercut and the commutator resurfaces by a qualified repairman. Do not use lubricants of any kind on the commutator.

Generator bearings should be subjected to careful inspection at regularly scheduled intervals. The frequency of inspection, including addition or changing of oil or grease, is best determined by a study of the particular operating conditions. Sealed bearings require no maintenance and must be replaced when worn or loose. When the generator is running, listen for/or record noise, and feel the bearing housing for vibration or excessive heat. Use equipment to obtain signature on antifriction bearings.

The failure of an insulation system is a common cause of problems in electrical equipment. Insulation is subject to many conditions that can cause failure, such as mechanical damage, vibration, excessive heat or cold, dirt, oil, corrosive vapors, and moisture from either processes or just humid weather. To aid in detecting any of these damaging effects, an insulation-resistance test is used to determine insulation quality. The test is simple, convenient, and non-destructive. A carefully controlled high-potential (hi-pot) test may be performed at less frequent intervals.

The location of the engine-generator set for an emergency or a standby power system is an important aspect of maintenance. If located indoors, provisions should be made to ensure there is space for repair/maintenance procedures to be accomplished. If located outdoors, dusty and corrosive environments should be avoided, and engines should be equipped with a lubricating heater and engine-coolant heater.

With proper preventive maintenance, a generator will provide reliable and lengthy service.

8.4.3 Typical maintenance schedule

NOTE—The following maintenance items or schedule are significant but not necessarily complete. Each system should have it's own schedule developed from experience and early test results. In addition, table A-6-3.1 (a) from ANSI/NFPA 110-1993 can be helpful.

The following typical maintenance schedule is presented as a guide:

a) *Weekly inspections.* The following checks should be made weekly. Corrective action shall be taken for any item found to be deficient.

    1) Check battery charging system.

    2) Start-run generator under full load for 30–60 min.

b) *Monthly inspections.* The following checks should be made monthly. Corrective action shall be taken for any item found to be deficient.

    1) Check/verify meter readings.

    2) Check intake filter.

    3) Check battery level.

    4) Check insulation resistance (surge arrestor must be disconnected).

c) *Semiannual inspections.* The following action shall be made semiannually.

    1) Check for leaks.

d) *Annual inspections.* The following action shall be made annually:

    1) Tighten mounting bolts.

    2) Perform hi-pot test of windings (includes polarization index and step voltage).

    3) Grease bearings.

    4) Tighten electrical connections and thermal scan under load.

8.5 Uninterruptible power supply (UPS) systems

8.5.1 General

UPS systems are installed because the load requires an uninterruptible source of power or a power source of specific quality. Therefore, precautions must be taken when isolating a UPS for maintenance. Be familiar with the critical loads supplied by the UPS and notify the appropriate personnel whenever the UPS must be removed from service for maintenance.

Whenever a shut-down of the system is required for maintenance, the UPS system should be placed in the bypass mode, or for redundant systems, the load should be transferred to the redundant units.The UPS system to be maintained should be completely isolated from input and output power, including batteries. Many UPS systems have a unique isolating procedure to prevent an outage to a critical load. These procedures, where available, should be followed. An additional safety precaution is required to ensure that stored energy capacitors are discharged.

8.5.2 Typical maintenance schedule for a static UPS system

A static UPS system is extremely reliable and requires minimal maintenance of the inverter and battery charger. See 8.7 for maintenance of batteries.

(The following maintenance items or schedule are significant but not necessarily complete. Each system should have its own schedule developed from experience and early test results.)

Preventive maintenance consists of cleaning and inspecting the UPS system periodically. Typical inspection intervals are daily, monthly, quarterly, and annually. In severe environments, intervals should be decreased. When performing maintenance, follow all safety procedures using appropriate tools, test equipment, and safety equipment. The following items should be included in the inspections:

a) *Weekly inspections.* The following checks should be made weekly. Corrective action shall be taken for any item found to be deficient.
   1) Check all lamps using the "lamp test" feature.
   2) Check all meters to ensure they are operating.
   3) Check input, output, and bypass voltage and current.
   4) Verify that the disturbance monitor is operable, if the UPS system is so equipped.

b) *Monthly inspections.* The following checks should be made monthly. Corrective action shall be taken for any item found to be deficient.
   1) Complete all daily inspections.
   2) Check the appearance and cleanliness of all equipment, the room/area.
   3) Inspect the HVAC equipment and measure the room/area temperature and humidity.
   4) Check all UPS equipment air intakes and exhausts, including all filters.

c) *Quarterly inspections.* The following checks should be made quarterly. Corrective action shall be taken for any item found to be deficient.

1) Complete all monthly inspections.
2) Inspect all parts for evidence of overheating.
3) Inspect all parts for evidence of physical damage, including worn insulation and corrosion.
4) Inspect terminals for loose or broken connections, burned insulation, etc.
5) Check for liquid contamination (battery electrolyte, oil from capacitors, etc.).
6) Clean the inside of all equipment enclosures and clean the components within.
7) Measure the phase and neutral currents with a true rms ammeter.

d) *Annual inspections.* The following checks should be made annually. Corrective action shall be taken for any item found to be deficient.
1) Complete all quarterly inspections.
2) Check all connections, e.g., retorque or thermal scan under load.
3) Check and test all circuit breakers (biannually only).
4) Perform a complete operational test of the system, including operation at full load, operation on batteries, overload checks, simulation of faults, loss of input, manual and automatic transfers, operation of redundant modules, and so forth (biannually only).
5) Check and adjust voltage output and frequency according to manufacturer's specifications.
6) Test alarm shutdown functions.

e) *System restoration.* If the UPS system has been removed from service for maintenance, follow procedures to place it back in service. After the UPS system has been reconnected and if an operational test was not performed as part of the maintenance, check the output voltage and frequency under load. Simulate a power failure and check for proper system operation.

8.5.3 Typical maintenance schedule for a rotating UPS system

Like the static UPS system, preventive maintenance for the rotating UPS consists of cleaning and inspecting the UPS system periodically. Typical inspection intervals are daily, monthly, semiannually, and annually. In severe environments, intervals should be decreased. When performing maintenance, follow all safety procedures and use appropriate tools, test equipment, and safety equipment. The following items should be included in the inspections.

a) *Weekly inspections.* The following checks should be made weekly. Corrective action shall be taken for any item found to be deficient.
1) Check all lamps using the "lamp test" feature.
2) Check all meters to ensure they are operating.
3) Check input, output, and bypass voltage and current.
4) Verify that the disturbance monitor is operable, if the UPS system is so equipped.

b) *Monthly inspections.* The following checks should be made monthly. Corrective action shall be taken for any item found to be deficient.
1) Complete all daily inspections.
2) Check the appearance and cleanliness of all equipment, the room/area.
3) Inspect the HVAC equipment and measure the room/area temperature and humidity.

4) Check all air intakes and exhausts, including all filters.
5) Run unit at full-load for minimum of 30–60 min.

c) *Semiannual inspections.* The following checks should be made semiannually. Corrective action shall be taken for any item found to be deficient.
1) Complete all monthly inspections.
2) Inspect all parts for evidence of overheating.
3) Inspect all parts for evidence of physical damage, including worn insulation and corrosion.
4) Inspect terminals for loose or broken connections, burned insulation, etc.
5) Check for connections for tightness.
6) Clean the inside of all equipment enclosures and clean the components within.
7) Check all bearings and their lubrication.
8) Run the unit at full-load and check all transfer functions.
9) Test alarm shutdown functions.

d) *Annual inspections.* The following checks should be made annually. Corrective action shall be taken for any item found to be deficient.
1) Complete all semiannual inspections.
2) Check all connections, e.g., retorque or thermal scan under load.
3) Check and test all circuit breakers (biannually only).
4) Perform a complete operational test of the system, including operation at full load, operation on batteries, overload checks, simulation of faults, loss of input, manual and automatic transfers, operation of redundant modules, and so forth (biannually only).

e) *System restoration.* If the UPS system has been removed from service for maintenance, follow procedures to place it back in service. After the UPS system has been reconnected and if an operational test was not performed as part of the maintenance, check the output voltage and frequency under load. Simulate a power failure and check for proper system operation.

8.6 Stationary batteries

8.6.1 General

The primary objective of any battery maintenance program is to ensure that the battery installation is able to meet the emergency requirements of the system to which it is connected, over its design life. Secondary objectives are to achieve optimum life of the battery and to determine when the battery requires replacement. To be effective, the maintenance must be both regular and consistent. In addition, since much of the analysis of the data relies upon comparison to previous data (i.e., trend analysis), the data must be corrected to standard references. For example, within the USA, the reference values are voltage and capacity at 25 °C, and electrolyte full charge specific gravity at 25 °C and at a specific level reference (e.g., the high-level line or the midpoint between the high- and low-level lines).

Maintenance of a battery usually begins at the time of installation. However, if the battery will be in storage for a period longer than that recommended by the battery manufacturer, maintenance should begin while the battery is in storage. IEEE Std 484 describes the data to be taken during installation as well as maintenance to be performed during storage, if required, for vented lead-acid batteries. IEEE Std 1187-1996 provides the same information for valve-regulated lead-acid (VRLA) batteries. (For a discussion of lead-acid batteries, including vented and valve-regulated types, refer to Chapter 5.)

IEEE Std 450-1995 describes the necessary maintenance and testing for vented lead-acid batteries. It also provides information on the corrective actions to be taken, the urgency of the need to take such actions, and the criteria for battery replacement. IEEE P1188 and IEEE Std 1106-1995 provide the same information for VRLA and nickel-cadmium batteries, respectively.

8.6.2 Typical maintenance schedule

A summary of maintenance inspections and tests are provided in table 8-1. Persons performing maintenance should be familiar with the appropriate standard(s) and battery manufacturer's instructions for the battery to be maintained. This is particularly true for VRLA cells since some testing is recommended that is designed to determine if dry-out of the cell is occurring. Dry-out can be caused by a number of factors, such as high float voltage and high temperature. When these factors are present in the installation, the oxygen recombination process within the cell is upset, and the cell will begin to vent oxygen and hydrogen. This loss of gas (i.e., actually the water in the immobilized electrolyte) from the cell causes it to dry out, since there is no way to add water to the VRLA cell. The effects of dry-out can range from loss of capacity to thermal runaway (i.e., catastrophic failure of the cell). These conditions can be detected by measurement of cell impedance (or conductance) and cell temperatures (in the case of thermal problems). Although a considerable amount of impedance/conductance testing is being performed, which is a good indicator of loss of capacity for VRLA cells, it should not yet be considered a replacement for regular battery capacity tests. Additional information on the subjects of impedance/conductance testing and thermal runaway can be found in IEEE Std 1187-1996.

8.6.3 Safety

All work performed on a battery shall be done only with proper and safe tools and with the appropriate protective equipment as listed:

— Goggles and face shield.
— Acid- or alkali-resistant gloves.
— Protective aprons and overshoes.
— Portable or stationary water facilities for rinsing eyes and skin in case of contact with electrolyte.
— Acid (or alkali) neutralizing solution.
— Class C fire extinguisher.

  NOTE—Some battery manufacturers do not recommend the use of CO_2 Class C fire extinguishers due to the potential of thermal shock, and possible cracking, of the battery containers.

— Tools with insulated handles.

Table 8-1—Battery maintenance inspection schedule

Description[a]	Vented lead-acid cells					Valve-regulated lead-acid cells					Vented nickel-cadmium cells				
	INITIAL[b]	GENERAL[c]	QUARTERLY	ANNUAL	SPECIAL	INITIAL[b]	GENERAL[c]	QUARTERLY	ANNUAL	SPECIAL	INITIAL[b]	QUARTERLY	SEMIANNUAL	ANNUAL	SPECIAL
Visual inspections															
General appearance: battery/rack/area	×	×	×	×	×	×	×	×	×	×	×	×	×	×	×
Dirt/electrolyte on jars/covers, etc.	×	×	×	×	×	×	×	×	×	×	×	×	×	×	×
Charger output voltage/current	×	×	×	×	×	×	×	×	×	×	×	×	×	×	×
Electrolyte level	×	×	×	×	×						×	×	×	×	×
Jar/cover cracks or leaks	×	×	×	×	×	×	×	×	×	×	×	×	×	×	×
Evidence of corrosion	×	×	×	×	×	×	×	×	×	×	×	×	×	×	×
Flame arrestor— clogged	×			×	×						×			×	×
Detailed rack inspection	×		×	×		×			×		×			×	
Insulating covers on racks	×			×		×			×		×			×	

[a] For additional information and correction actions, see IEEE Std 450-1995, IEEE Std 1106-1995, and IEEE P1188.
[b] Initial inspections are performed at the time of installation.
[c] The recommended frequency for general inspection is monthly.
[d] Read every other inspection (i.e., every six months).
[e] Sample 25% per quarter. If sample shows an increase in resistance, perform measurements on each connection.
[f] Check 10% of cells.
[g] Measure temperature at the negative terminal of each cell/module.

Table 8-1—Battery maintenance inspection schedule (*Continued*)

Description[a]	Vented lead-acid cells					Valve-regulated lead-acid cells					Vented nickel-cadmium cells				
	INITIAL[b]	GENERAL[c]	QUARTERLY	ANNUAL	SPECIAL	INITIAL[b]	GENERAL[c]	QUARTERLY	ANNUAL	SPECIAL	INITIAL[b]	QUARTERLY	SEMIANNUAL	ANNUAL	SPECIAL
Seismic rack parts/spacers	×			×		×			×		×			×	
Detailed cell inspection	×			×											
Plates: Cracks/sulfate/hydration	×			×	×										
Abnormal sediment accumulation				×	×										
Jar and post seals	×			×	×	×	×	×	×	×	×			×	
Excessive jar/cover distortion	×			×	×	×	×	×	×	×					
Excessive gassing	×			×	×										
Signs of vibration	×			×	×	×			×						
Measurements															
Battery float voltage	×	×	×	×	×	×	×	×	×	×	×	×	×	×	×
Pilot cell voltage	×	×	×	×	×										

[a] For additional information and correction actions, see IEEE Std 450-1995, IEEE Std 1106-1995, and IEEE P1188.
[b] Initial inspections are performed at the time of installation.
[c] The recommended frequency for general inspection is monthly.
[d] Read every other inspection (i.e., every six months).
[e] Sample 25% per quarter. If sample shows an increase in resistance, perform measurements on each connection.
[f] Check 10% of cells.
[g] Measure temperature at the negative terminal of each cell/module.

Table 8-1—Battery maintenance inspection schedule (*Continued*)

Description[a]	Vented lead-acid cells					Valve-regulated lead-acid cells					Vented nickel-cadmium cells				
	INITIAL[b]	GENERAL[c]	QUARTERLY	ANNUAL	SPECIAL	INITIAL[b]	GENERAL[c]	QUARTERLY	ANNUAL	SPECIAL	INITIAL[b]	QUARTERLY	SEMIANNUAL	ANNUAL	SPECIAL
Pilot cell electrolyte temperature	×	×	×	×	×						×	×	×	×	×
Pilot cell electrolyte specific gravity	×	×	×	×	×										
Individual cell voltage	×		×	×	×	×		×[d]	×	×	×		×	×	×
Individual cell electrolyte specific gravity	×		×[f]	×	×										
Cell temperature	×		×[f]	×	×	×[g]		×[g]	×[g]	×[g]					
Intercell connection resistance	×			×		×		×[e]	×	×					
Cell impedance/ conductance/ resistance						×		×	×	×					
Ac ripple current/ voltage						×			×	×					
Intercell connection torque											×			×	×

[a] For additional information and correction actions, see IEEE Std 450-1995, IEEE Std 1106-1995, and IEEE P1188.

[b] Initial inspections are performed at the time of installation.

[c] The recommended frequency for general inspection is monthly.

[d] Read every other inspection (i.e., every six months).

[e] Sample 25% per quarter. If sample shows an increase in resistance, perform measurements on each connection.

[f] Check 10% of cells.

[g] Measure temperature at the negative terminal of each cell/module.

Table 8-1—Battery maintenance inspection schedule (*Continued*)

Description[a]	Vented lead-acid cells					Valve-regulated lead-acid cells					Vented nickel-cadmium cells				
	INITIAL[b]	GENERAL[c]	QUARTERLY	ANNUAL	SPECIAL	INITIAL[b]	GENERAL[c]	QUARTERLY	ANNUAL	SPECIAL	INITIAL[b]	QUARTERLY	SEMIANNUAL	ANNUAL	SPECIAL
Other															
Ambient temperature	×	×	×	×	×	×	×	×	×	×	×				
Ventilation equipment adequacy	×	×	×	×	×	×	×	×	×	×	×	×	×	×	×
Check/retorque battery rack				×					×					×	
Check connections to ground	×			×		×			×		×			×	

[a] For additional information and correction actions, see IEEE Std 450-1995, IEEE Std 1106-1995, and IEEE P1188.
[b] Initial inspections are performed at the time of installation.
[c] The recommended frequency for general inspection is monthly.
[d] Read every other inspection (i.e., every six months).
[e] Sample 25% per quarter. If sample shows an increase in resistance, perform measurements on each connection.
[f] Check 10% of cells.
[g] Measure temperature at the negative terminal of each cell/module.

Since much of the maintenance performed on a battery is done with the battery in service, the work methods used should follow the protective procedures outlined in the appropriate reference listed in 8.9. In addition, these methods should preclude circuit interruption or arcing in the vicinity of the battery. One of the reasons for this is that hydrogen is liberated from all vented-cell-type batteries while they are on float or equalize charge, or when they are nearing completion of a recharge. VRLA cells will also liberate hydrogen whenever their vent opens. Therefore, adequate ventilation by natural or mechanical means must be available to minimize hydrogen accumulation. Additionally, the battery area should be mandated as a "no smoking" area.

8.7 Automatic transfer switches

Automatic transfer switches require maintenance, as do most components of electrical installations. The automatic transfer switch is usually applied where two sources of power are made available for the purpose of maintaining power to a critical load. The necessity of providing safe maintenance and repair of an automatic transfer switch requires shutdown of both power sources or installation of a bypass switch. The bypass switch is used to isolate the automatic transfer switch while maintaining power to the critical load. For periodic maintenance inspections where de-energization is impractical, a two-way bypass isolation switch combined with an automatic transfer switch as part of UPS system can be provided. Although more costly, this type of switch (covered in 4.3.10) allows for periodic testing and maintenance.

8.8 Conclusions

Maintenance is an essential requirement of any electrical installation. The critical nature of emergency and standby power systems applications dictate the importance of properly maintaining the equipment involved. A good preventive maintenance program will aid in maintaining a reliable system.

8.9 References

This chapter shall be used in conjunction with the following publications:

ANSI/NFPA 101-1994, Code for Safety to Life from Fire in Buildings and Structures.[2]

ANSI/NFPA 110-1993, Emergency and Standby Power Systems.

ANSI/NFPA 111-1993, Stored Electrical Energy Emergency and Standby Power Systems.

---

[2]NFPA publications are available from Publications Sales, National Fire Protection Association, 1 Batterymarch Park, P.O. Box 9101, Quincy, MA 02269-9101, USA.

IEEE Std 450-1995, IEEE Recommended Practice for Maintenance, Testing, and Replacement of Vented Lead-Acid Batteries for Stationary Applications.[3]

IEEE Std 484-1996, IEEE Recommended Practice for Installation Design and Installation of Vented Lead-Acid Batteries for Stationary Applications.

IEEE Std 1106-1995, IEEE Recommended Practice for Installation, Maintenance, Testing, and Replacement of Vented Nickel-Cadmium Batteries for Stationary Applications (ANSI).

IEEE Std 1187-1996, IEEE Recommended Practice for Installation Design and Installation of Valve-Regulated Lead-Acid Storage Batteries for Stationary Applications.

IEEE P1188, Draft Recommended Practice for Maintenance, Testing, and Replacement of Valve-Regulated Lead-Acid Batteries for Stationary Applications, Oct. 1995.[4]

NFPA 70B-1994, Electrical Equipment Maintenance.

NFPA 70E-1995, Electrical Safety Requirements for Employee Work Places.

8.10 Bibliography

Additional information may be found in the following sources:

[B1] Demont, R. F., "Preventive Maintenance of Standby Generator Sets," *Electrical Construction and Maintenance Magazine*, pt. 1, Mar. 1992; pt. 2, Apr. 1992.

[B2] Feder, D. O., et al., "Field and Laboratory Studies to Assess the State of Health of Valve-Regulated Lead-Acid Batteries: Part I—Conductance/Capacity Correlation Studies." in *Conference Record 92CH3195-5*, 1992 IEEE INTELEC Conference, pp. 218–233.

[B3] Gabriel, C. M., and Uhlir, K. W., "Battery Impedance—Single Cell Capacity Test Vs. Standard Every Cell Capacity Test," in *Proceedings of the American Power Conference*, vol. 55-I, 1993, pp. 38–43.

[B4] Harrison, A. I., "Thermal Management of High Energy Density Battery Equipments," in *Conference Record 92CH3195-5*, 1992 IEEE INTELEC Conference, pp. 28-34.

[B5] Markel, G. J., "AC Impedance Testing for Valve-Regulated Cells," in *Conference Record 92CH3195-5*, 1992 IEEE INTELEC Conference, pp. 212–217.

[B6] Migliaro, M. W., "Maintaining Stationary Batteries," *IEEE Transactions on Industry Applications*, vol. 1A-23, no. 4, pp. 765–772, Jul./Aug. 1987.

[3]IEEE publications are available from the Institute of Electrical and Electronics Engineers, 445 Hoes Lane, P.O. Box 1331, Piscataway, NJ 08855-1331, USA.

[4]This IEEE standards project was not approved by the IEEE Standards Board at the time this publication went to press. For information about obtaining a draft, contact the IEEE.

[B7] Migliaro, M. W., "Maintaining Maintenance-Free Batteries," in *Conference Record 89CH2738-3*, 1989 IEEE IAS Industrial & Commercial Power Systems Conference, pp. 69–73.

[B8] Migliaro, M. W., "Stationary Batteries-Selected Topics," in *Proceedings of the American Power Conference*, vol. 55-1, pp. 23–33, 1993.

[B9] Migliaro, M. W., and Mazzoni, O. S., "Battery Problems That Can Spell Disaster," Disaster Avoidance & Recovery '93 Conference, May 1993.

[B10] Misra, S. S., Noveske, T. M., and Williamson, A. W., "Thermal Effects in VRLA Cells and Comparison with Wet Lead-Acid Cells Under Different Operating Conditions," in *Conference Record 92CH3195-5*, 1992 IEEE INTELEC Conference, pp. 35–40.

[B11] Soileau, R. D., Jr., A Diagnostic Testing Program for Large Lead-Acid Storage Battery Banks, *Conference Record 92-CH3186-4*, IAS 39th Annual Petroleum and Chemical Industry Conference, pp. 27–35, Sept. 1992.

[B12] Vaccarok, F. J., and Landwehrle, R. E., "Experiments on Thermal Run-A-Way and Its Management for Electrolyte Immobilized Lead-Acid Batteries," in *Conference Record 91CH2970-2*, 1991 IEEE INTELEC Conference, pp. 20–25.

Chapter 9
Specific industry applications

9.1 General

This chapter summarizes needs for emergency or standby electric power observed in each of several industries. Industries that have not demonstrated general need for such power are not listed, although there is probably no industry that has not used standby power of some type at some place or time. Even certain general uses of specific applications are ignored. Battery control sources for electrical switchgear are not referenced since they are covered in IEEE C37.20-1969.[1] Use of the common flashlight is not referenced unless the need for standby lighting is generally significant.

It is the intent of this chapter to catalog where standby power has been used, to point out how such power can serve to fulfill certain needs, and to provide some guidance in evaluating the desirability of standby power. It is not the intent of this chapter to suggest or interpret legal requirements for standby or emergency power. Such requirements, as may be included in building or safety codes, are adopted and interpreted by authorities having jurisdiction over such matters. The significant reasons for adopting these requirements are far broader than the engineering considerations of the standby power system itself.

Needs for standby power appear to be growing as equipment and process complexities and costs increase. As more industries find that standby power generally can be economically justified, they will be added to the summaries.

It is sometimes difficult to establish the justification for standby power on an objective economic basis. Developing objective historical costing of power outages can be difficult, and projecting costs can be more difficult. Data on power system outages are available in IEEE Std 493-1980, but local conditions of weather or utility service can result in performance at considerable variance with the standard data. Infrequency of outages in some locations tends to restrict the data base and the accuracy of short-time predictions. Such data should be augmented with the user's and other local data. The American Insurance Association has adopted the National Building Code, which contains requirements for standby based upon types of buildings and occupancy classifications. Compliance with this code is encouraged through adjustment of insurance rates.

Needs for standby power affecting human safety should not be evaluated purely on an economic basis. Standby power should be made available if there is a reasonable possibility that loss of normal power could cause serious injury or loss of life. Emergency or standby power has been mandated by authorities in many situations, and such mandates will likely spread to other situations upon occurrence of injury or death.

---

[1]Information on references can be found in 9.2.

Electrical standby power is not recommended as the correct or only solution to all problems or hazards that result from loss of electrical power. There is risk that local electrical failure could forestall use of the standby power. Alternate solutions may be attractive from both an economic and reliability standpoint. For example, cement plants often supply rotational power for the kiln from a mechanically coupled engine during power outages. While avoiding the cost of a generator, this arrangement covers not only loss of utility power, but also the contingencies of loss of in-plant distribution or failure of the electric kiln drive. Many jurisdictions also demand this type of drive as a standby for the electric drive on a chair lift.

Systems that are inherently safe will provide greater reliability than those dependent upon a source of electrical power to maintain safety. Designers are encouraged to produce systems that will assume a safe posture upon loss of electric power. Managers are encouraged to invoke procedures that will avoid hazards when power is lost. In the case of a work force that is required to carry flashlights, or a process controller with built-in battery backup, it may be argued whether they are inherently safe systems or whether they are examples of standby power systems, but they are effective and economically attractive.

Standby power can more easily be justified if generators are also operated in the *cogeneration* mode. Cogeneration refers to obtaining a second form of energy from the generation process, usually heat, which increases the efficiency in the use of energy as well as the economics of the operation. By maintaining certain efficiencies and utilizations, a generator operator may become a qualifying facility under the auspices of PURPA (Public Utilities Regulatory Act of 1978), which will allow them to operate in parallel with the utility. Parallel operation normally increases the economic benefit to be derived from the generators, while allowing no-break standby power. Qualifying facility status can make the generator operator eligible for certain tax benefits. With proper design and certain relaying and control additions, the basic cogeneration system can provide standby power, and this is commonly done.

Tables 9-1 through 9-10 itemize emergency and standby power needs that are at least somewhat specific to the designated industry. There may be needs that are common to many industries, but these are listed only once, under the industry with which they are most commonly associated. For instance, most industries have offices or occupancies to which the items in table 9-3 (commercial buildings) would apply. Most industries have some form of data processing, usually with some power supply needs. For larger data-processing installations, refer to table 9-5 (financial data processing).

Process controllers are proliferating throughout industry, but the tables are intended to address the electrical needs of the process itself rather than the controller. The consideration of supplying power to a controller to prevent malfunction, damage, or loss of data is common to all industries.

NOTES TO TABLES 9-1 THROUGH 9-10:

NOTE A: Categories of purposes for emergency or standby power

1—*Human safety and health.* This includes preventing injury or death from causes such as falling, collisions, equipment operations or malfunctions, explosions, fire, release of toxic or explosive substances, failure of safety of life supporting devices, and actions of others. Emergency power uses include signaling, lighting, conveyances for evacuation, control of machinery, combating fire, and smoke or vapor dispersal.

2—*Environmental protection.* This includes prevention of damage to environment (temporary or permanent), which includes effects on water quality, wildlife, or vegetation that do not immediately or significantly threaten human life or health.

3—*Nonemergency evacuation.* This covers requirements of evacuation for convenience or for precautionary reasons where no immediate danger or urgency exists, and can include lighting and conveyances.

4—*Protection of equipment, product, material, and property.* This covers needs for orderly shutdown, limited operation or security, lack of which could result in economic loss due to repair or replacement costs or unavailability of equipment or material.

5—*Continuance of partial or full production.* This covers needs where cessation of production could result in inordinate economic loss due to extended restart times or requirements of timely product delivery.

NOTE B: Categories to types of standby or emergency power required

1—*Uninterruptible ac power.* Specially conditioned.

2—*Uninterruptible ac power.* Suitable for computer use (see 3.11.3 for guidelines to computer power requirements).

3—*Interruptible ac power.* Specially conditioned to eliminate sags, spikes, flicker, harmonics, or noise such as could be achieved with static or rotating power conditioner. Required for powering equipment with no inherent immunity to these power system defects.

4—*Interruptible ac power.* Commercial grade such as defined by ANSI C84.1-1989 or ANSI/NEMA MG 1-1993 motor requirements. Suitable for equipment satisfactorily powered from conventional utility source. Range of tolerable outage time to dictate whether fixed or portable, automatic or nonautomatic.

5—*Permanently installed dc power maintained at full capability.* Includes emergency lighting sources and internal or external battery backup for communications, computers, and processors.

6—*Portable dc power.* Includes power sources in flashlight, lanterns, and portable communicating devices, either installed or spare.

Table 9-1—Summary of possible or typical emergency or standby power needs for the agri-business industry

Power use	Application	Purposes (see Note A)	Range of tolerable outage time	Duration of need	Power sources (see Notes under 9.2.2)	Remarks
Ventilation, feeding	Confinement, housing	4, 5	1 h or less	Duration of outage	4	
Ventilation, heating, feeding, egg gathering, lighting	Poultry production	4, 5	10 min	Duration of outage	4	Production affected after 10 min. Death can occur after 1/2 h.
Computer	Data or process control	4 or 5	0–1 h	Duration of outage	3, 4, 2	
Milking machine	Milking	4, 5	1–2 h	2–4 h twice daily	4	Cows must be milked even though milk not saved.
Refrigeration	Food storage	4, 5	1/2–15 h	Duration of outage	4	Temperature can be maintained for many hours if doors not opened.
Pumps, heater	Water supply systems	4, 5	2–6 h	Duration of outage	4	Alternate solutions available not requiring electric power.

Table 9-2—Summary of possible or typical emergency or standby power needs for the cement industry

Power use	Application	Purposes (see Note A)	Range of tolerable outage time	Duration of need	Power sources (see Note B)	Remarks
Kiln drive	Rotation	4	5 min	Indefinite or intermittent, or both	4	Often accomplished by mechanical power.
Control	Shutdown and continuity	4	0	Short or indefinite	2, 5	
Plant	Production	5	0–10 min	Duration of outage	4	Cogeneration using waste heat may be economically justified, particularly with poor commercial supply.

Table 9-3—Summary of possible or typical emergency or standby power needs for the commercial building industry

Power use	Application	Purposes (see Note A)	Range of tolerable outage time	Duration of need	Power sources (see Note B)	Remarks
Emergency lighting	Hotels, apartments, stores, theaters, offices, assembly halls	1, 3, 4, 5	10–60 s or statutory requirement	1-1/2 h or statutory requirement or as needed	2, 4, 5 [a]	Building management or safety authorities to determine *as needed* requirements.
Elevators	Hotels, apartments, stores, offices	3, 5	10 s to 5 min	Evacuation completion	4 [b]	Other methods of evacuation may be available.
Phones in elevators	Signaling, switching, talking	3	10–60 s	Evacuation completion or extended occupancy	2, 4, 6	Many PBX or PAX systems no longer have batteries.
Other phones or PAs	Signaling, switching, talking	3	10–60 s	Evacuation completion or extended occupancy	2, 4, 5	Many PBX or PAX systems no longer have batteries.
HVAC	Space, process, or material	4, 5	1–30 min	Duration of outage	4	Negotiable with tenants.
Tenants' computers	Various	4, 5	Negotiable	Negotiable	2, 3, 4	Negotiable with tenants. For large systems, see table 9-5.
Fire fighting and smoke control	Fire pumps and ventilation control	1, 4	10 s	2 h or more	4	Pumps needed when high-rise exceeds water pressure capability.
Electric security locks	Access controls	4	10–60 s	Completion of evacuation	2, 4, [b] 5 [a]	Protection from theft of stock and evacuation.

[a] Where applicable, the National Electrical Code (NEC) (NFPA 70-1996), Section 700-12, requires 1-1/2 h battery supply.

[b] Where applicable, the NEC, Section 700-12, requires 2 h generator fuel supply.

Table 9-3—Summary of possible or typical emergency or standby power needs for the commercial building industry (*Continued*)

Power use	Application	Purposes (see Note A)	Range of tolerable outage time	Duration of need	Power sources (see Note B)	Remarks
Emergency lighting	Store lighting	4	10–60 s	Completion of evacuation	2, 4	Protection from theft and continuing operation are financially significant.
Emergency lighting and HVAC	Casino lighting and environment	3, 4, 5	1–10 s	Duration of outage	2, 4	Protection from theft and continuing operation are financially significant.

NOTE—Statements regarding commercial buildings have to be somewhat general due to wide variations in building construction and use, but certain standardization does apply.

Definitions are performance requirements of emergency and standby power systems appear in NEC, Articles 700, 701, and 702; and NFPA 99-1996. Standard requirements for use appear in NEC, Article 517; ANSI/NFPA 101-1994; the Uniform Building Code; and the Basic National Building Code. Legal requirements are established by authorities having jurisdiction, often by adopting one or more of the above codes. In addition, conformance with the National Building Code may be made a requirement for insurance by the underwriter. Nevertheless, emergency or standby power is not universally required for all commercial buildings. Notes to NEC, Articles 700 and 701, suggest some circumstances that may require such power.

The statutory requirements for standby or emergency power are the minimum permitted. It should not be presumed that they will be adequate for all occasions. If occupants are not evacuated during the mandated period of emergency lighting or power, there may be inadequate lighting for subsequent evacuation, inadequate heating or ventilation, and inadequate water pressure for fire fighting. In addition, tenants may have processes or process equipment, controlled environments, or other needs, some of which are listed in the summary. Thus a loss of power, or the necessity of evacuation if commercial power is lost, could be a hardship. Evacuation of residential facilities during inclement weather could be undesirable. Unless notified or evacuated, tenants may be unaware that commercial power is lost, and therefore unaware of impending loss of power or lighting for evacuation.

Tenants are advised to make themselves aware of power needs during loss of commercial power, and to make themselves aware of the power facilities installed in their building. Tenants with greater needs should either contract with the building management for additional power or supply the necessary facilities themselves. Building managements may find it commercially attractive to offer enhanced or extended emergency power services.

If the requirements are only for emergency lighting, for the minimum 1.5 h specified by NEC battery lights will usually suffice. If lighting needs are more extensive, or if operation of motors is required, an engine generator is normally required. Once this latter equipment is installed, the only limit on the duration of availability of the power is the size of the fuel tank

[a] Where applicable, the National Electrical Code (NEC) (NFPA 70-1996), Section 700-12, requires 1-1/2 h battery supply.

[b] Where applicable, the NEC, Section 700-12, requires 2 h generator fuel supply.

Table 9-4—Summary of possible or typical emergency or standby power needs for the communications industry

Power use	Application	Purposes (see Note A)	Range of tolerable outage time	Duration of need	Power sources (see Note B)	Remarks
Central office, switching or repeater stations	Traffic transmission	1, 2, 4, 5	0	Duration of outage	3, 4, 5	Battery is primary source with generator backup.
Satellite earth stations	Traffic transmissions	1, 5	0	Duration of outage	1, 2, 4, 5	Power requirements largely ac.
Public safety, radio links and terminals	Police and fire communication	1, 2, 3, 4	0–10 s	Duration of outage	2, 4, 5	Usually engine generator.
Military links and terminals	Defense and diplomatic	1, 4	0	Duration of outage	2, 4, 5	Normal requirements, 99.6% reliability.
Aircraft warning lighting	Towers	1	0	Duration of outage	4, 5	

NOTE—The communications industry includes both common and private carriers, and both point-to-point links and broadcast facilities. Traffic can include radio/television entertainment, data transfer, domestic and business, voice transmission, and public safety and national defense functions. These facets of communications are grouped, since in many cases all of the previously listed traffic may be transmitted through the same common carrier, whose performance standards must meet the standards of the most exacting traffic.

The immediate purpose of standby power from the carrier's standpoint is continued timely delivery of the product. The purposes of the timely delivery can include protection of life, property, or environment by police, fire, or defense departments. The purpose can include any aspect of business operation, such as marketing, production, purchasing, or financial transactions.

Table 9-5—Summary of possible or typical emergency or standby power needs for the financial data processing industry

Power use	Application	Purposes (see Note A)	Range of tolerable outage time	Duration of need	Power sources (see Note B)	Remarks
Data processing equipment	Any critical application	4, 5	0	Up to duration of outage	2	UPS can be supported with standby power.
UPS system	Data processing equipment power supply	4, 5	UPS ride-through (usually 10–30 min)	Up to duration of outage	4	This source should meet 10 s requirement if also used for emergency functions.
HVAC	Data processing equipment cooling	4, 5	1 min	Per above	4	To include direct equipment cooling.
UPS system bypass	Power to data processing equipment if UPS fails	4, 5	0	Per above	3, 4	See chapter 7 and NEC, Article 250, for proper grounding. Bypass connection may cause UPS to no longer be defined as a separately derived source.

NOTE—This is an industry where the economic benefits of continued production are substantial enough to justify uninterruptible power supplies (UPSs), and usually alternate power sources that can maintain operation past the stored energy capability of the UPS. The capital cost of the large data processing equipment is justified only with optimum usage, and the utter dependence industry on this equipment for timely conduct of business would make nonavailability a prohibitive expense.

The first premise in standby power consideration is the need when utility power is lost. It is becoming more apparent that electrical problems on the premises can also interrupt power to the data processing equipment. It is also becoming apparent that these on-premises problems will proliferate unless equipment can be maintained and repaired.

The above realizations have illustrated the necessity of redundant circuits and power supplies so that power can be maintained during maintenance work or in case of failures. In the latter situation, the system should be designed, and protective devices applied, so as to provide a realistic ability to provide a realistic ability to clear faults selectively.

This industry category includes not only those obvious members, such as banks and thrift institutions, but also any industry whose sales, billing, or other financial operations have caused the assembling of comparable data processing systems.

Table 9-6—Summary of possible or typical emergency or standby power needs for the health industry

Power use	Application	Purposes (see Note A)	Range of tolerable outage time	Duration of need	Power sources (see Note B)	Remarks
Life safety equipment			10 s		4	Legally required emergency power.
Critical equipment			10 s		4	Legally required emergency power.
Essential equipment			1 min			Legally required standby power.

NOTE—These facilities have some of the greatest and the most regulated needs for emergency power for the preservation of human life. This chapter recognizes this industry as a significant user of emergency power, but refers the reader to IEEE Std 602-1996, where complete coverage of this topic is provided, and also the Articles 517 and 700 of the NEC, plus any local codes or ordinances for detailed requirements.

Table 9-7—Summary of possible or typical emergency or standby power needs for the mining industry

Power use	Application	Purposes (see Note A)	Range of tolerable outage time	Duration of need	Power sources (see Note B)	Remarks
Hoists	Personnel	3	1–10 min	± 1 h	4	Requirements vary greatly between sites; safety-related requirements are covered under the CFR, Title 30.
Fans	Ventilation	1	1 min	1 h or more	4	Requirements vary greatly between sites; safety-related requirements are covered under the CFR, Title 30.
Pumps	Drainage	1, 4	1–60 min	Indefinite	4	Requirements vary greatly between sites; safety-related requirements are covered under the CFR, Title 30.

Table 9-8—Summary of possible or typical emergency or standby power needs for the petrochemical industry

Power use	Application	Purposes (see Note A)	Range of tolerable outage time	Duration of need	Power sources (see Note B)	Remarks
Purge air supply		1 or 4	10 s	As determined	4, 5	To prevent incursion of combustible or toxic gases into machinery, housed field instrumentation (analyzers, etc.), or personnel areas.
Lighting	Emergency evacuation	1	0–10 s	5 min minimum	1–6	Inspection of facilities following a blackout, prior to black start, or evacuation from imminently hazardous areas.
Process controllers	Continued operation or orderly shutdown or both	1, 2, 4, or 5	0–30 min	As determined (by process)	1–5	
Motor-operated valves for emergency use	Isolating of fires by blocking flow of hydrocarbons	1, 2, or 4	0	30 s maximum	2, 4, or 5	
Steam generation	Orderly shutdown or continued operation	1, 2, 4, or 5	0 to as determined	As determined	3, 4, or 5	See 3.5 in Chapter 3.
Flame detectors	Orderly shutdown	1, 2, or 4	0 to as determined	As required by specific process	4	

Table 9-9—Summary of possible or typical emergency or standby power needs for the ski resort industry

Power use	Application	Purposes (see Note A)	Range of tolerable outage time	Duration of need	Power sources (see Note B)	Remarks
Lifts	Uphill transport	3, 5	1–10 min	Until lift is empty— 5–20 min— or for continuous operation	4	Evacuation also can be accomplished using mechanical coupled standby engines. These are required in many jurisdictions.
Slope lights	Night skiing	1, 3	0–1 s	10 s to cease normal skiing; 15–30 min for evacuation	2, 4, 5	Skier can suffer injury from collision or fall with loss of light. Evacuation can tolerate lower light levels.
Lift emergency lighting	Night lift operation	1, 3	0–1 min	Until lift is empty— 5–20 min	2, 4, 5	Required by ANSI B77.1-1992 for unloading or evacuation.

Table 9-10—Summary of possible or typical emergency or standby power needs for the waste water industry

Power use	Application	Purposes (see Note A)	Range of tolerable outage time	Duration of need	Power sources (see Note B)	Remarks
Pumps	Influence, effluence, or processing of waste water	2, 4, 5	0–10 min	Duration of outage	4	EPA or local statues, or both, define bypassing restrictions.
Process controllers		2, 4, 5	0–10 min	Duration of outage	1, 2, 3, 4, 5	To meet above requirements.
Telephones	Signaling and talking	2, 4, 5	0–1 min	Duration of outage	2, 4, 5	The geographical dispersion in the typical facility requires a facility communication system.

NOTES—Local power generation sometimes accomplished with digestor gas.

Facilities are closely regulated and individually permitted under federal clean water laws. Loss of power could require gravity bypassing of processes that require pumping. These processes may exceed permitted allowances, and in no case is complete bypass allowed. Even permitted abnormal operation may receive extensive unfavorable publicity and may be unacceptable to local citizens. Lack of adequate gravity bypass capability or control thereof could cause flooding. It is usually necessary to maintain level, flow, and temperature monitors to oversee bypassing or other contingency operations.

Minimum standby power should be whatever is necessary to meet permit requirements. Many plants have achieved 100% standby capability through the use of digestor gas to operate generators.

Communication should be maintained to coordinate efforts involving manual control or monitoring at various locations. Many modern PBX systems depend upon commercial power for operation.

9.2 References

This chapter shall be used in conjunction with the following publications:

ANSI B77.1-1992, American National Standard Safety Requirements for Passenger Tramways—Aerial Tramways, Aerial Lifts, Surface Lifts, and Tows.[2]

ANSI C84.1-1989, American National Standard Voltage Ratings for Electric Power Systems and Equipment (60 Hz).

ANSI/NEMA MG 1-1993, Motors and Generators.[3]

ANSI/NFPA 101-1994, Code for Safety to Life from Fire in Buildings and Structures.[4]

IEEE Std C37.20.1-1993, IEEE Standard for Metal-Enclosed Low-Voltage Power Circuit Breaker Switchgear.[5]

IEEE Std C37.20.2-1993, IEEE Standard for Metal-Clad and Station-Type Cubicle Switchgear.

IEEE Std C37.20.2b-1994, Supplement to IEEE Standard for Metal-Clad and Station-Type Cubicle Switchgear: Current Transformer Accuracies.

IEEE Std C37.20.3-1987 (Reaff 1992), IEEE Standard for Metal-Enclosed Interrupter Switchgear (ANSI).

IEEE Std 493-1990, IEEE Recommended Practice for Design of Reliable Industrial and Commercial Power Systems (IEEE Gold Book) (ANSI).

IEEE Std 602-1996, IEEE Recommended Practice for Electric Systems in Health Care Facilities (IEEE White Book) (ANSI).[6]

NFPA 70-1996, National Electrical Code®.

NFPA 99-1996, Health Care Facilities Code.

---

[2]ANSI publications are available from the Sales Department, American National Standards Institute, 11 West 42nd Street, 13th Floor, New York, NY 10036, USA.

[3]NEMA publications are available from the Sales Department, American National Standards Institute, 11 West 42nd Street, 13th Floor, New York, NY 10036, USA.

[4]NFPA publications are available from Publications Sales, National Fire Protection Association, 1 Batterymarch Park, P.O. Box 9101, Quincy, MA 02269-9101, USA.

[5]IEEE publications are available from the Institute of Electrical and Electronics Engineers, 445 Hoes Lane, P.O. Box 1331, Piscataway, NJ 08855-1331, USA.

[6]As this standard goes to press, IEEE Std 602-1996 is approved but not yet published. The draft standard is, however, available from the IEEE. Anticipated publication date is December 1996. Contact the IEEE Standards Department at 1 (908) 562-3800 for status information.

Basic National Building Code, Building Officials and Code Administrators (BOCA International, Inc.).[7]

CFR (Code of Federal Regulations), Title 30: Mineral Resources (pts. 1–199), Mine Safety and Health Administration, Department of Labor, July 1986.[8]

National Building Code, American Insurance Association.[9]

Uniform Building Code, International Congress of Building Officials.[10]

[7]This publication is available from BOCA International, Inc., 4051 West Flossmoor Road, Country Club Hills, IL 60477-5795.

[8]This document is available from the Superintendent of Documents, U.S. Government Printing Office, Washington, DC 20402.

[9]This publication is available from the Publications Department, American Insurance Association, 85 John St., New York, NY 10038.

[10]This publication is available from the International Conference of Building Officials, South Workman Mill Rd., Whittier, CA 90601.

Chapter 10
Design and operation considerations for improving the reliability of emergency power systems

10.1 Introduction

There are numerous factors that contribute to the reliability of standby and emergency power systems. Many of these factors have been examined in the previous chapters of this standard.

Reliability, while frequently not a quantifiable value, is dependent on availability. The following definition of reliability reflects this dependence: The lack of unscheduled loss of availability. There are two quantifiable terms that are used to define reliability:

— Mean time between failures (MTBF)
— Mean time to repair after a failure (MTTR)

The common denominator for both of the above terms is *time*. By increasing MTBF and/or reducing MTTR, the system will obtain a higher *availability* due to reduced unscheduled system or component failures. This is greater *reliability*.

This chapter does not deal with rigorous analytical methods for improving reliability. IEEE Std 493-1990[1] should be consulted for an excellent detailed treatment of these methods. Although it is not the intent of this chapter to duplicate the information in IEEE Std 493-1990, some factors and concerns relating to reliability are addressed herein that should be considered by designers and users of standby and emergency systems in the application and use of these systems. The information presented in this chapter is specifically geared towards improving the time factors in the two reliability terms discussed above, MTBF and MTTR.

The factors that will be examined in this chapter are the following:

— Applications
— Environmental concerns
— Specification and acceptance testing
— Maintenance and training
— Failure modes
— Management awareness

10.2 Applications

The most basic factor that applies to the reliability of standby and emergency power systems is its application. Incorrect application of equipment will, sooner or later, lead to poor system reliability.

---

[1]Information on references can be found in 10.9.

The designer should discuss with the user the function the system is expected to perform. Designing a reliable system requires that all of the following questions be considered in relation to its function.

— What is user experience with specific types of equipment?

— What are possible locations for the equipment?

— What is the load profile and types of load the system must supply?

— What are the applicable codes and standards that will apply to the system, including local codes and insurance requirements, if any?

— What is current system configuration and existing margin within the system?

— Does the system impact a utility company? What are the utility company requirements that may exist?

— How will the system be used?

— Has a short-circuit study of the existing and proposed system been performed? What are the results?

— Has a protective coordination study of the proposed system been performed?

— Has the designer verified that all components of the proposed system are compatible with each other and the existing system? Specifically, are UPS and engine generator sets compatible? Solid-state UPS systems draw harmonic currents that can interfere with generator controls. In other cases, the generator may not be able to supply the required harmonics causing the UPS to malfunction.

— Have transient conditions been evaluated? Specifically, are there step loads on generators? Can the generator set safely handle this load? Have inrush currents from UPS systems and motor starts and their impact on the system been evaluated?

— What level of redundancy is required?

— What staff operating and maintenance skills are available?

In addition to considering these questions, the designer must also completely define total system performance requirements. The designer should not fall into the trap of expediency by simply adding a uninterruptible power supply (UPS) system or a diesel generator. For example, a mainframe computer generally requires substantial cooling to keep operating. A design that addresses only the power supply to the computer without addressing required support systems will lead to an unreliable design. Typically, the computer will shut down from overheat in about 15 min. Batteries that operate only the computer are useless at this point.

The proliferation of personal computers and application software has lead to an abundance of design tools. Applications programs now make it possible to fully model system performance, generator loading, transients, battery discharge, and other characteristics associated with standby systems. Full advantage should be taken of these during the design phase.

Designers of standby systems should also be aware of specific products that are available as well as industry trends and topics.

10.3 Environmental concerns

Of significant concern to both the designer and user of standby and emergency systems is the overall system environment. When equipment is not compatible with its operating environment, both MTBF and MTTR will suffer. There are a number of questions and concerns that need to be addressed that can all fall under the broad heading of environmental concerns.

The first of these might be, "What technology am I introducing into this facility?" The skilled design engineer is familiar and comfortable with many available technologies. However, does the end user have personnel that can adapt to the equipment? The system must be designed to fit the personality of the user. In addition, the abilities of the user/operators need to be factored into the design. If a new technology can be assimilated by the user, then it should by all means be used. If, however, assimilation poses a problem, then the equipment will most likely fall into disrepair and not be available when needed most. Further, a lack of understanding may mean that abuse, with its subsequent high maintenance costs, may make the new technology a poor investment.

Additional questions relative to the work rules within the facility should be asked. Who will be in control of the system? How will maintenance and operation be handled? These do not frequently pose significant problems; however, do they in this facility? The answers to these questions should always be determined before a new system is introduced into the workplace. Answers to these questions will aid in the ultimate design of a reliable system.

Another environmental concern is the physical surroundings of the equipment. There are specific precautions that must be taken for dirty, hot, cold, corrosive, explosive, tropical, and other environments. An engine generator set in a cold climate, for example, will probably require thermostatically controlled lubricating oil, coolant heaters, and radiator louvers. For advice on specific environmental requirements, such as the previous example, the equipment manufacturer should be consulted. All equipment manufacturers have requirements for temperature extremes, humidity, ventilation, etc., that need to be included in the design in order for their equipment to give satisfactory performance.

It is incumbent upon the design engineer to obtain all pertinent physical, electrical, and environmental recommendations and data from the manufacturer. These need to be properly addressed in the initial design of the facility for design of adequate support systems. For retrofits into existing facilities, these data need to be examined in detail to verify that an adequate environment will exist. If modifications need to be made, they should be identified early and factored into the economic analysis of the system. It is possible that these modifications may dictate the use of alternate technology or solutions.

As an example, the designer should obtain approximate weights of the proposed equipment. Batteries, chargers, inverters, generator sets, and other typical standby pieces of equipment can be quite heavy. The floor and structure should be checked to ensure that the new system will not cause structural problems. Required modifications should be planned ahead of time and factored into the project.

The designer also needs to determine approximate fuel consumption and requirements for adequate sizing of day tanks and storage tanks.

The design engineer should also consult applicable codes such as the National Electrical Code (NEC) (NFPA 70-1996), Code for Safety to Life from Fire in Buildings and Structures (ANSI/NFPA 101-1994), national fire codes, OSHA, etc. Is adequate space and lighting available for routine maintenance activities? Can the equipment be removed for replacement or major overhaul activities? Will the overhead steel support chain falls for the positioning of heavy items such as batteries? Will future modifications close off access to the equipment?

For engine generators, consideration should be given to either an overhead crane (large installations) or provisions for a portable crane (small installations). There should also be a way to remove and install large components from the building during major maintenance activities.

The designer should ask how maintenance will be performed. If provisions for maintenance activities are made by the designer ahead of time, the process can proceed smoothly when it occurs. As examples of problems that can occur when maintenance is not provided for, an automatic transfer switch without a maintenance bypass will probably require a system outage, with associated high costs, for routine maintenance, and an engine generator without an "auto-start lockout" can create a safety hazard during maintenance.

10.4 Specification and acceptance testing

The design engineer, having fully evaluated both the intended application and the operating environment, must now take great pains to specify the equipment that is needed for the application and must ensure that all of the considerations have been accounted for. The engineer should avoid the use of "typical" manufacturer specifications for custom-engineered and procured equipment. Specification and acceptance testing is crucial for the installation to be a reliable system.

The design engineer should insist on review and approval of all shop drawings, test reports, and documentation. Engineering approval should be required prior to manufacture or assembly of the equipment.

The design engineer must also specify the required shop tests that are to be done before the equipment is released for delivery. Reliance upon standard manufacturer tests and methods is frequently not enough for these systems. The design engineer should not be hesitant to request that all features specified are to be tested and verified before equipment is released from the factory. Consideration should be given to having the following tests made:

— Running all load tests at rated power factor and not on a pure resistive load.
— Using oscillographs on transfer switches to see if transfers are "bumpless."
— Having all equipment intended to be run together at the facility be run together at the factory before release. This is of particular importance on engineered systems.

— Requiring that all test running times be sufficient to test for heating, overheating, fuel supply, and the several load transfer steps, including transfer back to normal operation.

The following steps are suggestions for the testing process of a UPS system that uses lead acid batteries. These test steps are to be performed after final assembly and quality control (including all normal factory tests) are completed:

a) Add blocks of load in 25% increments at specified power factor and observe output wave form, voltage regulation, and voltage transients. These readings shall be recorded and transmitted to purchaser prior to shipment.

b) Using the static switch (by manual activation), transfer at no load and full load (at rated power factor) from the inverter to standby and then retransfer. All disturbances outside of specification limits shall be corrected, and this test shall be reperformed.

c) Operate the system (exclusive of battery and temporary testing dc power supply) at an elevated temperature of 40 °C for a period of 24 h under various load conditions with the following conditions:

1) Minimum to maximum dc voltage: minimum = 1.75 V × number of cells: maximum = 2.30 V × number of cells

2) Overcurrent limit (transfer and retransfer)

3) Automatic operation of static switch including transfer and retransfer at various load conditions a minimum of 24 times

It is strongly recommended that the specifier, or a technically competent substitute, witness all factory tests. Equipment should not be shipped until all tests are witnessed and satisfactory completion of the tests have been verified. This is of prime importance for custom-built equipment. Witnessed testing may not be practical for all items that go on the system; a balance between the cost of witnessed tests and the cost of site rework needs to be found. The more difficult or expensive to rework an item after leaving the manufacturer, the more desirable testing becomes.

The specifications should name the specifier as the final party in technical interpretations of specifications or contracts. Contract administrators and purchasing agents can and should handle the legal side of the purchase; but they should not interfere with the technical aspects of the purchase.

Another area of testing to consider in this process is the overall reliability of the system. If the user requires that the system has a given overall success rate, a single test will not be a statistically valid test to verify this requirement. For this requirement, a series of tests will need to be run. The test number will need to constitute a statistically valid population. The test (number of tests and allowable failures) will also need to be constructed in such a manner to minimize the chances of both statistical errors of type I (rejecting a good system) and type II (accepting a bad system). Koval 1990 [B3][2] is recommended as a guide in this endeavor.

_____
[2]The numbers in brackets preceded by the letter B correspond to those of the bibliography in 10.10.

Careful attention paid during the specification, assembly, and acceptance of the system equipment will go a long way towards having a reliable system.

10.5 Maintenance and training

It is axiomatic that standby systems, particularly engine generators, need maintenance. But this area is frequently neglected.

The reader is referred to Chapter 8 of this standard for discussions of maintenance. Many of the items listed below are addressed only from the reliability standpoint; Chapter 8 treats them from a more detailed perspective. As stated in 10.1, many factors that directly affect reliability are contained in this standard and they should all be read in addition to this chapter.

A reasonable maintenance budget needs to be established by the owner or operator of the system. Included in this budget should be some or all of the following items as appropriate:

a)   *An adequate supply of fuel and lubricants for exercise, maintenance, and standby use should be available at all times.* Engine generator exercise periods should be set in accordance with manufacturers recommendations, national codes such as ANSI/NFPA 110-1993, and local codes. Adequate records should be maintained of exercise periods, and a "squawk sheet" of problems should be kept and acted upon.

It is important to maintain a realistic exercise schedule. A balance should be struck between too much exercise, which will lead to premature wear of components, and too little exercise, which may cause the system to be unavailable when needed.

All moving parts need lubrication of some type, and lubricants should be replaced or reprocessed at regular intervals. An adequate supply of the proper lubricants needs to be on hand for routine lubrication and for occasional required unplanned lubrication. Maintenance requirements for engines and turbines depend upon the number of running hours and the quality of fuel burned.

The user should ensure that all fuel delivered is of good quality and has been properly specified for the local area. As an example, diesel fuel needs to have its pour point 6 °C below ambient temperature (ANSI/ASTM D975-92a). If you are using an outdoor storage facility, this can be a very important specification item. A bad delivery of fuel can cause major problems with an engine or turbine.

b)   *Maintenance and operations personnel need to be trained on the equipment.* In order for facility personnel to be able to maintain the system, they should be adequately trained on the equipment. Initial and recurrent training needs to be included within the maintenance budget. This is also true of operations personnel. They should have instruction in how the equipment should be operated, what it can and cannot do, etc. Adequate up-front instructions will help eliminate abuse from operations due to lack of understanding.

The results of good training will go beyond simply having better-educated mechanics on staff. Employees who are invested in by management feel a sense of pride and ownership in the system. This investment will repay its cost many times over in reduced downtime, fewer maintenance calls, and increased morale. It is virtually impossible to quantify the result of good training. However, the recent trend towards improved quality, Baldridge Awards, etc., lend credence to this frequently overlooked area in the reliability equation.

c) *Adequate tools and documentation should be kept on hand.* The budget should also include purchasing all required documentation and special tools. The best-educated maintenance person will still need to have proper equipment and documentation to do a proper job of maintaining the system. The engineer, when first putting the system out for bids should consider including the cost of at least two sets of required special tools and maintenance documents within the initial cost of the system. This will enable the end user to start with all necessary items. It is also possible that during the bidding process manufacturers will include these items at prices not normally available if procured separately.

d) *A preventive maintenance schedule should be established.* The owner/operator of the system needs to establish a firm preventive maintenance schedule for all equipment. This schedule should be based upon the recommendation of the equipment supplier. There are also other general guidelines for maintenance schedules when this information is not available or needs to supplemented.

e) *Maintenance records should be kept.* Accurate and detailed records of all maintenance activities should be kept that are current, readily understandable, and easy to retrieve. These records will enable the user to keep adequate supplies of spare parts, fuel coolant, and lubrication supplies in stock. Pieces of equipment that are becoming labor-intensive and thus candidates for replacement should also be recorded. A good set of records can form the starting point for a predictive maintenance schedule to further enhance system reliability. Lastly, these records are of vital importance for input to management in the budget and decision-making process.

f) *A clean environment should be considered mandatory for reliable operation.* Dirt contributes to the following:

1) Additional heating of components. Heat will contribute to shortened life of almost any part in a standby system. Cleanliness, along with its reduced heating, helps in this regard.

2) Infiltration of sensitive parts. When parts that have very tight tolerances, or are sensitive to infiltration by foreign objects, are not cleaned on a regular basis, failure will follow.

3) Hinderance of troubleshooting by maintenance personnel. It is difficult for anyone to perform work on equipment that is dirty. A clean system will aid in maintenance and reduce downtime during maintenance periods.

The presence of dirt acts as an indicator of how well the system is being maintained. Systems that receive regular maintenance will be cleaner and, hence, more reliable than dirty systems. No standby system should be considered operational until it is clean.

g) *Outside services should be used as appropriate.* There are some maintenance-related activities that need to be contracted to outside concerns. Spectrometric analysis for lubrication oil on engine or turbine generator sets is a good example of one of these activities. It will give a very good idea of the condition of the generator set so appropriate activities can be planned in advance. It should be done on a periodic basis; see Chapter 8.

Another example of routine outside testing is one that checks for water in diesel fuel. Water will cause sludge to form in the tank. Testing will help keep the user informed and aid in recovery activities.

h) *Instructions should be posted in a conspicuous location.* The owner/operator of the system should post complete mimics or system diagrams in a conspicuous location. Included on or near the mimic should be clear instructions for both operation and maintenance bypass of the system. The mimics should be either a single-line or a switching diagram. The operators level of understanding and skill should be factored into the making of the instructions. Do not make the instructions and mimics so complex that the average operations or maintenance mechanic has trouble reading or interpreting the information.

Other information that should be posted nearby is a troubleshooting chart. This is typically a chart from the manufacturer and gives step-by-step instructions for correcting a given malfunction. This is not usually a detailed operation instruction and does not take the place of an instruction manual. It should, however, give typical problems and corrections.

i) *An adequate supply of spare parts should be kept on hand.* There should be an adequate supply of required spares for both planned and unplanned maintenance. Included in this collection of spares should be filters, fuses, etc. Manufacturers should be consulted about the desirability of maintaining spare circuit boards, silicon-controlled rectifiers (SCRs), and various other items.

10.6 Failure modes

The designer of the system should anticipate certain failures. The following questions should be considered:

— Is the fuel oil transfer pump powered from the diesel generator?
— Will a fire in a riser cause the loss of both normal and emergency power?
— Will loss of power cause a computer control system in the plant to reboot?
— Will the system respond correctly to the restoration of normal power?
— Has the protective relaying been examined for its response to abnormal conditions?

The designer and user are encouraged to examine their systems for other potential failure modes.

10.7 Management awareness

None of the items discussed in this subclause can occur without the support of plant and company management. This support is critical for reliable operation.

It is perhaps the most challenging task for the user to make management aware of the costs involved with standby systems. It is the job of the user to work with management to establish realistic operating budgets and expectations. Both budgets and goals need to be balanced against the ultimate cost of a power loss. Management and the user need to make sure that each is providing the other with realistic expectations and budgets. It is in this area that maintenance records are of vital importance [refer to 10.5 e) for more detailed information]. They form the basis of accurately projecting cost estimates for the future based upon current actual costs. Items that are consuming too much maintenance budget can be singled out for replacement.

Use of standard engineering economic analysis for budgeting can be easily performed when accurate records of costs are available. Records kept of power outages and interruptions, and the costs avoided because of system availability, are also invaluable in this process.

10.8 Conclusions

This chapter has discussed some ways to improve the time factor in the terms generally used to describe reliability. This is not, and should not be considered, the final statement on reliable design and operation of standby power systems. There are many areas of this topic that warrant further review. There is also a significant lack of hard data on this subject, making empirical recommendations difficult to prove. For example, there is virtually no data on the trade-offs between maintenance and forced outages. It is axiomatic that some maintenance is required, but what is the optimum level? This question is not easily answered. However, there are certain common elements on both reliable and unreliable systems. This chapter has tried to list these. These traits, when seriously considered, will help to increase the reliability of the system.

10.9 References

This chapter shall be used in conjunction with the following publications:

ANSI/ASTM D975-92a, Specification for Diesel Fuel Oils.[3]

ANSI/NFPA 101-1994, Code for Safety to Life from Fire in Buildings and Structures.

ANSI/NFPA 110-1993, Emergency and Standby Power Systems.

NFPA 70-1996, National Electrical Code®.[4]

---

[3]ANSI/ASTM publications are available from the Sales Department, American National Standards Institute, 11 West 42nd Street, 13th Floor, New York, NY 10036, USA, or the Customer Service Department, American Society for Testing and Materials, 1916 Race Street, Philadelphia, PA 19103, USA.

[4]ANSI/NFPA publications are available from the Sales Department, American National Standards Institute, 11 West 42nd Street, 13th Floor, New York, NY 10036, USA, or from Publications Sales, National Fire Protection Association, 1 Batterymarch Park, P.O. Box 9101, Quincy, MA 02269-9101, USA.

10.10 Bibliography

Additional information may be found in the following sources:

[B1] IEEE Std 493-1990, IEEE Recommended Practice for the Design of Reliable Industrial and Commercial Power Systems (IEEE Gold Book) (ANSI).[5]

[B2] IEEE Std 500-1984 (Reaff 1991), IEEE Guide to the Collection and Presentation of Electrical, Electronic, Sensing Component and Mechanical Equipment Reliability Data for Nuclear Power Generation Stations.

[B3] Koval, Don O., "Testing Required to Demonstrate Reliability of Emergency and Standby Power Equipment," IEEE Paper 90CH2828-2/90/000-023.

---

[5]IEEE publications are available from the Institute of Electrical and Electronics Engineers, 445 Hoes Lane, P.O. Box 1331, Piscataway, NJ 08855-1331, USA.

INDEX

A

Absorbed electrolyte cell, definition of, 3
Absorbed glass mat (AGM) cell, 3
Ac motors, 162–163
Acceptance testing, reliability and, 290–292
AGM (absorbed glass mat) cell, 3
Agri-business industry applications, 119, 274
Air compressors, startup power, 18
Air conditioning, 11, 23, 46. *See also* HVAC
Air pollution control, 24
Air supply, generators, 91. *See also* Ventilation
Aircraft warning lights, emergency or standby power needs, 278
Alarms
    fire, 25, 72, 74–75
    for battery systems, 207
    ground fault, 243
    health care facilities, 74–75
    signal circuits. *See* Signal circuits
    space conditioning, 46
Aluminum wire, 226
Application of emergency and standby power systems
    need guidelines. *See* Need guidelines
    reliability and, 287–288. *See also* Reliability
    specific industries. *See* Industry applications
Armature winding protection
    harmonics, 198
    overcurrent protection, 191–196
    overvoltage protection, 196–198
Armor, cable, 206
Arson, 48
Automatic transfer switches, 182, 185–186
    definition of, 3
    engine-generator sets, 90
    maintenance, 268
    multiple utility services, 95–96
Auxiliary lighting, 25. *See also* Lighting

Auxiliary power systems. *See* Emergency power systems; standby power systems
Availability
    definition of, 3
    reliability and, 287

B

Batteries and battery systems, 33, 125–145. *See also* Battery/inverter systems
    chargers, protection of, 208–209
    charging, 93, 140–141
    definition of, 3
    emergency lighting, 142–145
        central battery supplied emergency lighting systems, 144
        emergency lighting units, 143–144
        selecting, 145
    for generators, charging, 93
    industrial batteries, 125
    installation design, 134
    lead acid batteries. *See* Lead-acid batteries
    lead-antimony batteries, 202–203
    lead-calcium batteries, 202–204
    maintenance, 139, 262–268
        safety, 263, 268
        typical maintenance schedule, 263
    motive power batteries, 125
    nickel-cadmium batteries. *See* Nickel-cadmium batteries
    overview, 125–126
    protection, 202–208
    railroad batteries, 125
    recharge/equalize charging, 140–141
        lead-acid batteries, 140
        nickel-cadmium batteries, 140–141
        operation, 141
    short-circuit calculation, 141–142
    sizing, 135–139
    SLI (starting, lighting, and ignition) batteries, 125
    standby batteries, 125–126

H

I

K

L

M

R

S